Welcome to the *EVERYTHING*® series!

These handy, accessible books give you all you need to tackle a difficult project, gain a new hobby, comprehend a fascinating topic, prepare for an exam, or even brush up on something you learned back in school but have since forgotten.

You can read an *EVERYTHING*® book from cover-to-cover or just pick out the information you want from our four useful boxes: e-facts, e-ssentials, e-alerts, and e-questions. We literally give you everything you need to know on the subject, but throw in a lot of fun stuff along the way, too.

We now have well over 100 *EVERYTHING*® books in print, spanning such wide-ranging topics as weddings, pregnancy, wine, learning guitar, one-pot cooking, managing people, and so much more. When you're done reading them all, you can finally say you know *EVERYTHING*®!

E FACTS
Important sound bytes of information

E-SSENTIALS
Quick handy tips

E ALERT
Urgent warnings

E QUESTIONS?
Solutions to common problems

THE EVERYTHING®

SLOW COOKER COOKBOOK

300 delicious, healthy meals that you can toss in your crockery and prepare in a snap!

Margaret Kaeter

Adams Media Corporation
Avon, Massachusetts

EDITORIAL
Publishing Director: Gary M. Krebs
Managing Editor: Kate McBride
Copy Chief: Laura MacLaughlin
Acquisitions Editor: Bethany Brown
Development Editor: Michael Paydos

PRODUCTION
Production Director: Susan Beale
Production Manager: Michelle Roy Kelly
Series Design: Daria Perreault, Colleen Cunningham
Cover Design: Paul Beatrice, Frank Rivera
Layout and Graphics: Brooke Camfield,
Colleen Cunningham, Rachael Eiben,
Michelle Roy Kelly, Daria Perreault

An Everything® Series Book.
Everything® is a registered trademark of Adams Media Corporation.

Published by Adams Media Corporation
57 Littlefield Street, Avon, MA 02322 U.S.A.
www.adamsmedia.com

ISBN: 1-58062-667-X
Printed in the United States of America.

J I H G F E D C B A

Library of Congress Cataloging-in-Publication Data
Kaeter, Margaret.
The everything slow-cooker cookbook : 200 delicious, healthy meals
that you can toss in your crockery and prepare in a snap! /
Margaret Kaeter.
p.   cm.   -- (Everything series)
Includes index.
ISBN 1-58062-667-X
1. Electric cookery, Slow. I. Title. II. Series.
TX827 .K34 2002
641.5'884–dc21
2002004629

Many of the designations used by manufacturers and sellers to distinguish their products are claimed as trademarks. Where those designations appear in this book and Adams Media was aware of a trademark claim, the designations have been printed in initial capital letters. Crock-Pot® is a registered trademark of Rival Corporation.

This publication is designed to provide accurate and authoritative information with regard to the subject matter covered. It is sold with the understanding that the publisher is not engaged in rendering legal, accounting, or other professional advice. If legal advice or other expert assistance is required, the services of a competent professional person should be sought.

—From a *Declaration of Principles* jointly adopted by a Committee of the
American Bar Association and a Committee of Publishers and Associations

Illustrations by Barry Littmann.

This book is available at quantity discounts for bulk purchases.
For information, call 1-800-872-5627.

Visit the entire Everything® series at everything.com

Dedication

To Michael, Gretchen, and Emma,
the essential ingredients in the Olesen family stew.

Acknowledgments

To Michael Olesen, Ann Johns, and Verla Olesen for their cooking expertise;
to my mother and my grandmothers for their secret recipes; to my husband's
grandmothers for their wonderful collections of church cookbooks.

Contents

Introduction

Cooking should be fun. It's a simple enough thought, but too many people turn it into drudgery. Perhaps they find a handful of recipes they like and keep repeating them, never savoring the chance to experiment with new spices or new combinations of flavors. In this increasingly hectic world some people simply resent the time it takes to prepare a good meal. Others just see food as fuel for the body and ignore its impact on the soul and its role in bonding family and friends.

Slow cooking can bring the joy back into food. Not only does the slow cooker offer limitless opportunities for experimentation, it is a surprisingly versatile appliance. Most people think of slow cookers as best suited to soups and stews, which they certainly excel at, but slow cookers also can bake breads and cakes as well as serve as a romantic fondue pot. They can roast meat, steam vegetables, and even keep hot apple cider at the perfect temperature for a holiday gathering.

And we really shouldn't be surprised. Virtually every culture on the planet has some sort of slow-cooked repertoire. In part, this is because people throughout history have been busy ensuring their survival—they couldn't spare time to stand over a fire. In part, it's because every culture has a "leftover" dish. From goulash and chili to shepherd's pie, soups, and spaghetti sauces, people have developed ways to recombine yesterday's meals into new, flavorful creations.

In fact, throughout history, slow cooking has had a prominent place. When people first discovered fire, they also discovered that burying the animal carcass and vegetables below a bed of coals helped it cook more evenly and thoroughly. Clay pots brought the opportunity to keep the food clean while providing an efficient way to heat it even in hot climates.

So now we are coming full circle in our experiences with food. Instead of looking for ever-faster ways to prepare tasteless meals that keep our bodies running, we are looking for ways to regain the advantages our ancestors found in slow cooking. The meals in this cookbook offer the chance to combine old foods in new, exciting ways. They take you beyond the slow-cooker box to tempt you to experiment with flavors you may never have dreamed of. And most important, they rekindle the spirit of food preparation, the fact that it should be a constant part of our daily existence instead of a too-quick interruption.

In that spirit, many of these recipes are downright fun. They provide the chance to experiment with ingredients many people pass by in the grocery store. Many also provide the opportunity to get a whole group of family and friends involved chopping, cleaning, and mixing ingredients. And, who can resist the fun of seeing a dish cook through the clear cover?

Also note that these recipes are extremely healthy. Most avoid high-fat, high-sugar contents while replacing salt with flavors derived directly from the meats, vegetables, and plant spices. The slow-cooking process also retains more nutrients than many other methods of cooking.

Even more exciting is the fact that these recipes are easy. They require only a few simple utensils, an occasional unique ingredient, and an extremely basic knowledge of cooking terms. The rest of the magic is achieved through the science of slow cooking—the fact that food is cooked evenly through indirect heat and doesn't dry out. Flavors meld, meats and vegetables blend, spices release their hidden aromas, and everyday ingredients become exciting adventures.

CHAPTER 1
The Slow Cooker

Although slow cooking was common throughout history, the invention of the cast-iron stove changed all that. Sure, people still put the occasional stew or soup "on the back burner," but they more often baked their bread and main dishes quickly in a hot oven. What they lost in flavor and control they made up for with convenience.

The Resurgence of the Slow Cooker

It wasn't until the 1960s that Americans and Europeans began to see the advantages of slow cooking again. One important factor was the women's movement. Suddenly meals had to be planned the evening before they would be eaten because Mom wasn't there to hover over the stove. If you wanted anything that took longer than a half-hour, it needed to be cooked during the day.

Enter the Crock-Pot®. The Rival Corporation, an appliance manufacturer, saw the need for a new appliance that would create healthy, home-cooked meals without infringing on free time. They went back to an earlier time in history and revisited the clay pot. By putting an electric plug in the pot and heating elements around the crock to substitute for hot coals, they created the first modern-day slow cooker.

FACTS

The slow cooker we know was first introduced in the 1960s as a response to women working outside the home in large numbers. It became more popular as an energy-saving device during the energy crisis of the 1970s.

How the Slow Cooker Works

Of course, the electric slow cooker also provided a few other advantages over the clay pot and hot coals. Today's slow cookers usually have two settings—high and low. The low setting is equivalent to about 200 degrees Fahrenheit, while the high setting is about 300 degrees. However, the reason they are listed as high and low is because the actual degrees don't matter. Because the food heats indirectly, absorbing the heat from the crockery, it will cook the same within a 50-degree temperature range.

The cover also is an important component of the slow cooker. It usually is a heavy glass or plastic cover that fits securely, creating a seal that holds the steam in the slow cooker. This is an important factor in creating those marvelous flavors—foods are cooked in their own steam, literally infusing the flavor back in through the cooking process. This keeps the food moist and works to tenderize the toughest cuts of meat and the most stubborn vegetables.

Slow cookers heat up slowly, usually taking two to three hours to get up to their highest temperature. This ensures that the food retains its nutrients while also preventing scorching or burning. It's also the reason you don't need to be home while the meal cooks.

The temperature of the cooked food on the low setting is about 200 degrees. This is hot enough to inhibit bacterial growth, yet it is low enough that stirring isn't necessary. Stirring is usually done to eliminate hot spots in a dish. Since the slow cooker never gets hot enough to burn the food, there are no hot spots to eliminate.

Because the food cooks slowly, the same dish can take a different amount of time on different days. The reason is that the size of the food pieces, the fat content, and the liquid content all conduct heat differently. The lean three-pound pork roast that took eight hours last week could take nine hours this week if it has more fat and you've added a few more vegetables to the pot this time.

QUESTIONS?

How often should I stir the food in the slow cooker?
Because it cooks by indirect heat, you never need to stir the food to make sure it's evenly cooked. However, you may want to stir it at first to make sure the ingredients are well mingled.

What Is a Real Slow Cooker?

Note that some companies have tried to pass off their "hot plate" appliances as slow cookers. While these imposters do allow slow cooking, they do not have the same effect as a true slow cooker. A real slow cooker has a crockery insert that warms up evenly, thus spreading the heat evenly throughout the food. A device that provides heat only from the bottom to a metal container is no different than putting a pot on the stove, no matter how low the temperature setting goes.

Since the early days of Crock-Pots®, many variations have developed. Today they come in all shapes and sizes. Some include separate compartments so vegetables and meat can be cooked at the same time without blending. Most even include special-purchase options such as bread bakers and meat roasters. And virtually all of them come in pleasing colors to fit in any kitchen décor.

Slow-cooker recipes need very little water because they "recycle" the water in the vegetables and meats via steam. If you're converting an oven recipe for the slow cooker, use about one-fourth the water.

How to Choose the Right Slow Cooker

With so many different styles from which to choose, how do you pick the one that's right for you? Well, if you're like most people, you probably got your first slow cooker as a housewarming or wedding present.

Relax, it will be just fine. Sure, there are small one-quart versions that are perfect for hot-dip appetizers and there are massive eight-quart models designed to make enough stew for a small army. There are versions with automatic timers and warming settings. Some have removable crockery inserts, while others have the crock built into the device. But a slow cooker remains a slow cooker. It's a relatively simple device that's hard to use incorrectly.

If you are lucky enough to plan your purchase of a slow cooker, define what you will be using it for. Do you have more than four people in your family? If so, you might want to go with a six-quart or even eight-quart version. Someone who does a lot of entertaining might want the larger version. And, if you like to freeze leftovers, by all means go for a bigger one.

If you're a small family, you might want to start with the midsize and most versatile type of slow cooker. The 2½-quart version—the one first introduced by the Rival Corporation—is still the most popular for first-time buyers. It is large enough to make meals for groups of up to eight people while small enough to remain energy efficient and to correctly cook small quantities of food.

Also take a look at how you plan to use your slow cooker. Are you routinely gone for more than nine hours during the day? If so, you might want to consider the automatic timer and warming function because even a slow cooker can overcook some food. Do you want to make entire meals? The two-compartment model would provide more options.

If you don't like to spend a lot of time washing pots and pans, consider a slow cooker with a removable crockery insert. These can be cleaned in the dishwasher while self-contained units must be sponge cleaned.

If this is your first slow cooker and you aren't sure how you will be using it, choose a reasonable middle ground. That removable crock is a real time saver. Likewise, 3½ to 4 quarts adds enough flexibility to cook large meals without being too large to store in your cupboard or to properly cook a small meal.

Note that most of the recipes in this book are well suited to slow cookers in the three- to six-quart size range. However, that is simply the optimal size for the dish mentioned. Most can also go into slightly smaller or larger slow cookers without severely affecting the food quality.

ALERT

Because a slow cooker uses indirect heat to cook food, it needs to be filled at least halfway and no more than three-quarters full. Any more or less will cause food to cook unevenly.

Why the Prices Vary

As a general rule, the pricing on slow cookers is relatively easy to decipher. The more options they offer and the larger the capacity, the more expensive they run. A basic 2½-quart model with a built-in crock and two temperature settings will sell for under $10 at a discount store. Add a quart more space, a warming setting, and removable crock, and it will sell for $30 to $40.

When you start getting larger and fancier, the prices go up quickly. The eight-quart slow cooker with removable crock, automatic timer, digital readout, warming function, and two compartments will sell for about $80.

Many slow cookers also offer special utensils such as bread baking inserts, vegetable steamers, meat roasters, and insulated carrying cases. As a rule, you need to special order these directly from the manufacturer. However, if you do find them at the store, resist the urge to purchase them until you are sure you need them. These inserts can cost as much as a basic slow cooker, yet they can easily be re-created using aluminum cans and simple utensils you already own.

The good news is that it's hard to go wrong when buying a slow cooker. If you buy an inexpensive slow cooker and find you need a bigger one with more options, you likely will find plenty of times you can use them both at once. And, since they're an extremely durable appliance, you can always pass your smaller, simpler slow cooker on to your oldest child when he rents his first apartment!

What You Can Do with a Slow Cooker

Slow cookers are extremely versatile. They gained their reputation as the perfect appliance for cooking soups and stews, but they also do an excellent job with pot roasts and whole chickens. They are a natural choice for long-cooking vegetables such as squash and potatoes and are an absolute necessity for potluck events and entertaining because they keep food warm for long periods without overcooking.

But those uses are just the beginning. Think of your slow cooker as both a pot and an oven that never goes above 350 degrees Fahrenheit. It can be used to melt cheeses for fondue or candy coatings for special desserts. It is a convenient way to cook rice or beans without having to worry about the bottom scorching. It also does a superb job baking cookies, cakes, and breads. It even does a good job on dishes requiring a little more attention, such as fresh fish.

Just think of your slow cooker as something other than the appliance you use when you'll be gone all day, and suddenly you will find all sorts of uses for it.

One hour on high equals about two hours on low. Most recipes respond well to either temperature setting, although flavors tend to meld better when cooked on the low setting.

What You Shouldn't Do with a Slow Cooker

Still, there are a few things that a slow cooker can't do. Because it cooks foods over several hours, it won't brown meats and vegetables. For that reason, some recipes ask you to brown the meat, garlic, and onions, for example, in a skillet before putting them into the slow cooker. Others use spices and vegetables as a substitute for that browned taste.

In fact, any recipe that requires quick cooking or high heat isn't well suited to a slow cooker. You can't deep-fry or parboil anything.

Milk products also offer special challenges for slow cookers. Some cheeses will separate when cooked over the long term and most milk products will turn brown. There's a reason many slow-cooker recipes call for condensed cream soups instead of "real" cream or whole milk—the cooking process in canned soups stabilizes the milk so it doesn't react to lengthy cooking times.

Rice and pastas also add special challenges when slow cooking, because they tend to absorb too much water when cooked over long periods. As a result, many recipes ask you to add these items later in the cooking process. If you put them in for a full eight-hour cooking period, you may find them a little mushy.

Basic Techniques for Slow Cooking

Even the most inexperienced cook can quickly master slow-cooker recipes. Just keep the following things in mind:

- Cut meat and vegetables to the same size to ensure even cooking in soups and stews.
- Place slow-cooking items such as hard vegetables—rutabagas, turnips, potatoes—on the bottom of the slow cooker.
- Don't peek. Every time you lift the cover of the slow cooker, valuable steam escapes, reducing the internal temperature several degrees. Every time you lift the cover, plan to add at least twenty minutes to your cooking time.

- Slow-cooker recipes don't like water. Because the food is infused with steam, very little water escapes. When converting a recipe from a regular cookbook, use about half the water and add more during the last hour of the cooking cycle if necessary.

- Don't preheat the slow cooker. A few recipes ask you to preheat the slow cooker, usually because you will be melting cheese or chocolate in it. However, most are designed to start with both the crock and the food at room temperature. This ensures even heating of the food and prevents thermal shock from adding cold food to a warm crock. (The result could be a cracked crock.)

- Most traditional slow-cooker recipes take seven to nine hours on the low setting. The high setting takes about half that time but doesn't tenderize the meat as much.

- Spices and aromatic vegetables have different characteristics when slow cooked. Some, such as green peppers and bay leaves, increase in intensity when slow cooked. Others, such as onions and cinnamon, tend to lose flavor over the long cooking process. Most slow-cooker recipes reflect this difference, although you may have to adjust for your own tastes.

- When cooking traditional slow-cooker meals such as soups, stews, and meats, make sure the slow cooker is at least half full and the food does not extend beyond one-inch below the top. This ensures even cooking.

- Don't bother stirring. Remember, the steam from the food permeates the other foods in the slow cooker, so there is no need to stir. The flavors will blend anyway. Some recipes call for stirring at the beginning or the end of the process to accentuate this blending, but very few recipes require stirring midprocess.

- Throw away the timer. In our harried lives, we look for exact measurements in everything, yet slow cookers are very forgiving appliances. Dishes usually taste about the same within a two-hour window. If a recipe calls for eight hours, rest assured that seven to nine hours of cooking time is probably fine. Even breads and cakes will have fifteen- to thirty-minute windows because of the slow cooking process.

- Don't thaw food in the slow cooker. While it may seem a natural use, frozen food actually heats up too slowly to effectively prevent bacterial growth when in a slow cooker. It's better to thaw food overnight in a refrigerator or use the microwave.

How to Clean and Care for Your Slow Cooker

Slow cookers are very simple appliances. However, they do need some special care. If you follow these rules your slow cooker will produce healthy meals for many years:

- Never, never, never immerse the slow cooker in water. If it's plugged in at the time, you could receive a shock. If it isn't plugged in, you could damage the heating element.
- Always check for nicks or cuts in the electrical cord before plugging it into the outlet. This is especially important because you may be leaving the slow cooker on for several hours with no one in the house.
- If the crockery container is removable, it can be washed in the dishwasher. If not, use a soft cloth or sponge to wash it out. Always use a damp cloth to wash the metal housing.
- Remove baked-on food from the crockery container with a nonabrasive cleaner and a damp sponge. Do not scrub with abrasives, as these can scratch the crock, creating areas for bacteria to reside.

ALERT

Parts of the slow cooker can be cleaned in a dishwasher. If you have a removable crockery core, place it on the bottom rack. If you have a plastic cover, be sure to place it in the top rack of the dishwasher so it doesn't warp.

CHAPTER 2
Appetizers

Broccoli Dip

Cooking time: 3–4 hours

Preparation time: 15 minutes

Attention: Minimal

Pot size: 1–2 quart

Serves 12 as an appetizer

1 small yellow onion
2 celery ribs
8 ounces (1 cup) fresh mushrooms,
   sliced
2 garlic cloves

2 cups fresh broccoli, chopped
¼ cup butter
1 (10¾-ounce) can cream of
   mushroom condensed soup

1. Peel the onion and chop into ¼-inch pieces. Chop the celery into ¼-inch pieces. Clean the mushrooms by wiping with a damp cloth, then slice paper-thin. Peel the garlic and chop into ⅛-inch pieces. Chop the broccoli florets into ¼-inch pieces.
2. Combine all the ingredients in the slow cooker. Cover and cook on low setting for 3 to 4 hours.

Serve with premium gourmet crackers.

Roasted Garlic

Cooking time: 4–5 hours

Preparation time: 15 minutes

Attention: Minimal

Pot size: 1–2 quart

Serves 8

3 bulbs of premium garlic

3 tablespoons olive oil

Cut off the tops of the garlic bulbs and discard tops. Spread olive oil on the bottom of the slow cooker. Place the garlic bulbs (right side up) in the slow cooker. Drizzle remaining olive oil on top of the garlic. Cover and cook on low setting for 4 to 5 hours. Ready when tender and golden. Squeeze cloves to remove softened garlic; discard skins

Use roasted garlic as a spread for French bread. Because the garlic sweetens as it roasts, there is no need for butter.

Cooking time: 6–7 hours

Preparation time: 15 minutes

Attention: Minimal

Pot size: 5–6 quarts

Serves 12 as an appetizer

Honey-Pineapple Chicken Wings

3 pounds chicken wings
1 garlic clove
1 cup fresh or canned pineapple, cubed
½ teaspoon salt
½ teaspoon ground black pepper
1 cup honey
½ cup soy sauce
2 tablespoons vegetable oil

1. Cut the wing tip off each chicken wing and discard tips. Mince the garlic with a sharp kitchen knife. Cut the pineapple into 1 inch cubes.
2. Combine the salt, pepper, honey, soy sauce, pineapple, vegetable oil, and garlic in a bowl and mix well. Place the wings in the slow cooker. Pour the sauce over the wings and cook covered on low setting for 6 to 7 hours.

To keep the wings from drying out during a party, mix in a half cup of water every hour.

Handling Raw Chicken

Chicken is perhaps the most dangerous raw meat. To prevent salmonella and other bacteria from being transmitted, thoroughly wash your hands and all utensils before and after handling it.

Li'l Baby Reubens

Cooking time: 2 hours
Preparation time: 10 minutes
Attention: Medium
Pot size: 2–4 quarts
Serves 12–24 as an appetizer

½ pound corned beef
1 medium onion
1 (16-ounce) can sauerkraut
2 cups Swiss cheese, shredded
1 cup Cheddar cheese, shredded
1 cup mayonnaise (do not substitute low-fat mayonnaise)
Thousand Island dressing
Rye crackers

1. Shred the corned beef with a fork. Peel and chop the onion into ¼-inch pieces. Drain and rinse the sauerkraut. Combine the corned beef, sauerkraut, Swiss cheese, onion, Cheddar cheese, and mayonnaise in the slow cooker. Cook covered on low setting for 2 hours, stirring every 15 minutes.
2. Serve each appetizer with rye crackers and a small dollop of Thousand Island dressing.

Spicy dill pickles are a perfect complement to this full-bodied appetizer.

Preventing Food from Sticking

Because it uses slow, indirect heat, food will not burn in a slow cooker. However, some dishes will stick a little bit. Simply spray the container with vegetable oil cooking spray before adding ingredients.

Cooking time: 1 hour

Preparation time: 10 minutes

Attention: Constant

Pot size: 1–3 quarts

Serves 6 as an appetizer

Artichoke Dip

6 ounces (1½ cups) marinated artichoke hearts
1 clove fresh garlic
⅓ cup light mayonnaise
½ cup Parmesan cheese, grated
⅓ cup light sour cream

1. Drain the artichoke hearts and chop into pieces about the size of a penny. Finely mince the garlic with a sharp kitchen knife.
2. Combine the mayonnaise, grated Parmesan, sour cream, and garlic. Mix in the chopped artichoke hearts. Put mixture in the slow cooker, cover, and cook on low setting for 1 hour. Mix periodically while it is cooking.

For a truly unique appetizer, spread a thin layer of olive oil on pocket bread and bake in a conventional oven for 10 minutes. Cut each half circle of pocket bread into eight triangles and let guests scoop the dip with the bread.

Storage Tip

Store the slow cooker with the lid alongside instead of on top to prevent the chance that mold will grow if you don't use it for several weeks.

Barbecued Turkey Meatballs

Cooking time: 4–6 hours
Preparation time: 20 minutes
Attention: Medium
Pot size: 3–6 quarts
Serves 12 as an appetizer

1 egg
1 clove garlic
3 tablespoons fresh onion, chopped
1 slice bread
1 medium-sized apple
1 pound ground turkey
¼ teaspoon salt
2 small cans tomato sauce
¼ cup brown sugar
1 tablespoon vinegar

1. Beat the egg lightly with a fork. Peel the garlic and chop finely. Peel the onion and chop finely. Toast the bread in a toaster and break into pieces no larger than ¼ of a penny to make crumbs. Mince the apple with a sharp kitchen knife.
2. Use your hands to mix the ground turkey with the egg, garlic, onion, salt, and bread crumbs. Make sure all the ingredients are mixed well. The mixture should be sticky. Form the mixture into meatballs about the size of a golf ball. Place them on a cookie sheet and brown in a 350-degree oven for 20 minutes.
3. Transfer all the meatballs into the slow cooker. Combine the tomato sauce, brown sugar, minced apple, and vinegar in a bowl and stir until mixed well. Pour this sauce over the meatballs and cook covered on low setting for 4 to 6 hours.

Prepare several servings of the meatballs and store them in the freezer. Then simply put them in the slow cooker frozen and pour the sauce on top for a quick, no-attention appetizer.

Cooking time: 8 hours
Preparation time: 20 minutes
Attention: Minimal
Pot size: 3–6 quarts
Serves about 30

Green Apple Salsa

6 large tomatoes
3 large, tart green apples
1 large Vidalia onion
1 large green bell pepper
1 large red bell pepper
1 small green jalapeño pepper
1 (5-ounce) can tomato paste
1½ cups packed brown sugar

1½ cups cider vinegar
½ teaspoon lime juice
2 tablespoons chili powder
2 teaspoons mustard seeds
½ teaspoon cayenne pepper
1 teaspoon salt
1 tablespoon vegetable oil

1. Crush the tomatoes in the bottom of the slow cooker with a wooden spoon. Peel and chop the apples into ¼-inch pieces. Peel and chop the onion into ¼-inch pieces. Remove the stems and seeds from the green, red, and jalapeño peppers; chop into ¼-inch pieces.
2. Combine all the ingredients in the slow cooker and cook covered on low heat for 8 hours. If the sauce seems too runny, remove the cover for the last hour.

This tasty salsa is wonderful served with baked tortilla chips. It also makes an excellent addition to meat loaf or hamburgers.

Preparing a Day Ahead
If you're preparing the food the evening before you will be cooking it, add the dry ingredients to the slow cooker that evening. Add the water or other liquid right before turning it on.

Mock Stuffed Grape Leaves

Cooking time: 2–4 hours

Preparation time: 30 minutes

Attention: Minimal

Pot size: 2–4 quart

Serves 12–24 as an appetizer

1 cup cooked white rice
½ cup golden raisins, plus extra for garnish
¼ cup apple jelly, plus extra for garnish
⅛ teaspoon saffron
½ teaspoon salt
1 bunch fresh Swiss chard leaves

1. Combine the cooked white rice, raisins, apple jelly, saffron, and salt. Mix with a spoon until all ingredients are evenly distributed.
2. Wash the Swish chard leaves in cold water. Using a large melon scoop, place one scoop of rice mixture in the center of each leaf. Fold ends in and roll up tightly, as you would an egg roll. Place them in layers in the slow cooker. Cook covered on low setting for 2 to 4 hours.

Add a small dollop of apple jelly and a raisin on the top of each appetizer for a sweeter taste.

Heat Retention

Because slow cookers use porous stoneware "crocks" to cook the food, the heat is absorbed and retained. You will notice that the crock stays warm for an hour or more after you unplug it.

Spicy Shrimp and Cheese Dip

Cooking time: 1–2 hours
Preparation time: 20 minutes
Attention: Minimal
Pot size: 1–3 quarts
Serves 12–24 as an appetizer

1 slice bacon
1 cup popcorn shrimp, cooked
3 medium-sized yellow onions
2 garlic cloves
1 medium tomato
3 cups Monterey jack cheese, shredded
¼ teaspoon Tabasco sauce
¼ teaspoon cayenne pepper
¼ teaspoon ground black pepper

1. Cook the bacon in a frying pan until crisp; keep grease in pan. Lay bacon on a paper towel to cool. When cool, crumble it with your fingers. If the shrimp is not precooked, boil it in water for 10 minutes.
2. Peel and chop the onions into ¼-inch squares. Peel the garlic and mince with a sharp kitchen knife. Peel and chop the tomato into ¼-inch squares. Add the onion and garlic to the bacon drippings in the frying pan and sauté on medium-low heat until they are limp.
3. Combine all the ingredients in the slow cooker; stir well. Cook covered on low setting for 1 to 2 hours, or until the cheese is fully melted.

Cooking tip: If the dip is too thick, add milk in half-cup increments until it's the consistency you like.

Cleaning

Use a rough sponge to remove any dried-on food from the slow cooker when cleaning it. A scouring pad could scratch the surface, creating a place for bacteria to grow.

Creamy Refried Bean Dip

Cooking time: 2 hours

Preparation time: 10 minutes

Attention: Medium

Pot size: 2–4 quarts

Serves 12–24 as an appetizer

1 cup shredded Monterey jack cheese
1 cup shredded Cheddar cheese
1 (12-ounce) can refried beans
1 cup picante sauce
⅓ cup sour cream
3 ounces cream cheese
1 tablespoon chili powder
¼ teaspoon ground cumin
tortilla chips

1. Combine the refried beans, picante sauce, shredded cheeses, sour cream, cream cheese, chili powder, and cumin in a medium-sized bowl; mix well with a large spoon.
2. Place the mixture in the slow cooker and cook on low setting for 2 hours, stirring every 15 minutes.

Serve with tortilla chips and a bowl of Green Apple Salsa (page 17) for additional flavor.

Converting Recipes

Don't translate quick recipes. The best recipes for slow cookers are those that take about an hour of time or more in the oven or simmering on a stove top. Others likely contain ingredients that need to be cooked fast.

Baked Brie with Strawberry Chutney

Cooking time: 4–5 hours
Preparation time: 10 minutes
Attention: Medium
Pot size: 1–3 quarts
Serves 8–12 as an appetizer

1 cup strawberries
½ cup brown sugar
⅓ cup cider vinegar
⅛ teaspoon nutmeg
2 tablespoons grapefruit juice
1 (8-ounce) piece of Brie cheese
1 tablespoon sliced almonds, toasted

1. Remove the green tops from the strawberries and slice berries in quarters. Combine the strawberries, brown sugar, vinegar, nutmeg, and grapefruit juice in slow cooker. Cover and cook on low setting for 4 hours. Remove top, turn heat to high and cook 30 minutes, stirring every few minutes. Put mixture in refrigerator to cool.
2. Place the Brie on an ovenproof plate and cover with sliced almonds; bake uncovered in 350-degree oven for about 10 minutes. Cheese should be partially melted but not fully melted. Remove from the oven and top with room-temperature chutney.

Serve with raw celery sticks and a dry white wine.

Add a Little Vino

A half cup of wine adds an elegant taste to many dishes without adding many calories. And, since the alcohol evaporates in the cooking process, you get all the flavor without the hangover!

Cooking time: 1–2 hours	
Preparation time: 15 minutes	
Attention: Minimal	
Pot size: 1–3 quarts	
Serves 12–24 as an appetizer	

Southwestern Apricot Salsa

2 tablespoons red onion, chopped
½ teaspoon fresh jalapeño pepper, minced
2 cups canned apricots in light syrup, chopped
½ tablespoon olive oil
1 tablespoon fresh cilantro
½ teaspoon white vinegar
½ tablespoon lime juice
¼ teaspoon lime peel, grated
¼ teaspoon ground cumin
½ teaspoon garlic salt
½ teaspoon ground white pepper

1. Peel and chop the onion into ¼-inch pieces.
2. Remove the stem from jalapeño pepper and mince.
3. Drain and rinse the apricots and cut into ¼-inch pieces.
4. Combine all the ingredients in the slow cooker. Cook uncovered on low setting for 1 to 2 hours.

This salsa is excellent served hot or cold with baked taco chips.

CHAPTER 3
Soups

Hamburger Vegetable Soup

Cooking time: 7–8 hours

Preparation time: 15 minutes

Attention: Minimal

Pot size: 3–6 quarts

Serves 6

½ pound lean ground beef
4 medium-sized fresh tomatoes
1 large yellow onion
½ cup celery, sliced
3 medium carrots
6 cups beef broth
½ teaspoon table salt
½ teaspoon ground black pepper
1 cup fresh peas
1 cup fresh green beans

1. Brown the ground beef in a medium-sized skillet on medium-high heat; drain off grease.
2. Cut the tomatoes into ½-inch cubes. Peel the onion and cut into ¼-inch pieces. Cut the celery into ¼-inch-thick slices. Peel the carrots and slice them into ¼-inch-thick pieces.
3. Place the ground beef, beef broth, tomatoes, onion, celery, carrots, salt, and pepper in slow cooker. Cover and cook on low setting for 6 hours.
4. Add the peas and green beans. Cover and cook on low 1 to 2 more hours.

Garnish with fresh parsley before serving.

Hold the Cream, Please
To create a dairy-free cream soup, remove some of the cooked vegetables from the broth and puree them in a blender. Stir them back into the soup.

Cooking time: 9–11 hours

Preparation time: 30 minutes

Attention: Medium

Pot size: 3–6 quarts

Serves 8

Minestrone Soup

1 pound beef stewing meat
1 (28-ounce) can tomatoes
1 medium onion
6 cups water
1 beef bouillon cube
2 tablespoons dried parsley
1½ teaspoon table salt
1½ teaspoon dried thyme
½ teaspoon ground black pepper
1 medium zucchini
2 cups cabbage, chopped
1 (16-ounce) can garbanzo beans, drained
1 cup uncooked shell macaroni

1. Cut the meat into 1-inch cubes. Cut the tomatoes into ½-inch cubes; reserve liquid. Peel the onion and cut into ¼-inch pieces. Combine the beef, water, tomatoes with their liquid, bouillon cube, onion, parsley, salt, thyme, and pepper in slow cooker. Cover and cook on low for 8 to 10 hours.
2. Cut the zucchini into ¼-inch thick slices. Chop the cabbage into ¼-inch pieces. Add the zucchini, cabbage, beans, and macaroni to soup. Cover and cook on high for 1 hour.

Sprinkle with Parmesan cheese right before serving.

De-Meating Your Dish

Substitute vegetable bouillon or broth for a meat broth in any soup recipe. It adds a cleaner, lighter flavor with none of the fat. Add beans in place of meat to create a vegetarian dish.

Day-After Thanksgiving Turkey Soup

Cooking time: 6–8 hours	
Preparation time: 20 minutes	
Attention: Minimal	
Pot size: 3–8 quarts	
Serves 6	

1 large yellow onion
1 fresh green pepper
1 cup carrots, sliced
1 cup celery, diced
1 cup fresh mushrooms, sliced
1 pound leftover turkey, shredded
¼ teaspoon pepper
¼ teaspoon oregano
¼ teaspoon basil
1 tablespoon chicken bouillon
3 cups boiling water
1 cup tomato sauce
1 tablespoon soy sauce

1. Peel the onion and carrots, and remove the seeds and stem from the green pepper. Cut the celery, carrots, onion, and green pepper into ¼-inch pieces. Wash the mushrooms by wiping with a damp cloth; slice paper-thin with a sharp paring knife.
2. Add all ingredients to the slow cooker. Cover and cook on low setting 6 to 8 hours.

What else but Halloween Is Here Pumpkin Bread (page 78) as a complement to this soup?

Bell Peppers

Bell peppers have different flavors depending on their color. Green is the most acidic and sour tasting. Red has the most peppery flavor. Yellow and orange have a gentle flavor. Combine them to create unique flavors and a beautiful dish.

Split Pea and Ham Soup

Cooking time: 8–10 hours

Preparation time: 20 minutes

Attention: Minimal

Pot size: 3–8 quarts

Serves 6

1 medium-sized yellow onion
3 carrots
2 stalks celery, leaves included
2 garlic cloves
1 (16-ounce) package dried green split peas, rinsed
2 cups diced ham
1 bay leaf
¼ cup fresh parsley, chopped
1 tablespoon salt
½ teaspoon ground black pepper
1½ quarts hot water

1. Peel and chop the onion into ¼-inch pieces. Peel the carrots and slice into ¼-inch rounds. Chop the celery ¼-inch thick. Mince the garlic with a sharp paring knife.
2. Add all ingredients to the slow cooker, pouring water on top; do not stir. Cover and cook on low 8 to 10 hours. Remove bay leaf before serving.

Serve with Honey Oatmeal Bread (page 82) as a nice complement of flavors.

Freezing Your Food

When planning to freeze a soup or stew after it's cooked, under-cook the vegetables so they don't get mushy when reheated. If possible, leave the potatoes out and add them fresh when reheating.

Fancy Golden Potato Soup

Cooking time: 7–9 hours

Preparation time: 30 minutes

Attention: Medium

Pot size: 3–6 quarts

Serves 6

6 medium-sized golden potatoes

1 yellow onion

1 large celery stalk

1 large carrot

4 chicken bouillon cubes

1 tablespoon dried parsley flakes

5 cups water

1 tablespoon salt

1 teaspoon ground black pepper

⅓ cup butter

1 (13-ounce) can evaporated milk

1. Peel the potatoes and cut into 1-inch squares. Peel the onion and chop into ¼-inch pieces. Chop the celery into ¼-inch pieces. Peel the carrot and chop into ¼-inch pieces.
2. Place all the ingredients except the milk into slow cooker. Cover and cook on low setting for 7 to 8 hours.
3. Add the milk and cook an additional half-hour, covered, on low setting.

Serve as a complement to a grilled steak.

Save the Skin!

Potato skins contain many vitamins not found in the "meat" of the potato. Unless your recipe calls for a clean, "white" look, leave the skins on and savor the extra nutrition.

Cooking time: 8–9 hours
Preparation time: 20 minutes
Attention: Minimal
Pot size: 3–6 quarts
Serves 6

Cauliflower and Ham Chowder

2 cups ham, diced
3 cups fresh cauliflower, chopped
1 small white onion
1 cup canned evaporated milk
2 tablespoons flour
1 cup Swiss cheese, grated
2 cups water
1 cup light cream

1. Cut the ham into ½-inch pieces. Cut the cauliflower into ½-inch pieces. Peel the onion and chop finely.
2. Mix the evaporated milk and flour in the slow cooker.
3. Add the ham, cauliflower, onion, Swiss cheese, and water. Cover and cook on low setting for 8 to 9 hours.
4. Ten minutes before serving, stir in the cream.

Serve with an array of pickled vegetables to offset the creamy sweet flavor of this soup.

The Squash Bowl

Use squash as a soup bowl. Many small squash make excellent complements to soups and stews. Cut them in half, remove the seeds and prebake in the microwave or oven. Ladle your soup or stew into the squash for a festive look.

A Bit of Everything Soup

Cooking time: 8–10 hours
Preparation time: 30 minutes
Attention: Minimal
Pot size: 4–8 quarts
Serves 8

6 slices bacon
1 pound ham
1 pound beef
2 skinless chicken breasts
6 medium carrots
3 celery ribs
1 large yellow onion
1 cup fresh green beans
1 cup fresh peas
1 cup fresh corn

1 pound crabmeat,
  chunks or shredded
1 teaspoon table salt
¼ teaspoon ground black
  pepper
6 cups water

1. Brown the bacon in a medium-sized skillet on medium-high heat; place on paper towels to cool, then break into crumbles. Cut ham, beef, and chicken into 1-inch cubes. Peel the carrots and slice into ¼-inch thick discs. Slice the celery ¼-inch thick. Peel the onion and slice into ¼-inch pieces. Remove the stems from the green beans.
2. Add all ingredients except peas and crabmeat to the slow cooker. Cover and cook on low setting for 7 to 9 hours. Add peas and crab-meat, and cook for 1 to 2 hours.

Serve with an assortment of crackers and cheeses.

Brown Scum

Don't fear, this is a natural product of slow cooking, especially when chicken with bones is used. It's simply the bone marrow combined with the spices and fat. Just skim it off and serve your tasty soup.

Pork, Pea, and Spinach Curry Soup

Cooking time: 10–12 hours
Preparation time: 20 minutes
Attention: Minimal
Pot size: 3–6 quarts
Serves 8

1½-pound pork roast
1 cup baby carrots
1 celery rib
1 medium-sized white onion
1 cup yellow split peas, rinsed
6 cups chicken broth
2 teaspoons curry powder
½ teaspoon paprika
¼ teaspoon ground cumin
¼ teaspoon ground black pepper
2 cups fresh spinach, torn

1. Trim the fat from the pork roast and cut into ½-inch cubes.
   Cut the baby carrots in half. Chop the celery into ¼-inch pieces.
   Peel and chop the onion into ¼-inch pieces.
2. Add all the ingredients except the spinach to slow cooker. Stir well.
   Cover and cook on low setting for 10 to 12 hours.
3. Tear the spinach into 1-inch pieces; stir into soup right before serving.

Serve with Slightly Seedy White Bread (page 84).

Curry, Please
Curry powder is not one spice, but a combination of anywhere from 15 to 50 different spices. Madras curry typically has the fullest, richest flavor.

Cousin Jimmy's Favorite Lima Bean Soup

Cooking time:	8–10 hours
Preparation time:	20 minutes
Attention:	Minimal
Pot size:	3–6 quarts
Serves 8	

1 large yellow onion
2 ribs celery
3 large potatoes
3 medium carrots
2 cups kielbasa, sliced
1-pound bag large dry lima beans
1 tablespoon table salt
1 teaspoon pepper
1 teaspoon dried oregano
2 bay leaves
6 cups beef broth
4 cups water

1. Peel the onion and chop into ¼-inch pieces. Chop the celery into ¼-inch pieces. Peel the potatoes and cut into ½-inch cubes. Peel the carrots and cut into ¼-inch pieces. Slice the kielbasa into ¼-inch rounds. Rinse the lima beans.
2. Add all ingredients to the slow cooker; stir well. Cover and cook on low setting for 8 to 10 hours. Remove the bay leaves before serving.

Serve with Heavy Brown Bread (page 85) and an assortment of cheeses.

How Much Water Do I Use?
When cooking soup, add only enough water to cover the ingredients. More water can be added a few minutes before serving if a thinner soup is desired.

Cooking time: 4–5 hours

Preparation time: 30 minutes

Cheesy Broccoli Noodle Soup

Attention: Minimal

Pot size: 3–6 quarts

Serves 6

2 cups noodles

2 cups fresh broccoli, chopped

1 medium-sized white onion

2 cups processed cheese, cubed

2 tablespoons butter

1 tablespoon flour

½ teaspoon table salt

5½ cups skim milk

1. Cook the noodles in boiling water in a saucepan until they are limp but still crunchy in the middle. Chop the broccoli into 1-inch pieces. Peel and chop the onion into ¼-inch pieces. Cut the cheese into ½-inch cubes.

2. Combine all ingredients in the slow cooker. Cover and cook on low setting for 4 to 5 hours.

Serve as a first course for Beef Roast with Dried Fruit (page 102).

Slow-Cooker Buffet

Don't forget the slow cooker at your next large buffet. Add a soup or hot hors d'oeuvre to the menu for a fast and easy way to serve a crowd.

Cooking time: 7–9 hours

Preparation time: 30 minutes

Attention: Minimal

Pot size: 3–8 quarts

Ham and Chicken Gumbo

Serves 8

1½ pounds chicken breasts
½ pound smoked ham
1 tablespoon oil
1 cup fresh okra, sliced
2 medium-sized white onions
1 medium-sized green bell pepper
4 large red tomatoes
¼ cup canned or fresh green
   chilies, diced

2 tablespoons fresh cilantro,
   chopped
6 cups chicken broth
3 (16-ounce) cans navy beans **or**
   3½–4 cups dry navy beans,
   cooked
½ cup dry white rice
¾ teaspoon table salt
½ teaspoon ground black pepper

1. Remove the bones and skin from the chicken and discard. Cut the chicken and ham into 1-inch pieces. Place the oil, ham, and chicken in medium-sized skillet and cook on medium heat until chicken is no longer pink inside. Cut the okra into ¼-inch pieces. Peel the onions and cut into ¼-inch pieces. Remove the stem and seeds from the green pepper and chop into ¼-inch pieces. Cut the tomatoes into ½-inch pieces. Dice the green chilies with a sharp paring knife. Chop the cilantro into ¼-inch pieces.
2. Combine all the ingredients except the cilantro in the slow cooker. Cover and cook on low setting for 7 to 9 hours. Stir in cilantro right before serving.

Serve with Slightly Seedy White Bread (page 84) and an assortment of cheeses.

Cooking rice

Processed white rice typically needs less water added than long-grain brown rice or wild rice, which can take up to six cups of water per cup of dry rice. If in doubt, read the package directions.

Clam, Chicken, and Ham Chowder

Cooking time: 8–10 hours
Preparation time: 30 minutes
Attention: Minimal
Pot size: 3–8 quarts
Serves 8

4 chicken breasts
1 pound bacon
½ pound ham
2 large yellow onions
4 medium carrots
4 celery ribs
4 medium potatoes
1 cup clams, with juice
2 cups whole kernel corn,
   with liquid

4 cups chicken broth
½ teaspoon table salt
½ teaspoon ground black pepper
1 bunch green onions
¾ cup flour
4 cups milk
4 cups Cheddar cheese, shredded
½ cup whipping cream

1. Remove the skin and bones from the chicken breasts and cut meat into 1-inch pieces. Cut the bacon into 1-inch pieces. Cut the ham into ½-inch cubes. Peel the yellow onions and chop into ¼-inch pieces. Peel the carrots and chop into ¼-inch rounds. Chop the celery into ¼-inch pieces. Peel the potatoes and cut into ½-inch cubes.

2. Put the bacon, ham, and chicken meat in a large skillet with the celery and yellow onions; sauté on medium heat until the bacon is crisp. Drain grease off and put the mixture in the slow cooker. Add the carrots, potatoes, clams, corn, salt, pepper, and chicken broth. Cover and cook on low setting for 7 to 9 hours.

3. Remove the roots and first layer of peel from the green onions and chop the onions, including the green stems, into ¼-inch pieces. In a medium mixing bowl combine the flour, milk, cheese, and cream. Whisk quickly until slightly frothy; stir into soup. Cover and cook on low setting for 1 hour. Stir in the green onions right before serving.

Serve with an assortment of pickled vegetables and cheeses.

Cooking time: 4 hours

Preparation time: 15 minutes

Attention: Minimal

Pot size: 3–8 quarts

Serves 6

Beer Soup

2 ½ tablespoons butter
1 ½ tablespoons flour
2 cups pilsner beer
½ cinnamon stick
½ teaspoon sugar
2 egg yolks
½ cup milk

1. Melt the butter in a medium-sized skillet on medium heat. Add the flour and cook until the flour browns; transfer the flour mixture to the slow cooker. Add the beer, cinnamon, and sugar. Cover and cook on high setting for 4 hours.
2. Turn slow cooker down to low setting. Whisk together the egg yolks and milk; stir into the soup. Cook 15 minutes uncovered on high setting. Strain before serving.

Serve as a first course for Sparkling Beef Tips (page 109)

Problems with Cinnamon

While it tastes wonderful, cinnamon is a tricky spice. It can kill yeast, causing bread not to rise. It also does not permeate a soup or stew but tends to remain on top of the liquid.

Italian Vegetable Soup

Cooking time: 6–8 hours
Preparation time: 20 minutes
Attention: Minimal
Pot size: 3–6 quarts
Serves 6

2 pounds hamburger
1 small zucchini
3 medium potatoes
1 can corn
1 (16-ounce) can tomato sauce
2 tablespoons ground oregano
⅛ teaspoon basil
½ teaspoon garlic salt
3 bay leaves

1. Brown the hamburger in a medium-sized skillet on medium-high heat on the stove; drain off the grease.
2. Cut the zucchini into ½-inch pieces. Peel and cut the potatoes into ½-inch squares.
3. Add all ingredients to the slow cooker. Cook covered on low setting for 6 to 8 hours.

Serve with a side of garlic buttered linguine.

Removing Bay Leaves

Bay leaves add flavor to a dish, but be sure to remove them before serving food. The leaves can be sharp.

Cooking time: 7–9 hours

Preparation time: 20 minutes

Attention: Minimal

Pot size: 3–8 quarts

Serves 8

Barley Lamb Soup

2½ pounds lamb
2 medium-sized white onions
3 celery ribs
3 cups parsley, chopped
3 tablespoons butter
1 cup medium-sized barley
½ teaspoon table salt
½ teaspoon ground black pepper
1 bay leaf
6 cups water

1. Cut the lamb into 1-inch cubes, trimming off the fat as you cut. Peel and chop the onions into ¼-inch pieces. Chop the celery, including leaves, into ¼-inch pieces. Chop the parsley into ½-inch pieces.
2. Heat the butter in a large skillet on medium heat until brown; add the lamb and sauté for about 10 minutes. Using a slotted spoon, remove the meat from the skillet and put it into the slow cooker. Add the onion to the skillet and sauté until translucent. Drain off the grease and add the onion to the slow cooker. Add the celery, parsley, barley, salt, pepper, bay leaf, and water to the slow cooker. Cover and cook on low setting for 7 to 9 hours.

Serve with a fresh green salad and hard-boiled eggs.

How to Sauté

When a recipe calls for sautéing, cook the food on medium-high to high heat in a frying pan. Oil is the most common ingredient in which to sauté although water and flavored vinegar are good, low-fat alternatives.

Cooking time: 8–10 hours

Preparation time: 30 minutes

Attention: Minimal

Pot size: 3–8 quarts

Curried Tomato Soup

Serves 8

1 medium-sized white onion
2 garlic cloves
12 plum tomatoes
4 cups chicken broth
1 tablespoon curry powder
¼ teaspoon cinnamon
½ teaspoon table salt
4 cups dry egg noodles

1. Peel the onion and chop into ¼-inch pieces. Peel the garlic and mince with a sharp kitchen knife. Chop the tomatoes into ¼-inch pieces.
2. Combine all the ingredients except the egg noodles in the slow cooker. Cover and cook on low setting for 7 to 9 hours.
3. Add the egg noodles. Cover and cook on low setting 1 additional hour.

Use as a first course for East Indian Green Curried Chicken (page 212).

Cooking with Tomatoes

When using fresh tomatoes in a recipe, be sure to cook them for at least four hours on the low setting. This will release the acid and the dish will taste much more mellow. It also will prevent your guests from getting heartburn.

Golden Potato, Ham, and Vidalia Onion Soup

Cooking time: 8–10 hours

Preparation time: 15 minutes

Attention: Minimal

Pot size: 3–8 quarts

Serves 8

1 cup ham

2 large Vidalia onions

½ small red bell pepper

4 large golden potatoes

2 cups chicken broth

½ teaspoon ground black pepper

1 cup skim milk

1 cup ricotta cheese

1. Cut the ham into ½-inch pieces. Peel and cut the onions into ¼-inch pieces. Remove the stem and seeds from the red pepper and cut into ¼-inch pieces. Peel the potatoes and cut into ½-inch pieces.

2. Add the ham, onions, bell pepper, potatoes, chicken broth, and black pepper to the slow cooker. Cover and cook on low setting for 8 to 10 hours. A half-hour before serving, add skim milk and ricotta cheese; mix in. Cover and continue to cook on low setting.

Serve with gourmet crackers and fresh vegetables such as red pepper, carrot and celery sticks.

Wisconsin Cheesy Beer Soup

Cooking time: 1–2 hours

Preparation time: 10 minutes

Attention: Frequent

Pot size: 3–8 quarts

Serves 8

1 large onion

1 cup sharp Cheddar cheese

½ cup vegetable broth

1 cup pilsner beer

2 cups 1 percent milk

½ teaspoon garlic powder

½ teaspoon ground black pepper

Peel the onion and chop into ¼-inch pieces. Shred the cheese with a vegetable grater. Combine all ingredients in the slow cooker. Cover and cook on low setting for 1 to 2 hours, stirring every 10 minutes. Do not overcook, as the cheese will begin to separate.

Serve sprinkled with freshly made white popcorn.

Easy Corn and Cheese Chowder

Cooking time: 8–9 hours

Preparation time: 15 minutes

Attention: Minimal

Pot size: 3–6 quarts

Serves 6

1 medium-sized yellow onion
4 medium carrots
4 celery ribs
1½ cups shredded Cheddar cheese
¾ cup water
1 teaspoon table salt
1 teaspoon ground black pepper
2 cups whole kernel corn, canned or fresh
2 cups canned creamed corn
3 cups milk

1. Remove peel and chop the onion into ¼-inch pieces. Peel the carrots and chop into ¼-inch slices. Chop the celery into ¼-inch slices.
2. Combine the water, onions, carrots, celery, salt, and pepper in slow cooker. Cover and cook on low setting for 8 to 9 hours. One hour before serving, add the corn, milk, and cheese. Cover and cook on low setting for 1 more hour.

Using Frozen Corn

Substitute canned or frozen corn in any recipe calling for fresh corn. It holds up well even over several hours of cooking. And because the kernels are small, even frozen corn heats up quickly.

Creamy Asparagus and Leek Soup

Cooking time: 8–10 hours

Preparation time: 20 minutes

Attention: Medium

Pot size: 3–8 quarts

Serves 6

2 medium potatoes
2 large leeks
3 medium carrots
2 celery ribs
2 pounds asparagus
2 teaspoons thyme
4 cups chicken broth
2 cups 1 percent milk

1. Peel and chop the potatoes and leeks into ¼-inch pieces. Chop the carrots and celery into ¼-inch pieces. Remove the tips from the asparagus and set aside. Chop the green part of the stalks into ¼-inch pieces.
2. Put the carrots, celery, potatoes, leek, thyme, asparagus stalks, and chicken broth in slow cooker. Cover and cook on low setting for 7 to 9 hours.
3. Put the mixture into a blender and purée until creamy. Stir in the milk and add the asparagus tips. Cover and cook on low setting for 1 additional hour.

Serve with Zucchini Bread (page 79) for a nice blend of flavors.

Too-Thin Soups

Try adding half the recommended water. If it's still runny, remove the cover from the slow cooker for an hour or two before serving.

Cooking time: 8–10 hours
Preparation time: 30 minutes
Attention: Minimal
Pot size: 3–8 quarts
Serves 8

Swedish Fruit Soup

1 cup dried apricots
1 cup dried apples
1 cup dried prunes
1 cup dried pears
1 cup dried peaches
1 cup canned dark, sweet cherries, pitted
½ cup sweet red wine
1 cup orange juice
¼ cup lemon juice
½ cup brown sugar
½ cup quick-cooking tapioca

1. Cut dried fruit into 1-inch pieces.
2. Add all the ingredients to the slow cooker; stir well. Cover and cook on low setting for 8 to 10 hours.
3. Check after 5 hours to determine if water needs to be added (it should have the consistency of a light syrup—if it is thicker than that, add ½ cup water).

This is excellent served warm over a traditional white cake with vanilla ice cream.

Low-Fat Sautéing

For a fat-free alternative, add flavored vinegars when sautéing meats and vegetables. They will add a light flavor to the dish and tend to blend well with almost any recipe.

Danish Pork and Pea Soup

Cooking time: 8–10 hours

Preparation time: 30 minutes

Attention: Minimal

Pot size: 3–8 quarts

Serves 8

1 pound yellow split peas
2 pounds lean bacon
1 pound pork sausage links
4 medium leeks
3 medium carrots
2 celery ribs
1 teaspoon salt
1 teaspoon ground black pepper
6 cups vegetable stock

1. Rinse the split peas. Chop the bacon and sausage into 1-inch pieces. Peel the leeks and chop into ¼-inch pieces. Cut the celery and carrots into ¼-inch pieces.
2. Put the bacon and sausage into a large skillet and cook on medium-high heat until meat is brown on all sides; drain off the grease. Spread out the meat on paper towels to absorb more grease.
3. Add all ingredients to the slow cooker. Cover and cook on low setting for 8 to 10 hours.

Serve with open-faced cucumber and cream cheese sandwiches on rye toast.

De-Fatting Meat

To remove most of the fat from ground beef or bacon, cook it in the microwave, then lay it on several paper towels to drain. Lay a paper towel on top of the meat and pat it lightly before adding to the slow cooker.

CHAPTER 4
All-In-One Meals

Hamburger Potato Casserole

Cooking time: 7–9 hours

Preparation time: 20 minutes

Attention: Minimal

Pot size: 4–6 quarts

Serves 4

1 pound lean ground beef
3 medium potatoes
4 medium carrots
1 medium-sized yellow onion
1 cup fresh peas
2 tablespoons dry white rice
1 teaspoon table salt
½ teaspoon ground black pepper
1 cup tomato juice

1. Brown the beef in a medium skillet on medium-high heat; drain off the grease. Peel the potatoes and cut into ¼-inch slices. Peel the carrots and slice into ¼-inch rounds. Peel the onion and cut into ¼-inch pieces.

2. Combine all ingredients except peas in the slow cooker; stir well. Cover and cook on low setting for 5 to 7 hours. Add peas and cook for 2 hours.

Serve with Hot Fruit Medley (page 302) for dessert.

Save the Veggies for Last

Add quick-cooking vegetables no more than two hours before serving. Peas especially can become too mushy if added early, so if you don't want them like that, add them later.

Cooking time: 5–6 hours
Preparation time: 20 minutes
Attention: Medium
Pot size: 3–6 quart
Serves 8

Spinach, Cheese, and Egg Casserole

2 bunches fresh spinach
2 cups cottage cheese
1½ cups Cheddar cheese, grated
3 eggs
¼ cup flour
1 teaspoon table salt
½ cup butter, melted

1. Clean the spinach in cold water and remove the stems. Tear the leaves into 1-inch pieces. Place the spinach leaves, cottage cheese, and Cheddar cheese in a large mixing bowl.
2. In a small bowl, combine the eggs, flour, table salt, and butter, mixing well until all the ingredients are melded; pour over the spinach mixture. Mix well with a wooden spoon.
3. Pour mixture into the slow cooker and cook covered on high setting for 1 hour. Stir well after the hour is up and reduce heat to low setting.
4. Cover and cook 4 to 5 additional hours.

Try this for an elegant Sunday brunch. Complement it with champagne and buttery croissants. Your guests will never believe you made it in the slow cooker!

Hold the Yolk

Egg yolks contain all of the fat and cholesterol in an egg. Use egg whites instead of whole eggs when making pasta, cakes and other dishes. Usually two egg whites can be substituted for one whole egg.

Cooking time: 8–9 hours

Preparation time: 20 minutes

Attention: Minimal

Pot size: 4–6 quarts

Serves 6

Corned Beef Dinner

2 yellow onions
6 small potatoes
12 carrots
1 rutabaga, peeled and
*   quartered*
6 ribs celery

1 head cabbage
3 pounds corned beef brisket
2 bay leaves
20 black peppercorns
2 cups water

1. Peel the onions and slice into quarters. Peel the potatoes and slice in halves. Peel the carrots and cut into quarters. Peel the rutabaga and slice into eight pieces. Cut the celery ribs into quarters. Cut the cabbage into eight pieces.
2. Place the corned beef brisket in the bottom of the slow cooker. Put the bay leaves and peppercorns on top. Layer the vegetables in the following order: onions, potatoes, celery, carrots, cabbage, and rutabaga. Add water. Cook covered on low setting for 8 to 9 hours, or until the rutabaga is soft.
3. Remove the bay leaves before serving. Cut the meat into thin slices across the grain.

Arrange the meat and vegetables on a large platter. Use the juice left in the bottom of the slow cooker as you would gravy.

Hard Potatoes

Try cooking them for less time; add them later in the cooking process. Or, if you're making a pot roast, put them into the slow cooker whole.

Sausage and Fall Vegetable Harvest

Cooking time: 6–8 hours
Preparation time: 20 minutes
Attention: Minimal
Pot size: 3–6 quarts
Serves 4

1 pound acorn squash
2 medium potatoes
4 carrots
4 ribs celery
¼ cup green bell pepper, chopped
2 yellow onions
1 cup zucchini, sliced
1 cup fresh or frozen peas
1 cup fresh or frozen green beans

2 cups fresh or canned beef broth
2 tablespoons red wine
¼ teaspoon ground black pepper
1 teaspoon dried, crushed rosemary
*½ pound sausage in large round links **or** patties*
2 tablespoons flour
½ cup warm water

1. Peel the squash and cut into ½-inch cubes. (Squash has a very tough skin so use a large, sharp knife and work on a hard surface.) Peel the potatoes and cut into ½-inch cubes. Peel the carrots and cut into 1-inch lengths. Cut the celery ribs into 1-inch lengths. Core the green pepper and chop with a medium-sized knife into pieces about ¼-inch square. Peel the onions and quarter. Cut the zucchini into slices about ¼-inch thick.

2. Combine the squash, potatoes, carrots, celery, zucchini, green beans, broth, wine, black pepper, and rosemary in slow cooker.

3. Cut the sausage into ½-inch slices. If using sausage patties, break them into marble-sized chunks. Combine the sausage, green peppers, and onions in a frying pan and cook on medium-high heat until the sausage and onions are browned. Drain off the grease and lay the mixture on paper towels for 2 minutes to soak up additional grease. Add the sausage, onions, and green peppers to the vegetables in the slow cooker. Cook covered on low heat for 6 to 8 hours.

4. One hour before serving, add the peas, and use a fork to mix 2 tablespoons flour and ½ cup water in a small bowl until the mixture is smooth; add this to the vegetables and sausage, stirring until it is well mixed. Cook covered for 1 additional hour.

Serve with Heavy Brown Bread (page 85) and cream cheese.

Cooking time: 6–8 hours	
Preparation time: 30 minutes	
Attention: Minimal	
Pot size: 4–6 quarts	
Serves 8	

Mixed Meat Tetrazzini

1 bunch small green onions
1 cup celery
½ cup pimiento-stuffed green olives, chopped
1 green bell pepper
½ pound fresh mushrooms

1 cup chicken, precooked and cubed
1 cup turkey, precooked and cubed
1 cup ham, precooked and cubed
1 pound package spaghetti
1 tablespoon dried parsley
3 cups chicken broth

1. Peel and chop the green onions into ¼-inch pieces. Chop the celery and olives into ¼-inch pieces. Remove the stem and seeds from the green pepper and chop pepper into ¼-inch pieces. Clean the mushrooms by wiping them with a damp cloth, then slice paper-thin. Precook meat in the microwave or use leftover meats; cut into 1-inch cubes. Break the spaghetti noodles into approximately 1-inch lengths.
2. Layer ingredients in the slow cooker in the following order:
   1. Spaghetti
   2. Meats
   3. Onions
   4. Olives
   5. Celery and parsley
   6. Pepper
   7. Mushrooms
3. Pour the chicken broth over the top. Cover and cook on low setting for 6 to 8 hours.

Scoop out of the slow cooker with a large serving spoon and sprinkle with Parmesan cheese before serving.

Pasta Twist

For a different taste in your next pasta dish, experiment with vegetable pastas such as tomato or spinach. They frequently have a more substantial consistency and more nutrients than regular pasta.

Cooking time: 4–6 hours

Preparation time: 15 minutes

Attention: Minimal

Pot size: 3–6 quarts

Serves 4

Smoky Beef and Beans Dinner

1 pound lean ground beef
1 large yellow onion
¾ pound bacon
2 cans pork and beans
1 can lima beans
1 can kidney beans
1 cup ketchup
¼ cup brown sugar
1 tablespoon liquid smoke flavoring
3 tablespoons white vinegar
1 teaspoon salt
½ teaspoon ground black pepper

1. Place the ground beef in a medium-sized skillet on the stove; cook on medium-high heat, stirring until the meat is brown. Drain off grease and place the meat in the slow cooker.
2. Peel and chop the onion into ¼-inch pieces. Slice the bacon into 1-inch pieces. Place the bacon and onion in skillet and cook on medium-high heat, stirring until the bacon is crisp.
3. Put all ingredients in the slow cooker; stir well. Cook covered on low setting 4 to 6 hours.

Serve with Raisin Bread Pudding (page 310) for dessert.

The Interchangeable Bean

Substitute beans at will. Go to your local food co-op and try those different-looking beans in your next chili or bean soup. All beans taste fairly mild so you can't make a drastic mistake and you may find a new favorite.

New Orleans–Style Jambalaya

Cooking time: 7–8 hours

Preparation time: 45 minutes

Attention: Medium

Pot size: 4–8 quarts

Serves 8

1 (3-pound) chicken

1 pound hot smoked sausage

3 tablespoons olive oil

1 cup celery, chopped

¾ cup fresh parsley, chopped

1 large yellow onion

⅔ cup green pepper, chopped

2 garlic cloves

8 whole tomatoes

1 cup green onions, chopped

2 cups chicken broth

1 (6-ounce) can tomato paste

1½ teaspoons thyme

2 bay leaves

2 teaspoons oregano

1 teaspoon chili powder

1 teaspoon salt

½ teaspoon cayenne pepper

1 teaspoon ground black pepper

1 teaspoon garlic powder

2 cups uncooked long grain rice, washed and rinsed

3 pounds raw shrimp

New Orleans–Style
Jambalaya (continued)

1. Place the chicken in a large pot on the stove; cover with water and boil for 1 hour. Remove the chicken and cut the meat off the bones; discard the skin. Cut the meat into bite-size pieces and place in the slow cooker.

2. Cut the sausage into ¼-inch-thick pieces. Place in a large frying pan with the olive oil on the stove and cook on medium heat until brown. Remove the meat with a slotted spoon and place it on paper towels to absorb remaining grease.

3. Chop the celery and parsley into ¼-inch pieces. Peel the onion and chop into ¼-inch pieces. Remove the seeds and stem from the green pepper and chop the pepper into ¼-inch pieces. Mince the garlic using a sharp kitchen knife. Place the celery, parsley, onion, green pepper, and garlic in the frying pan and sauté in the sausage grease on medium heat for five minutes. Drain grease.

4. Cut the tomatoes into quarters. Remove the roots and outer layer of skin from the green onions and chop into ¼-inch pieces, including the green stems. Place all the ingredients except the shrimp in slow cooker; stir to combine and cook covered on low setting 6 to 7 hours.

5. One hour before serving, boil the shrimp in water for 10 minutes. Remove shells and devein by running a fork tine up the back of the shrimp. Add shrimp to slow cooker; stir well. Cook covered on low setting for 1 hour.

Serve with a light dessert such as Swedish Fruit Soup (page 43) over vanilla ice cream.

Cooking time: 8½–10½ hours

Preparation time: 15 minutes

Attention: Minimal

Pot size: 4–6 quarts

Chicken and Dumplings

Serves 4

1 (3-pound) chicken, cut up
½ cup chicken broth or bouillon
2 teaspoons salt
½ teaspoon ground black
  pepper
½ teaspoon poultry seasoning

3 stalks celery
3 medium carrots
1 small yellow onion
2 cups packaged biscuit mix
¾ cup milk
1 teaspoon dried parsley flakes

1. Wash the chicken pieces and cut away excess fat. Place the chicken pieces in the slow cooker. Add broth. Sprinkle with salt, pepper, and poultry seasoning.
2. Chop the celery and carrots into 1-inch lengths. Peel and chop the onion into ¼-inch pieces; place celery, carrots, and onion on top of the chicken. Cover and cook on low setting 8 to 10 hours.
3. About a half-hour before serving, combine the biscuit mix, milk, and parsley flakes; stir until all the biscuit mix is moistened. Drop by tea-spoonfuls onto top of the mixture in the slow cooker. Cover and cook for 30 minutes.

Serve immediately after the dumplings are cooked to ensure they don't become rubbery and tasteless. Sprinkle parsley flakes over individual servings.

Layering Ingredients

For best results, layer meals with heavy vegetables such as potatoes and carrots on the bottom then lighter vegetables such as corn and peas on top. Add the meat above the vegetables. Add liquid and spices to the top of the mixture.

Cooking time: 7–9 hours

Preparation time: 15 minutes

Attention: Minimal

Pot size: 3–6 quarts

New England Dinner

Serves 6

6 medium carrots
2 medium-sized yellow onions
4 celery ribs
1 small head cabbage
3-pound boneless chuck roast
½ teaspoon table salt
½ teaspoon ground black pepper
1 envelope dry onion soup mix
2 cups water
1 tablespoon vinegar
1 bay leaf

1. Clean the carrots and cut in half. Peel the onions and slice into quarters. Cut the celery ribs in half. Remove outer leaves from the cabbage, then cut the head into eighths.
2. Place the carrots, onion, and celery in the slow cooker. Put the roast on top. Sprinkle with salt and pepper, then add the soup mix, water, vinegar, and bay leaf on top. Add the cabbage. Do not mix ingredients. Cover and cook on low setting for 7 to 9 hours.

Serve with a dip made of half horseradish and half sour cream.

Spicing It Up

Instead of a marinade, rub meat with dry seasonings before placing in the slow cooker. You can buy prepared mixes or experiment with some of your favorites. Dried garlic, onion, and parsley are a good place to start.

Ten-Story Casserole

Cooking time: 4 hours

Preparation time: 20 minutes

Attention: Minimal

Pot size: 3–6 quarts

Serves 6

1½ pounds ground turkey
6 medium potatoes
2 medium-sized white onions
½ teaspoon table salt
½ teaspoon ground black pepper
1 (15-ounce) can corn
1 (15-ounce) can peas
1 (10¾-ounce) can cream of celery condensed soup
¼ cup water

1. Brown the turkey in a medium-sized skillet on medium-high heat. Drain off grease and spread the turkey on paper towels to cool. Peel the potatoes and cut into ¼-inch slices. Peel the onions and slice into ¼-inch rings.
2. Place ingredients in the slow cooker in the following layers:
    1. One-fourth of potatoes, half of onions, sprinkle of salt, sprinkle of pepper
    2. Half can of corn
    3. One-fourth of potatoes
    4. Half can peas
    5. One-fourth of potatoes, remaining half of onions, sprinkle of salt, sprinkle of pepper
    6. Half can corn
    7. One-fourth of potatoes
    8. Half can peas
    9. Turkey
    10. Cream of celery soup and water
3. Cover and cook on high setting for 4 hours.

Serve with a dessert of Strawberry Rhubarb Sauce (page 313) over vanilla ice cream.

Black Forest Sausage and Sauerkraut

Cooking time: 8–9 hours

Preparation time: 20 minutes

Attention: Minimal

Pot size: 3–6 quarts

Serves 6

2½ pounds fresh Polish sausage
6 medium carrots
6 medium potatoes
2 medium yellow onions
3 cloves garlic
4 cups sauerkraut
1½ cups dry white wine
1 teaspoon caraway seeds
½ teaspoon ground black pepper

1. Cut the Polish sausage into 3-inch pieces. Peel the carrots and cut into 3-inch lengths. Peel the potatoes and cut into 1-inch cubes. Peel the onions and cut into ¼-inch rings. Peel the garlic and mince with a sharp kitchen knife. Rinse and drain the sauerkraut.
2. Brown the sausage in a skillet at medium-high heat; drain off grease and transfer sausage to the slow cooker. Add remaining ingredients to the slow cooker. Cover and cook on low setting for 8 to 9 hours.

Serve with Scalloped Fruit Cocktail (page 309) for dessert.

Lower-fat Sausage

Pre-cook sausage in the microwave to reduce the fat content. If you like crispy sausage in recipes, brown it beforehand and add it to the recipe during the last half hour.

Wyoming Cowboy Casserole

Cooking time: 4 hours

Preparation time: 15 minutes

Attention: Minimal

Pot size: 3–6 quarts

Serves 4

1 pound lean ground beef

1 cup Colby cheese, cubed

1 (10¾-ounce) can condensed tomato
  soup

1 (16-ounce) can whole kernel corn

1 (16-ounce) can red kidney beans

¼ cup milk

1 teaspoon dry onion flakes

½ teaspoon chili powder

1. Brown the beef in a medium-sized skilled on medium-high heat; drain off grease. Spread the beef on paper towels to cool. Cut the cheese into ½-inch cubes.
2. Add all ingredients to the slow cooker. Cover and cook on low for 4 hours.

Serve over biscuits.

Shepherd's Pie

Cooking time: 6–8 hours

Preparation time: 15 minutes

Attention: Minimal

Pot size: 3–6 quarts

Serves 4

1 pound beef steak

3 medium carrots

1 cup fresh green beans

1 medium-sized yellow onion

1 cup fresh peas

1 cup canned or frozen sweet corn

1 teaspoon table salt

1 teaspoon ground black pepper

2 cups beef gravy

6 cups leftover mashed potatoes

1. Cut the meat into 1-inch cubes. Peel and chop the carrots into ¼-inch rounds. Remove the stems from the beans and cut the beans in half. Peel the onion and chop into ¼-inch pieces.
2. Combine the vegetables, salt, pepper, meat, and gravy in the slow cooker. Top with mashed potatoes. Cover and cook on low setting for 6 to 8 hours.

Serve with Raisin and Orange Baked Apples (page 304) for dessert.

Kielbasa and Cabbage Dinner

Cooking time: 7–8 hours

Preparation time: 15 minutes

Attention: Minimal

Pot size: 4–6 quarts

Serves 6

1½ pounds kielbasa
2 medium yellow onions
4 medium potatoes
1 red bell pepper
4 large ripe tomatoes
2 garlic cloves
1½ heads green cabbage
1 cup dry white wine
1 tablespoon Dijon mustard
¾ teaspoon caraway seeds
½ teaspoon ground black pepper
¾ teaspoon table salt

1. Cut the kielbasa into 3-inch pieces. Peel the onions and chop into ¼-inch pieces. Peel the potatoes and cut into 1-inch cubes. Remove the stem and seeds from the red pepper and chop into ¼-inch pieces. Chop the tomatoes into ½-inch pieces. Peel the garlic and mince with a sharp paring knife. Shred the cabbage into ¼-inch strips with a sharp kitchen knife.
2. Combine all ingredients in the slow cooker. Cover and cook on low setting for 7 to 8 hours.

Serve with Rice Pudding (page 306) for dessert.

Slicing Meat

To slice thin strips of meat, position a cleaver or large knife at a 45-degree angle to the meat and slice it across the grain into strips.

Smoky Little Sausage Hot Dish

Cooking time: 6–7 hours

Preparation time: 15 minutes

Attention: Minimal

Pot size: 3–6 quarts

Serves 4

1 pound smoky wieners

2 cups cooked macaroni

1 medium-sized yellow onion

¾ cup American cheese

3 tablespoons pimientos, chopped

3 tablespoons flour

¾ teaspoon table salt

¼ teaspoon ground black pepper

1 cup milk

1 cup water

½ tablespoon vinegar

1 cup fresh peas

1 teaspoon dry parsley

1. Cut the wieners into 1-inch lengths. Cook the macaroni in boiling water until soft but not mushy. Peel the onion and chop into ¼-inch pieces. Grate the cheese using a vegetable grater. Chop the pimientos into ¼-inch pieces.

2. Combine the cheese, flour, salt, pepper, milk, water, and vinegar in a medium-sized saucepan on the stove; cook on medium heat, stirring frequently, until the mixture is smooth and thick. Pour into the slow cooker. Add the wieners, macaroni, peas, onions, parsley, and pimientos; stir well. Cover and cook on low setting for 6 to 7 hours.

Serve with Grandma's Apples and Rice (page 305) for dessert.

CHAPTER 5

Vegetarian

Mexican-Style Stuffed Red Peppers

Cooking time:	4–6 hours
Preparation time:	30 minutes
Attention:	Minimal
Pot size:	4–6 quarts
Serves 4	

4 large red bell peppers
2 cloves garlic
½ cup green chives, chopped
1 large tomato
2 sprigs fresh cilantro
½ cup cooked rice
½ cup cooked black beans
　(fresh or canned)

½ cup fresh, canned, or
　frozen corn
½ teaspoon dried crushed basil
¼ teaspoon ground black pepper
½ teaspoon chili powder
½ cup tomato sauce
2 cups water
¼ cup Cheddar cheese, shredded

1. Remove the stem and seeds from the red peppers. Peel the garlic and mince with a sharp kitchen knife. Chop the chives into ¼-inch pieces. Chop the tomato into ¼-inch pieces. Crush the cilantro or mince with a sharp knife.
2. Combine the rice, beans, chives, corn, diced tomatoes, garlic, cilantro, basil, black pepper, and chili powder in a bowl; mix well with a large spoon. Use an ice cream scoop to spoon a portion of the mixture into each red pepper. The mixture should come to the top of the peppers but should not overflow.
3. Pour the tomato sauce and water into the slow cooker. Place the stuffed red peppers in the slow cooker so they stand upright. Cook covered on low setting for 4 to 6 hours. Five minutes before serving, sprinkle Cheddar cheese on the top of each red pepper. Cover and cook on low setting until cheese melts.

Spread butter on flour tortillas, sprinkle on garlic salt, and bake in a 350-degree oven for 10 minutes to create a crunchy complement to this meal.

Mushrooms for Meat

To turn any meat dish into an instant vegetarian entrée, substitute Morel mushrooms for the meat. Be sure to substitute by volume, not weight because even these heavier mushrooms weigh less than meat.

Cooking time: 8–10 hours

Preparation time: 20 minutes

Attention: Medium

Pot size: 5–6 quarts

Serves 8

Garlicky Red Beans

1 pound red beans
3 cups water
1 medium-sized yellow onion
1 bunch green onions
7 cloves garlic
1 celery rib
1 green bell pepper
½ cup fresh parsley

½ cup ketchup
1 tablespoon Worcestershire sauce
2 tablespoons Tabasco sauce
2 bay leaves
1 teaspoon thyme
½ teaspoon table salt
½ teaspoon ground black pepper

1. Soak the beans overnight in six cups water. Drain and rinse the beans. Place them in slow cooker and add 3 cups of fresh water. Cook covered on low setting for 3 hours.
2. Peel and chop the yellow onion into ¼-inch pieces. Clean and cut the green onions into ½-inch lengths. Be sure to use all of the green stems. Peel and slice the garlic paper-thin, using a sharp paring knife. Chop the celery into ¼-inch pieces. Remove the seeds from the bell pepper and cut the pepper into ¼-inch pieces.
3. Add the yellow onion, green onion, garlic, celery, bell pepper, parsley, ketchup, Worcestershire, Tabasco, bay leaves, thyme, salt, and pepper to slow cooker; stir until ingredients are well mingled with beans. Cook covered on low setting for 5 to 7 hours.

Serve over brown rice with a side of fresh-steamed broccoli for a complete, healthy meal.

Garlic in Jars?

Beware of prepared garlic. While preminced garlic looks like a good buy and certainly sounds easier, after being chopped it releases an oil while stored. This affects both the taste and consistency in your recipes. Fresh garlic is always best.

Caribbean Black Beans and Rice

Cooking time: 7–9 hours
Preparation time: 30 minutes
Attention: Medium
Pot size: 3–6 quarts
Serves 6

1 large red bell pepper
Olive oil for basting red pepper,
    plus 1½ teaspoons more
½ green bell pepper
2 cloves garlic
1 cup raw white rice (yields 3
    cups cooked)

2 (16-ounce) cans of black beans
2 tablespoons white vinegar
2 teaspoons Tabasco or other
    hot sauce
3 tablespoons cilantro, chopped
1 teaspoon table salt
½ teaspoon ground black pepper

1. Remove the stems and seeds from the red bell pepper and cut into quarters. Lightly cover the inside "meat" of the pepper with olive oil. Bake in 350-degree oven for 1 hour; remove and cut into ¼-inch-long strips. Remove the seeds from the green bell pepper and cut into ¼-inch-long strips. Peel and slice the garlic paper-thin with a sharp paring knife. Prepare the rice according to package directions to yield 3 cups of cooked rice.

2. Sauté the red pepper, green pepper, and garlic in 1½ teaspoons olive oil for 2 minutes on medium-high heat in a large skillet on the stove. Drain off the oil; combine with cilantro, salt, and black pepper and place mixture in the slow cooker. Drain and rinse the black beans; add them to the slow cooker. Add vinegar, Tabasco, and rice to slow cooker. Stir until all ingredients are well mingled. Cook covered on low setting for 6 to 8 hours. Because this meal does not have a great deal of liquid, you may need to add ¼ to ½ cup water about halfway through the cooking process.

Serve with Slightly Seedy White Bread (page 84).

Spinach, Rice, and Vegetable Casserole

Cooking time: 6–8 hours

Preparation time: 20 minutes

Attention: Medium

Pot size: 3–6 quarts

Serves 8

1 large yellow onion
3 cloves of garlic
1 bunch parsley
2 bunches spinach
1 cup fresh tomatoes, chopped
2 tablespoons olive oil

3 cups water
2 tablespoons tomatopaste
⅛ teaspoon table salt
⅛ teaspoon ground black pepper
1 cup uncooked white rice

1. Peel and chop the onion into ¼-inch pieces. Peel and slice the garlic paper-thin with a sharp paring knife. Chop the parsley into ¼-inch lengths. Wash the spinach and remove the stems. Chop the tomatoes into ¼-inch pieces.

2. Heat the oil over medium-high heat in a medium-sized skillet. Add the onions, parsley, and garlic; sauté for 3 to 5 minutes, until the onions are translucent. Drain off oil and transfer the mixture to the slow cooker. Add the water, tomato paste, chopped tomatoes, salt, and pepper. Mix well so ingredients are well mingled. Add spinach and rice; stir. Cook covered on low setting for 6 to 8 hours, or until rice is done.

Pair this meal with fresh cantaloupe and honeydew melon cubes to offset the robust tomato flavor.

Sautéing with Water

For a healthy alternative, sauté onions and garlic in a few tablespoons of water instead of oil or butter. They tend to get a little crisper this way but this cooking method saves many grams of fat.

Creamy Roasted Corn with Rice

Cooking time: 7–9 hours
Preparation time: 20 minutes
Attention: Medium
Pot size: 3–6 quarts
Serves 6

3 tablespoons olive oil
1 cup uncooked white rice
4 cups chicken broth
½ cup skim milk
½ cup dry white wine
½ teaspoon table salt
½ teaspoon ground black pepper
½ teaspoon nutmeg
2 cups fresh or frozen corn, cooked
⅓ pound cream cheese
4 fresh scallions

1. Heat the olive oil on medium-high in a medium-sized skillet.
   Sauté the rice, stirring constantly for 3 to 5 minutes, until slightly
   browned. Drain and place in the slow cooker.
2. Add the chicken broth, milk, white wine, salt, pepper, and nutmeg
   to the slow cooker. Cook covered on low setting for 6 to 8 hours,
   or until rice is soft.
3. Cut the cream cheese into ½-inch cubes. Peel and slice the scallions
   paper-thin, using a sharp paring knife.
4. Add the corn, scallions, and cream cheese to the slow cooker;
   stir well. Cook covered 30 to 60 minutes, stirring every 10 minutes.
   The cheese should be fully melted and integrated into the sauce.

Preparing Frozen Veggies

Thaw frozen vegetables in the refrigerator the night before
you will use them. If you have more than 2 cups of frozen vegetables in your recipe, it could cause the food to heat too
slowly at the beginning of the cooking process.

Cooking time: 6–9 hours

Preparation time: 30 minutes

Attention: Medium

Pot size: 3–6 quarts

Serves 6

Lemony Bulgur Garbanzo Pilaf

1 cup medium-grind bulgur

*2 cups cooked chickpeas, **or** 1 cup dried*

½ teaspoon table salt

½ teaspoon ground black pepper

2 cups vegetable stock or bouillon

1 small yellow onion

1 small green bell pepper

3 cloves garlic

1 tablespoon olive oil

½ teaspoon cumin

⅓ cup fresh lemon juice

1 cup fresh parsley, chopped

1. Wash the bulgur and chickpeas, then place them in the slow cooker along with the salt, pepper, and vegetable stock. Cook covered on low setting for 2 to 3 hours.
2. Peel and chop the onion into ¼-inch pieces. Remove the seeds from the green pepper and chop into ¼-inch pieces. Peel and mince the garlic, using a sharp kitchen knife.
3. Heat the olive oil to medium-high heat in a medium-sized skillet. Add the onion, green pepper, and garlic; sauté for 3 to 5 minutes, stirring constantly, until the onions are translucent. Drain off oil. Add the onions, green pepper, garlic, and cumin to the slow cooker; mix well. Cook covered on low setting for 4 to 6 additional hours.
4. Add the lemon juice and parsley to the slow cooker; mix well. Cook uncovered for 30 minutes more on low setting.

For a creamy alternative, add half a cup of grated mild Cheddar cheese and eliminate the parsley and lemon juice.

Eggplant and Tomatoes with Pasta

Cooking time: 3½–5 hours

Preparation time: 45 minutes

Attention: Frequent

Pot size: 3–6 quarts

Serves 4

¾ cup yellow onion, chopped

3 cloves garlic

¾ pound of eggplant, cubed

2 tablespoons fresh basil, chopped

1 (16-ounce) can Italian plum tomatoes with juice

2 tablespoons olive oil

2 tablespoons balsamic vinegar

½ cup chicken broth

1 tablespoon tomato paste

½ teaspoon dried oregano

⅛ teaspoon hot red pepper flakes

½ teaspoon table salt

12 ounces pasta shells or pieces (rotini, wagon wheels, bow ties, etc.)

1. Peel and chop the onion into ¼-inch pieces. Peel and mince the garlic. Peel and cut the eggplant into 1-inch cubes. Chop the fresh basil into ¼-inch lengths. Pour the canned tomatoes into a medium-sized bowl and break into approximate quarters, using a wooden spoon.
2. In a small skillet, heat the olive oil on a medium-high heat; sauté the onions and garlic for 3 to 5 minutes, stirring constantly, until the onions are translucent. Drain and place in the slow cooker.
3. Add the eggplant, balsamic vinegar, chicken broth, tomato paste, and oregano to the slow cooker; stir well so that all the ingredients are well mingled. Cook uncovered on high setting for 3 to 4 hours, or until the sauce is slightly thickened.
4. Reduce the temperature setting to low. Add the basil and red pepper flakes to the sauce in the slow cooker; stir to incorporate. Boil the pasta in water with the ½ teaspoon of salt in a pot on the stove for 10 minutes. Drain off the water and add the pasta to the slow cooker; stir well so that all of the pasta is covered with sauce. Cover and cook on low setting for 30 to 60 minutes, or until the pasta is soft but not overcooked.

Complement this meal with tomato slices topped with goat cheese and fresh basil.

Minted Lentil and Tofu Stew

Cooking time: 8–9 hours	
Preparation time: 10 minutes	
Attention: Minimal	
Pot size: 3–6 quarts	
Serves 6	

2 cups dry yellow lentils

6 cups salted water (add 1 tablespoon table salt to water and stir until dissolved)

¼ cup fresh spearmint, chopped

1 tablespoon fresh peppermint, chopped

2 cups firm tofu, cubed

½ teaspoon soybean oil

1 teaspoon lemon juice

1 cup water

1 teaspoon table salt

1. Soak the lentils overnight in 6 cups salted water. Wash and drain. Cut the spearmint and peppermint into ¼-inch pieces. Cut the tofu into 1-inch cubes.
2. Add all ingredients except tofu to the slow cooker; stir until ingredients are well mixed. Cook covered on low setting 7 to 8 hours. Add tofu and cook 1 to 2 more hours.

Substitute 2 tablespoons of Italian seasoning for the spearmint and peppermint to create an herbed version of this lentil stew.

Fresh vs. Dry Pasta

Fresh pastas typically contain more egg than dried pastas. This accounts for the creamier flavor but also adds cholesterol and fat to your diet. Make up for the flavor by adding more spices to your sauce.

Creamy Vegetarian Chili

Cooking time: 8–9 hours

Preparation time: 15 minutes

Attention: Minimal

Pot size: 3–6 quarts

Serves 6

2 cups dried red kidney beans
2 cups firm tofu, cubed
2 large carrots
2 large yellow onions
1 tablespoon chili powder
1 teaspoon garlic salt
1 teaspoon ground black pepper
1 cup fresh or frozen corn
½ cup low-fat sour cream

1. Soak the beans overnight in 6 cups water. Cut the tofu into 1-inch cubes. Peel and slice the carrots into ¼-inch rounds. Peel and slice the onions into ¼-inch squares.
2. Drain and wash the beans. Add all ingredients except tofu to the slow cooker; mix with a wooden spoon until all the ingredients are well mingled. Cook covered on low setting 7 to 8 hours. Add tofu cook 1 to 1½ hours. Approximately 30 minutes before serving, stir the chili, then add the sour cream; stir well. Cook uncovered on low setting for the remaining half-hour.

Serve this chili with Corn Bread in the Round (page 76) to create an almost-authentic Tex-Mex treat.

Cooking time: 6 hours

Preparation time: 20 minutes

Attention: Medium

Pot size: 3–6 quarts

Serves 4

Nutty Barley Pilaf

1¾ cup pearl barley

½ cup butter, divided

2 medium-sized yellow onions

8 ounces (1 cup) fresh
   mushrooms, sliced

4 cups vegetable broth

¼ cup toasted macadamia nuts,
   chopped

¼ cup toasted pecans, chopped

½ cup fresh parsley, chopped

1. On the stove, sauté the barley in four tablespoons of the butter in a medium-sized skillet on medium heat until the barley is golden; stir often. Pour the mixture into the slow cooker.

2. Peel and chop the onions into ¼-inch pieces. Clean the mushrooms by wiping with a damp cloth; slice paper-thin with a sharp paring knife. Put the onions and mushrooms in the skillet and sauté, stirring often, in the remaining butter on medium heat for about 5 minutes. Add this to the slow cooker and stir well. Pour 2 cups of vegetable broth over the mixture. Cover and cook on low setting for 4 hours.

3. Add the remaining broth and cook uncovered for 2 hours, stirring occasionally.

4. Chop the nuts finely with a sharp paring knife. Place on a cookie sheet in the oven and heat for 15 minutes at 350 degrees. Roughly chop the parsley. Fifteen minutes before serving, stir the nuts and parsley into the mixture.

Serve with fresh apple and orange slices to complement the nutty flavors in this dish.

Keeping Cut Fruit from Browning

Apples and bananas won't get brown if you cover them with a thin layer of half lemon juice and half water. The acidic lemon juice also will add a slight tang to blander fruit.

Cooking time: 7–9

Preparation time: 40 minutes

Attention: Medium

Pot size: 3–6 quarts

Buddhist Monk's Soup Serves 6

1 pound butternut squash
1 large sweet potato
1 quart water
½ cup raw peanuts, shelled and skinned
⅓ cup dried mung beans
3 tablespoons vegetable oil
1 square of tofu
1 quart unsweetened coconut milk
1 teaspoon table salt
1 (12-ounce) package cellophane noodles

1. Peel the squash and sweet potato and cut into 3-inch pieces. Put them into the slow cooker with 1 quart of water and salt. Cook covered on high setting for 6 to 8 hours or until soft.
2. Soak the mung beans and peanuts in water until soft, about 30 minutes. Sauté the tofu in the vegetable oil on medium-high heat until brown; drain off grease and cut the tofu into ¼-inch strips. Add beans, peanuts, tofu, coconut milk, salt, and cellophane noodles. Cover and cook on low setting for 1 hour.

Serve with Heavy Brown Bread (page 85) and three-year-old Cheddar cheese for an authentic monastery meal.

Making Your Own Pasta

Use semolina flour to make homemade noodles. It is made from high gluten wheat and is more finely ground. The pasta is slightly stiffer than that made with regular flour so it holds up better to slow cooking.

Vidalia Onion and Lentil Casserole

Cooking time: 6 hours

Preparation time: 15 minutes

Attention: Minimal

Pot size: 3–6 quarts

Serves 4

1 large Vidalia onion, chopped
2 cups dried lentils
1 teaspoon table salt
3 cups water

2 cups tomato sauce
¼ cup brown sugar
2 tablespoons Dijon mustard
⅓ cup dark molasses

Peel the onion and chop into ¼-inch pieces. Rinse the lentils and place in the slow cooker. Add the onion, salt, water, tomato sauce, brown sugar, mustard, and molasses; stir well. Cover and cook on low setting for 6 hours.

Peel and slice another onion into ¼-inch rings. Sauté rings until crisp and place them on top of the casserole before serving.

Root Vegetable Soup

Cooking time: 6–8 hours

Preparation time: 15 minutes

Attention: Minimal

Pot size: 3–8 quarts

Serves 6

2 medium-sized yellow onions
3 medium carrots
1 medium rutabaga
1 large beet
1 medium turnip

3 medium potatoes
¼ teaspoon ground black pepper
1 teaspoon ground nutmeg
3 cups vegetable broth

Peel all the vegetables and chop into ¼-inch cubes. Combine all ingredients in the slow cooker. Cover and cook on low setting for 6 to 8 hours.

This is an excellent complement to hot beef sandwiches.

Portobello-Stuffed Artichokes

Cooking time: 7–9 hours

Preparation time: 30 minutes

Attention: Minimal

Pot size: 3–8 quarts

Serves 4

4 large artichokes

4 large portobello mushrooms

3 garlic cloves

2 tablespoons grated Parmesan cheese

½ teaspoon ground black pepper

1 tablespoon olive oil

1 teaspoon salt

1. Remove the stems from the artichokes and discard the outer 2 to 3 layers of leaves. Trim the base so that the artichokes stand flat. Cut off the top of the artichoke and hollow out the center, removing all purple-tinged leaves and fuzzy material.

2. Chop the mushrooms into ¼-inch pieces. Peel the garlic and mince with a sharp kitchen knife. Combine the mushrooms, garlic, Parmesan cheese, black pepper, and olive oil in a medium-sized mixing bowl. Stuff the mixture into the artichoke centers.

3. Pour water into the slow cooker (so it is about 1½ inches deep) and stir in the salt. Set the artichokes in the water. Cover and cook on low setting for 7 to 9 hours. The leaves should be tender when done.

Sweet Potato and Apple Bake (page 274) makes a nice complement to this meal.

Releasing Garlic's Potential

Get the most out of garlic by "popping" the clove before adding it to a dish. Hold a large knife on its side and place the peeled clove under it. Push down until you hear the clove pop. You'll release all the wonderful oils without having to chop.

CHAPTER 6
Breads

Corn Bread in the Round

Cooking time: 2 hours

Preparation time: 10 minutes

Attention: Minimal

Pot size: 4–8 quarts

Serves 12–16

1¼ cups bread flour
¾ cup yellow cornmeal
¼ cup sugar
4½ teaspoons baking powder
1 teaspoon salt
1 egg
1 cup skim milk
⅓ cup melted butter
3 empty aluminum cans, approximately 12 ounces each
½ teaspoon vegetable oil

1. Mix together the flour, cornmeal, sugar, baking powder, and salt; set aside. Lightly beat the egg and combine with milk and butter. Add this mixture to the dry mixture and stir until all the dry ingredients are moistened; do not mix too much. Batter should remain lumpy.
2. Grease the insides of three empty cans using the ½ teaspoon vegetable oil. Pour ⅓ of the mixture into each can. Cover each can with aluminum foil that has been greased on the inside. Place the cans on a trivet in the bottom of the slow cooker. Cook on high for 2 hours or until a long wooden skewer inserted into the bread comes out clean. Let stand for 5 minutes before removing from the cans.

Serve corn bread, ham steaks, and Northwestern Baked Beans (page 253) for a traditional farm-style meal.

Bread Baking Inserts

Many slow cookers have bread baking inserts available. You can use these or use metal vegetable and coffee cans instead. Three soup cans will make the equivalent of a loaf and give you fun, individual little loaves of bread.

Traditional Dressing for Poultry or Red Meat

Cooking time: 6 hours

Preparation time: 20 minutes

Attention: Medium

Pot size: 3–6 quarts

Serves 8

1 loaf of corn bread
8 slices dry white bread
1 medium-sized yellow onion
2 stalks celery
4 eggs, beaten
2 cups chicken broth
2 (10 ¾-ounce) cans cream of chicken condensed soup
1 teaspoon sage
½ teaspoon black pepper
2 tablespoons butter

1. Tear the bread into pieces about the size of a quarter.
2. Peel and chop the onion into ¼-inch pieces. Chop the celery into ¼-inch pieces.
3. Mix together all the ingredients except the butter. Place in the slow cooker. Dot the butter on top. Cover and cook on high setting for 2 hours.
4. Keep covered and cook on low setting for 4 additional hours.

This makes an excellent complement to Dilled Turkey Breast (page 118).

Halloween Is Here Pumpkin Bread

Cooking time: 3–4 hours

Preparation time: 15 minutes

Attention: Minimal

Pot size: 4–6 quarts

Serves 12

1 cup vegetable oil

1 cup white sugar

1 cup brown sugar

4 eggs

2 cups canned pumpkin

3 cups flour

2 teaspoons salt

1 teaspoon cinnamon

1 teaspoon nutmeg

2 teaspoons baking soda

2 cups chopped walnuts

1. Blend the oil and white and brown sugars in a medium-sized mixing bowl using a wooden spoon. Beat the eggs with a fork until they are frothy. Stir the eggs and pumpkin into the oil and sugar mixture. Combine the flour, salt, cinnamon, nutmeg, and soda in a medium-sized bowl and mix well. Add this mixture to the batter and stir well. Chop the walnuts into ⅛-inch pieces with a sharp paring knife, then stir them into the batter.

2. Grease the inside of a 2-pound coffee can, then sprinkle the greased area lightly with flour. Add the batter to the can and cover with aluminum foil. Poke 3 sets of holes into the aluminum foil with a fork. Place the coffee can into the slow cooker. Cook covered on high setting for 3 hours. Test the bread before removing it by inserting a long wooden skewer. If it comes out clean, the bread is done. If there is batter on it, cook for an additional half-hour.

Serve this instead of rolls at your next fall holiday gathering.

Testing Bread

To test bread or cake to see if it's done, insert a toothpick into the center. If it comes out clean, it's done. If crumbs or batter stick to it, it needs to bake longer.

Cooking time: 3–4 hours
Preparation time: 20 minutes
Attention: Minimal
Pot size: 4–6 quarts
Serves 12

Zucchini Bread

2 eggs
⅔ cup vegetable oil
2 tablespoons sugar
1½ cups zucchini, peeled and grated
2 teaspoons vanilla
2 cups flour
¼ teaspoon salt
½ teaspoon baking powder
1 teaspoon cinnamon
½ teaspoon nutmeg
1 cup chopped walnuts

1. Beat the eggs in a medium-sized mixing bowl with a fork until foamy. Add oil, sugar, grated zucchini, and vanilla; mix well with a wooden spoon. Stir remaining ingredients into the batter; mix well.
2. Grease the inside of a 2-pound coffee can and lightly sprinkle with flour. Pour the mixture into the coffee can. Cover with a piece of aluminum foil. Poke 3 sets of holes in the aluminum foil with a fork. Put the coffee can in the slow cooker. Cover and cook on high setting 3 to 4 hours. Test after 3 hours by inserting a long wooden skewer into the bread. If it comes out clean, the bread is done.

Cooking tip: Avoid the temptation to peak at your bread before the minimum cooking time is up. Even breads that don't contain yeast can be affected by sudden changes in humidity or temperature.

Cooking time: 4–5 hours	
Preparation time: 20 minutes	
Attention: Minimal	
Pot size: 4–6 quarts	
Serves 12	

Banana Nut Bread

3 very ripe bananas
½ cup walnuts, chopped
2 large eggs, beaten
1 cup sugar
½ teaspoon salt
1 teaspoon baking soda
½ cup melted shortening
2 cups flour

1. Grease a 2-pound coffee can by putting a small amount of shortening on a paper towel and rubbing it inside the can. Sprinkle the inside of the can with a small amount of flour.
2. Mash the bananas. Cut the walnuts into $1/16$-inch pieces. Add the eggs, sugar, salt, baking soda, shortening, flour, and walnuts to mashed bananas. Mix well by stirring with a wooden spoon. Place the mixture in the coffee can. Cover the can with aluminum foil. Poke 3 sets of holes in the aluminum foil with a fork. Put the coffee can in the slow cooker. Cover and cook on low setting 4 to 5 hours.

Serve with Earl Grey teal as a dessert after a heavy mea.

Cheddar and Onion Bread

Cooking time: 4–6 hours
Preparation time: 15 minutes
Attention: Medium
Pot size: 4–6 quarts
Serves 12

2 tablespoons white onion,
   grated
½ cup Cheddar cheese, grated
2 teaspoons active dry yeast

1 cup warm water
3 cups bread flour
1 teaspoon salt

1. Grate the onion using the finest side of a vegetable grater. Grate the cheese using the coarser side of the grater. Grease a 2-pound coffee can by putting shortening on a paper towel and rubbing the inside of the coffee can.

2. Dissolve the yeast in half a cup of warm water. In a large bowl, combine the flour, yeast, salt, and remaining warm water. If the dough is too dry, add more water. Stir in the Cheddar cheese and onions. Roll the dough into a ball and place in the coffee can. Cover lightly with a paper towel and place in a warm place for 1 to 2 hours. Dough should rise to twice its original size.

2. Cover the coffee can with aluminum foil. Poke 3 sets of holes in the aluminum foil with a fork. Place the coffee can in the slow cooker. Cook, covered, on low setting for 4 to 6 hours. Bread is fully cooked when it bounces back when lightly touched.

This is an excellent complement to Beef Roast with Dried Fruit (page 102).

Yeast

Yeast is a live entity that grows when it gets warm. However, if it's added to boiling water, you can kill it. You can make a heavy, dense bread by leaving out the yeast and substituting baking soda.

Honey Oatmeal Bread

Cooking time: 4–6 hours

Preparation time: 15 minutes

Attention: Medium

Pot size: 4–6 quarts

Serves 12

2 teaspoons dry active yeast
1¼ cups warm water
½ cup honey
2 tablespoons vegetable oil
1 cup quick-cooking oats
1½ teaspoons salt
3 cups bread flour

1. Grease a 2-pound coffee can by putting shortening on a paper towel and rubbing it on the inside of the coffee can.
2. Dissolve the yeast in half a cup of the warm water. In a large bowl, combine all ingredients. If the dough is too dry, add more water. Roll the dough into a ball and place in the coffee can. Cover lightly with a paper towel and place in a warm place for 1 to 2 hours. Dough should rise to twice its original size.
3. Cover the coffee can with aluminum foil. Poke 3 sets of holes in the aluminum foil with a fork. Place the coffee can in the slow cooker. Place the lid on the slow cooker and cook on low setting for 4 to 6 hours. Bread is fully cooked when it bounces back when lightly touched.

Serve with Congo Stew (page 200) for a unique juxtaposition of flavors.

Grandma Margaret's Summer Dill Bread

Cooking time: 4–6 hours
Preparation time: 20 minutes
Attention: Medium
Pot size: 4–6 quarts
Serves 12

2 tablespoons grated onion
2 teaspoons dry active yeast
¼ cup warm water
3 cups flour
½ teaspoon baking soda
1 teaspoon salt
2 tablespoons dill weed
1 cup cottage cheese
1 tablespoon milk, if needed

1. Grate the onion using the finest side of a vegetable grater. Grease a 2-pound coffee can by putting shortening on a paper towel and rubbing it on the inside of the coffee can.
2. Dissolve the yeast in warm water. In a large bowl, combine all the ingredients **except** the onion. If the dough is too dry, add 1 tablespoon of milk. Stir in the onions. Roll the dough into a ball and place it in the coffee can. Cover lightly with a paper towel and put in a warm place for 1 to 2 hours. Dough should rise to twice its original size.
3. Cover the coffee can with aluminum foil. Poke 3 sets of holes in the aluminum foil with a fork. Place the coffee can in the slow cooker. Cover the slow cooker and cook on low setting for 4 to 6 hours. Bread is fully cooked when it bounces back when lightly touched.

This is excellent served with Spicy Pot Roast (page 106).

Slightly Seedy White Bread

Cooking time: 4–6 hours

Preparation time: 15 minutes

Attention: Medium

Pot size: 4–6 quarts

Serves 12

2 teaspoons dry active yeast
1½ cups warm water
3 cups bread flour
1 tablespoon nonfat dry milk
2 tablespoons olive oil
1½ teaspoons salt
¼ cup poppy seeds
¼ cup sesame seeds
½ cup sunflower seeds

1. Grease a 2-pound coffee can by putting shortening on a paper towel and rubbing it on the inside of the coffee can.
2. Dissolve the yeast in half a cup of warm water. In a large bowl, combine the flour, dry milk, oil, remaining water, salt, and yeast. If the dough is too dry, add more water 1 tablespoon at a time. Stir in the seeds. Roll the dough into a ball and place it in the coffee can. Cover lightly with a paper towel and place in a warm place for 1 to 2 hours. The dough should rise to twice its original size.
3. Cover the coffee can with aluminum foil. Poke 3 sets of holes in the aluminum foil with a fork. Place the coffee can in the slow cooker. Cover the slow cooker and cook on low setting for 4 to 6 hours. Bread is fully cooked when it bounces back when lightly touched.

Serve as a complement to Wild Duck Gumbo (page 144).

Cooking time: 4–6 hours

Preparation time: 15 minutes

Attention: Medium

Pot size: 4–6 quarts

Serves 12

Heavy Brown Bread

1 cup stone-ground rye flour

1 cup stone-ground whole wheat flour

1 cup stone-ground cornmeal

½ teaspoon baking soda

4 teaspoons baking powder

1 teaspoon salt

¾ cup molasses

1¾ cups milk

1 cup raisins

3 cups water

1. Grease a 2-pound coffee can by putting shortening on a paper towel and rubbing it on the inside of the coffee can.

2. In a large bowl, combine the flours, cornmeal, baking soda, baking powder, and salt; mix well. Add the molasses and milk. Mix until all ingredients are well combined. Stir in the raisins. Place the batter in the coffee can. Cover the coffee can with aluminum foil. Poke 3 sets of holes in the aluminum foil with a fork. Put 3 cups of water in the slow cooker. Place the coffee can in the slow cooker. Cover the slow cooker and cook on low setting for 4 to 6 hours. Bread is fully cooked when it bounces back when lightly touched.

3. Empty the water from the slow cooker and remove the foil from the coffee can. Put the coffee can back in slow cooker with the cover slightly ajar, so that steam can escape. Cook on low setting for 15 additional minutes.

This is perfect served with Beef Roast (page 102).

Baking Bread

When baking bread in soup, vegetable, or coffee cans, cover the can with aluminum foil and poke a few holes in it with a fork. Also use the slow cooker cover.

Almond and Chocolate Chip Bread

Cooking time: 4–6 hours

Preparation time: 15 minutes

Attention: Medium

Pot size: 4–6 quarts

Serves 12

1½ teaspoons dry active yeast

1 cup water, plus extra as needed

3 cups bread flour

1 tablespoon nonfat dry milk

¾ teaspoon salt

3 tablespoons sugar

½ teaspoon vanilla

2 tablespoons butter, softened

¾ cup semisweet chocolate chips

⅓ cup almond slivers

1. Grease a 2-pound coffee can by putting shortening on a paper towel and rubbing it on the inside of the coffee can.
2. Dissolve the yeast in half a cup of the warm water. In a large bowl, combine the flour, dry milk, yeast, remaining water, salt, sugar, vanilla, and butter. If the dough is too dry, add more water 1 tablespoon at a time. Stir in the chocolate chips and almonds. Roll the dough into a ball and place it in the coffee can. Cover lightly with a paper towel and place in a warm place for 1 to 2 hours. Dough should rise to twice its original size.
3. Cover the coffee can with aluminum foil. Poke 3 sets of holes in the aluminum foil with a fork. Place the coffee can in the slow cooker. Cover the slow cooker and cook on low setting for 4 to 6 hours. Bread is fully cooked when it bounces back when lightly touched.

Toast the bread and spread with peanut butter for a nutritious, tasty breakfast treat.

CHAPTER 7
Stews

Tomato and Bean Stew

Cooking time: 8–10 hours

Preparation time: 20 minutes

Attention: Minimal

Pot size: 4–8 quarts

Serves 6

2 medium potatoes
1 large white onion
1 medium-sized red bell pepper
1 medium-sized green bell pepper
2 medium carrots
1 (15-ounce) can garbanzo beans
1 (15-ounce) can kidney beans
1 cup dry lentils
1 (10-ounce) package chopped
    frozen spinach

1 (14½-ounce) can Italian
    stewed tomatoes
4 cups tomato juice
2 cups water
2 tablespoons dried parsley
2 tablespoons chili powder
2 teaspoons dried basil
2 teaspoons garlic powder
1 teaspoon ground cumin

1. Wash the potatoes but do not peel them; cut into 1-inch cubes. Peel the onion and cut into ¼-inch pieces. Remove the stem and seeds from the red and green peppers and cut into ¼-inch pieces. Wash the carrots and chop them into ¼-inch rounds. Drain and rinse the beans. Rinse the lentils.
2. Add all ingredients to the slow cooker; mix lightly. Cover and cook on low setting for 8 to 10 hours.

Serve with Italian Beets (page 285) to add some sharp flavors to the mellowness of this dish.

Hold the Foil When Freezing

When freezing soups and stews remember not to wrap tomato-based dishes in aluminum foil. The acid in the tomatoes will react with the aluminum.

Cooking time: 8–10 hours

Preparation time: 15 minutes

Attention: Minimal

Pot size: 6 quarts

Serves 8

Cuban Black Bean Stew

1 large yellow onion
1 green bell pepper
4 garlic cloves
8 ounces (1 cup) peeled baby carrots
2 celery stalks
4 fresh tomatoes
2 tablespoons olive oil
1 teaspoon ground black pepper

1 teaspoon cayenne pepper
1 teaspoon dried thyme
1 bay leaf
2 cups dried black beans, rinsed
2 chicken bouillon cubes
4 cups water
4 tablespoons balsamic vinegar

1. Peel and chop the onion into ½-inch pieces. Remove the stem and seeds from the green pepper; chop the pepper into ½-inch pieces. Peel the garlic cloves and mince with a sharp kitchen knife. Cut the baby carrots in half. Chop the celery into ¼-inch pieces. Chop the tomatoes into ½-inch pieces.
2. Heat the olive oil in a large skillet on medium-high heat on the stove. Add the onion, green pepper, garlic, and ground spices. Sauté, stirring constantly, until the onions are soft, about 5 minutes. Drain off the oil and place the mixture in the slow cooker.
3. Add the carrots, celery, black beans, bay leaf, tomatoes, and crumbled bouillon cubes to the slow cooker. Add the water; stir until all ingredients are mixed. Cook covered on low setting for 8 to 10 hours.
4. 10 minutes before serving, stir in the balsamic vinegar.

Serve pan-fried plantain slices for an authentic Cuban meal.

Moravian Ham, Tomato, and Green Bean Stew

Cooking time: 5–6 hours
Preparation time: 10 minutes
Attention: Minimal
Pot size: 3–6 quarts
Serves 6

2 cups precooked ham, chopped
4 medium-sized yellow onions
4 cups diced fresh tomatoes

6 cups fresh green beans
¾ teaspoon table salt
½ teaspoon ground black pepper

1. Chop the ham into 1-inch cubes. Peel and chop the onions into ½-inch pieces. Peel the tomatoes with a sharp paring knife, gently lifting the peel from the flesh. and dice the tomatoes in ¼-inch pieces. Snap the ends off the green beans and discard the ends.
2. Add all ingredients to the slow cooker. Stir 2 or 3 times with a wooden spoon. Cook covered on low setting 5 to 6 hours.

Serve over mashed potatoes with a side of squash for a fall harvest treat.

Polish Stew

Cooking time: 8–9 hours
Preparation time: 20 minutes
Attention: Minimal
Pot size: 3–6 quarts
Serves 4

1½ pounds Polish sausage
2 medium-sized onions
4 medium potatoes
1 cup shredded Monterey jack
  cheese

4 cups sauerkraut
1 (10¾-ounce) can cream
  of celery condensed soup
⅓ cup brown sugar

1. Cut the Polish sausage into ½-inch-thick slices. Peel the onions and chop into ¼-inch pieces. Peel the potatoes and cut into 1-inch cubes. Shred the cheese using a vegetable grater. Drain the sauerkraut.
2. Combine the soup, brown sugar, sauerkraut, sausage, potatoes, and onions in the slow cooker. Cover and cook on low for 8 to 9 hours. Stir in the cheese 10 minutes before serving.

Cooking time: 10 hours

Preparation time: 30 minutes

Attention: Medium

Pot size: 6–8 quarts

Serves 8

Fruity Beef Stew

2 pounds beef round roast

2 cups chopped yellow onions

6 cloves garlic

2 teaspoons crushed, dried red
   peppers

¾ teaspoon turmeric

¾ teaspoon ground cinnamon

¾ teaspoon ground ginger

½ teaspoon salt

2 tablespoons extra-virgin
   olive oil

2 cups beef broth

1 cup dried pitted dates

1 cup dried apricots

1 tablespoon cornstarch

2 tablespoons water

1. Cut the meat into 1¼-inch pieces. Peel the onion and chop into ¼-inch pieces. Peel and mince the garlic. In a small mixing bowl, combine the red peppers, turmeric, ginger, cinnamon, and salt; coat the meat with this seasoning mixture. In a large skillet heat the olive oil over medium heat until hot, then brown the meat; drain off grease.

2. Place the meat in the slow cooker the with onions, beef broth, dates, and apricots. Cover and cook on low setting for 9 hours. Remove the meat, onions, and fruit. Make a paste out of the cornstarch and water and stir into the juice in the slow cooker. Cook on high setting, stirring periodically, until mixture thickens into a gravy.

3. Add the meat, vegetables, and fruit back into slow cooker. Cover and cook on low setting for 1 more hour.

Serve with Minnesota Wild Rice (page 281) for a nice mix of flavors.

When Roasting Meat

When making a large pot roast, cut the meat into four or six smaller pieces. It will cook faster and get up to the bacteria-killing temperature quicker. Try adding onions between each layer of meat so their flavor saturates the meat.

Savory Garlic Chicken Stew

Cooking time: 6–8 hours

Preparation time: 30 minutes

Attention: Minimal

Pot size: 3–6 quarts

Serves 4

5 cups canned or frozen chicken broth

2 cups water

¼ cup all-purpose flour

8 garlic cloves

½ teaspoon low-fat oil

2 cups fresh carrots, sliced

6 medium golden potatoes

1 medium-sized yellow onion

1 cup fresh celery, sliced

2 pounds fresh or frozen boneless, skinless chicken breasts

1 teaspoon salt

¼ teaspoon white pepper

1. Put the chicken broth, water, and flour in a mixing bowl and whisk quickly until smooth.
2. Peel the garlic cloves and mash individually by placing the side of a large knife over each clove and pressing until the clove "pops," allowing the juice to come out. The cloves do not need to be cut into pieces. Sauté the mashed garlic in oil on medium heat until lightly golden.
3. Peel and cut the carrots and potatoes into 1-inch chunks. Dice the onion with a paring knife until pieces are smaller than ⅛-inch square. Cut the celery into ¼-inch slices. Cut the chicken into 1-inch cubes.
4. Combine all ingredients except the pepper in the slow cooker Stir until ingredients are well mixed and covered with liquid. Cook 6 to 8 hours covered on low heat. Remove cover 15 minutes before serving. Stir well and add pepper.

Although it is excellent served alone, to create a complete meal, ladle the stew over Heavy Brown Bread (page 85). Add color to the plate with a garnish of fresh orange slices and purple grapes.

Cooking time: 8–9 hours

Preparation time: 30 minutes

Attention: Minimal

Pot size: 3–6 quarts

Traditional Beef Stew

Serves 6

2 pounds beef chuck

6 medium carrots

6 medium-sized yellow onions

6 medium potatoes

6 celery ribs

1 (10¾-ounce) can condensed
   tomato soup

1 cup water

¼ cup flour

2 beef bouillon cubes

½ teaspoon salt

½ teaspoon pepper

1. Cut the beef into 1-inch cubes, trimming off all fat. Peel the carrots, onions, and potatoes. Slice the celery and carrots into 1-inch pieces. Quarter the onions and potatoes.

2. Mix the soup, bouillon cubes, water, and flour together in a medium-sized bowl with a fork until the mixture is smooth and the bouillon cubes have dissolved. Place the beef in the bottom of the slow cooker. Cover with the liquid mixture. Add the carrots, onions, celery, and potatoes. Sprinkle with salt and pepper. Cook on low setting for 8 to 9 hours.

Serve with Dilly Mashed Potatoes (page 283) for a flavorful and nutritious meal.

Why the Variations in Cooking Times?

The size of the slow cooker and the quality of meat or the water content of the vegetables can cause food to take more or less time to cook.

New Brunswick Chicken Stew

Cooking time: 6–8 hours

Preparation time: 20 minutes

Attention: Minimal

Pot size: 3–6 quarts

Serves 6

1 stewing chicken
2 quarts (8 cups) water
2 large yellow onions
4 cups fresh tomatoes, chopped
3 medium potatoes
2 cups okra, chopped
2 cups lima beans

4 cups fresh sweet corn
 (about 8 ears)
3 tablespoons table salt
1 teaspoon pepper
1 tablespoon sugar

1. Cut the chicken into pieces and put them in the slow cooker with two quarts of water. Cook covered on high setting for 2 hours. Remove the chicken and set aside to cool.
2. Peel and slice the onions into ¼-inch-thick rings. Cut the tomatoes into ½-inch cubes. Peel and cut the potatoes into ½-inch cubes. Cut the sweet corn from the cob. Chop the okra into ½-inch pieces. Remove the meat from the chicken bones.
3. Add the meat, onions, tomatoes, potatoes, sweet corn, okra, lima beans, salt, pepper, and sugar to slow cooker. Cook covered on low setting for 6 to 8 hours.

The flavor of this stew improves when it is refrigerated overnight and reheated the following day.

Using Aromatics

Turnips, onions, celery, and carrots are known as aromatic vegetables because they smell wonderful when cooked and add a great deal of flavor to meat-based recipes.

Cooking time: 10–12 hours

Preparation time: 15 minutes

Attention: Minimal

Pot size: 3–6 quarts

Serves 6

Apple Cider Beef Stew

2 pounds stewing beef
8 carrots
6 medium potatoes
2 Granny Smith apples
1 small white onion
2 teaspoons salt
½ teaspoon thyme
2 cups apple cider
¼ cup flour

1. Cut the beef into ½-inch cubes. Peel and slice the carrots ⅛ inch thick. Peel the potatoes and cut into ½-inch cubes. Peel the apples and cut into ½-inch pieces. Peel the onion and finely chop.

2. Place the carrots, potatoes, and apples in the slow cooker. Add the meat and sprinkle with salt, thyme, and onion. Pour the cider over the top. Cover and cook on low setting for 10 to 12 hours. Before serving, mix the flour with enough water to make a paste and add mixture to the stew; stir in. Cover and cook on high setting until thickened, about 15 minutes.

Ladle over Dilly Mashed Potatoes (page 283) for an unusual blend of flavors.

Best Meat Cuts to Use

The best cuts of beef for stew meat are chuck, flank, or brisket. The slow cooking tenderizes even the toughest meat while these cuts tend to be well marbled, allowing the flavorful fat juices to permeate the stew.

Cooking time: 9–10 hours

Preparation time: 20 minutes

Attention: Minimal

Pot size: 3–6 quarts

Serves 6

Layered Beef Stew

2½ pounds beef stewing meat

1 large yellow onion

6 medium carrots

4 celery ribs

4 large ripe tomatoes

10 small new potatoes

2 tablespoons Worcestershire sauce

¼ cup red wine

3 tablespoons brown sugar

1 teaspoon table salt

½ teaspoon ground black pepper

¼ teaspoon allspice

¼ teaspoon dried marjoram

¼ teaspoon dried thyme

2 bay leaves

6 tablespoons quick-cooking tapioca

1. Cut the beef into 1-inch cubes. Peel the onion and cut into ¼-inch-thick slices. Peel the carrots and cut in half lengthwise. Remove the leaves from the celery and cut ribs in half. Chop the tomatoes into ¼-inch pieces.

2. Layer all ingredients in the slow cooker in the following order: beef, onions, potatoes, carrots, celery, Worcestershire sauce, red wine, brown sugar, salt, pepper, allspice, marjoram, thyme, bay leaves, tapioca, tomatoes. Cover and cook on low setting for 9 to 10 hours.

Serve with Grandma Dorothy's Peas and Rice (page 279) for a complete meal.

French Countryside Chicken and Pork Stew

Cooking time: 8–9 hours

Preparation time: 20 minutes

Attention: Minimal

Pot size: 3–6 quarts

Serves 4

3 pounds pork chops

4 chicken breasts

10 pearl onions

8 ounces (1 cup) fresh
mushrooms, quartered

4 garlic cloves

1 tablespoon olive oil

2 cups beef broth

¼ cup dry white wine

2 tablespoons Dijon mustard

1 teaspoon flour

1 teaspoon warm water

1. Remove the bones from the pork and cut the meat into ½-inch cubes. Remove the bones and skin from the chicken and discard; cut the chicken into ½-inch cubes. Peel the pearl onions. Clean the mushrooms by wiping with a damp cloth; cut into quarters. Peel the garlic and mince.

2. Sauté the pork, chicken, onions, and garlic in olive oil over medium heat in a large skillet until the meat is browned. Drain off grease and add mixture to the slow cooker. Combine beef broth, wine, and mustard in a medium-sized bowl and pour mixture into the slow cooker. Add mushrooms on top. Cover and cook on low setting for 8 to 9 hours.

3. About 30 minutes before serving, make a paste of the warm water and flour; add to the slow cooker, stirring well. Cook uncovered, stirring occasionally, until a gravy develops.

Top with chopped parsley right before serving.

Preparing Pearl Onions

When using pearl onions, cook them first in boiling water for 3 minutes. Plunge them into cold water. Remove them from the water and cut off the ends before easily removing the stems.

Chicken Peanut Stew

Cooking time: 4–6 hours

Preparation time: 15 minutes

Attention: Minimal

Pot size: 3–6 quarts

Serves 4

4 chicken breasts
1 green bell pepper
1 red bell pepper
2 medium-sized yellow onions
1 (6-ounce) can tomato paste
¾ cup crunchy peanut butter
3 cups chicken broth
1 teaspoon table salt
1 teaspoon chili powder
1 teaspoon sugar
½ teaspoon ground nutmeg

1. Remove the skin and bones from the chicken breasts and discard; cut the meat into 1-inch cubes. Remove the stems and seeds from the peppers and cut into ¼-inch rings. Peel the onions and cut into ¼-inch rings.
2. Combine all the ingredients in the slow cooker; stir until all the ingredients are well mingled. Cover and cook on low setting for 4 to 6 hours.

Sprinkle with chopped peanuts and flaked coconut before serving over freshly cooked rice.

Don't Eat Bay Leaves

Remember, bay leaves add lots of flavor, but you should always remove them before serving a dish. Bay leaves are sharp and dangerous to eat.

Stewed Mushrooms, Peppers, and Tomatoes

Cooking time: 8–9 hours

Preparation time: 20 minutes

Attention: Minimal

Pot size: 3–6 quarts

Serves 8

12 plum tomatoes
2 red bell peppers
2 yellow bell peppers
2 green bell peppers
2 large yellow onions
12 ounces (1½ cups) oyster mushrooms, quartered
6 garlic cloves
2 tablespoons olive oil
3 bay leaves
2 teaspoons dried basil
1 teaspoon salt
1 teaspoon ground black pepper

1. Chop the tomatoes into ½-inch pieces. Remove the stems and seeds from the peppers and cut into ¼-inch-thick strips. Peel the onions and cut into ¼-inch rings. Clean the mushrooms by wiping with a damp cloth; cut into fourths. Peel the garlic and cut into eighths.
2. Heat the olive oil in medium-sized skillet on medium heat. Add the peppers, onions, garlic, and mushrooms and sauté for 5 minutes. Drain off grease. Transfer the vegetables to the slow cooker. Add the spices and tomatoes; stir well. Cover and cook on low setting for 8 to 9 hours.

Serve this to complement Lean, Mean Meat Loaf (page 107).

Shrimp and Clam Stew with Tomatoes

Cooking time: 6–9 hours
Preparation time: 20 minutes
Attention: Minimal
Pot size: 4–8 quarts
Serves 6

½ pound small to medium shrimp
3 cups canned or shelled fresh
    clams
2 medium-sized yellow onions,
    chopped
4 medium-sized ripe tomatoes
2 medium-sized white potatoes
1 medium-sized green bell
    pepper

2 celery ribs
2 medium carrots
4 garlic cloves
1 tablespoon olive oil
1 cup tomato sauce
1 teaspoon dried thyme
½ teaspoon ground black pepper
1 tablespoon hot pepper sauce

1. Boil the shrimp for 10 minutes. Drain and rinse in cool water. Remove the shells and tails. Remove the black veins by running the tine of a fork along the back of each shrimp. If using fresh clams, remove the shells. Peel the onions and chop into ¼-inch pieces. Chop the tomatoes into ½-inch pieces. Peel the potatoes and chop into ½-inch pieces. Remove the seeds and stem from the green pepper and chop the pepper into ¼-inch pieces. Chop the celery into ¼-inch pieces. Peel and chop the carrot into ¼-inch rounds. Peel and mince the garlic.

2. Sauté the onion and garlic in olive oil in a large skillet on medium heat until the onion is translucent and limp. Add the tomatoes, potatoes, green pepper, celery, carrots, tomato sauce, thyme, pepper, and hot sauce; sauté for 5 minutes.

3. Transfer mixture to the slow cooker. Cover and cook on low setting for 6 to 8 hours. Add the shrimp and clams. Cover and cook on high setting for 30 additional minutes.

Chop one bunch of green onions into ¼-inch pieces, including the green stems, and sprinkle on top of the soup before serving with French bread..

CHAPTER 8
Beef

Cooking time: 6–8 hours
Preparation time: 15 minutes
Attention: Minimal
Pot size: 3–6 quarts
Serves 8

Beef Roast with Dried Fruit

2 medium-sized yellow onions
1 clove garlic
3–4 pound boneless pot roast
1½ cups mixed dried fruit
1½ cups dried apple rings
¾ cup pale ale
1 cup water
¼ cup packed brown sugar
1 bay leaf
¼ teaspoon ground cinnamon
2½ teaspoons salt
¼ teaspoon ground black pepper

1. Peel and slice the onions about ¼-inch thick. Peel and mince the garlic using a sharp kitchen knife.
2. Place the onions in bottom of the slow cooker. Place the roast on top. Cover with the mixed dried fruit. Mix together the beer, water, garlic, brown sugar, bay leaf, cinnamon, salt, and pepper; pour over the roast. Cover and cook on low setting 6–8 hours.

Remove the bay leaf and top with the apple rings before serving.

Sweetening with Soda

Substitute Coca-Cola® or 7-Up® for the liquid when making your next roast. The sugar adds a caramel-like texture while the flavors meld well with meat and vegetables.

Cajun Vegetable Beef Soup

Cooking time: 8–10
Preparation time: 30 minutes
Attention: Minimal
Pot size: 4–6 quarts
Serves 8

1½ pounds beef brisket
1½ cups chopped green onions
1 cup chopped celery
½ cup chopped fresh parsley
1 teaspoon fresh, chopped mint
1½ cups fresh green beans
3½ cups potatoes, chopped
1½ cups fresh tomatoes, chopped
2 cups fresh green bell pepper,
  chopped
3 cups turnips, chopped
3 garlic cloves
2 cups Brussels sprouts
1½ cups fresh corn
3½ cups dry white wine
16 cups water
2 tablespoons hot pepper sauce
1 tablespoon soy sauce
1 tablespoon salt

1. Cut the brisket into 1-inch cubes. Remove the roots and the first layer of peel from the onions. Chop the onions, celery, parsley, and mint into ½-inch pieces. Cut the stems off of green beans. Peel and cut the potatoes into ¼-inch-thick slices. Peel the tomatoes and cut into ½-inch pieces. Remove the seeds and stem from the green pepper and cut the green pepper into ¼-inch pieces. Peel the turnips and cut into ¼-inch pieces. Peel the garlic and mince with a sharp paring knife.
2. Combine all ingredients in the slow cooker. Cover and cook on low setting for 8 to 10 hours.

Corn Bread in the Round (page 76) is a must to make this an authentic Cajun dish.

Using Veggies in Converted Receipes

When using strong vegetables such as turnips and rutabaga, reduce the amount in an oven recipe to half for the slow cooker. The slow cooking tends to draw out these flavors, which can overpower the dish.

Grandma Opal's Vegetable Oxtail Soup

Cooking time: 6–8 hours

Preparation time: 20 minutes

Attention: Minimal

Pot size: 3–6 quarts

Serves 6

1 small yellow onion
1 cup carrots, diced
½ cup celery, diced
2 cups white potatoes, cubed
1 pound (16 ounces) canned tomatoes, liquid retained
2 turnips

2 pounds oxtail
2 quarts (8 cups) water
1 teaspoon salt
1 teaspoon celery salt
1 pound (16 ounces) canned whole kernel corn, liquid retained

1. Peel and chop the onion into ¼-inch pieces. Peel the carrots with a potato peeler and cut into ¼-inch pieces. Cut the celery into ¼-inch pieces. Peel the potatoes and cut into ½-inch pieces. Cut the tomatoes into ½-inch pieces, reserving the liquid. Peel and chop the turnips into ¼-inch pieces.
2. Place the meat bones, water, salts, onions, carrots, turnips, and celery in the slow cooker. Cover and cook on low setting for 5 to 6 hours. Take the oxtail out of the slow cooker and remove the meat from the bones; discard the bones and return the meat to the slow cooker. Add the potatoes, tomatoes, and corn, including the liquid from the corn and tomatoes. Cover and cook on low setting for 1 to 2 additional hours.

Slightly Seedy White Bread (page 84) is a good complement to this traditional soup.

Slow to Cook Veggies

Dense root vegetables such as potatoes, carrots, turnips, and rutabagas take longer to cook than meat or other vegetables. Cut them into small pieces and line them on the bottom and along the sides of the food crock to ensure they receive the most heat.

| Cooking time: 7–8 hours |
| Preparation time: 20 minutes |
| Attention: Minimal |
| Pot size: 3–6 quarts |
| Serves 6 |

Porcupine Meatballs

½ cup chopped yellow onion
½ cup chopped green bell pepper
1½ cups lean ground beef
½ cup uncooked white rice
1 egg
1 teaspoon table salt
½ teaspoon ground black pepper
1 (10¾-ounce) can condensed tomato soup

1. Peel and chop the onion into ⅛-inch pieces. Remove the stem and seeds from the green pepper and chop into ⅛-inch pieces. In a mixing bowl, combine the ground beef, rice, onion, green pepper, egg, salt, and pepper; mix well with your hands until well blended.
2. Shape the mixture into about 24 golf ball–sized balls. Place in the slow cooker. Pour the soup over the meatballs. Cover and cook on low setting for 7 to 8 hours.

Serve with Brussels Sprouts à la Orange (page 259) for a complete meal.

Turkeyloaf?

For a lean alternative, substitute ground turkey for ground beef in your next meatball, chili or meatloaf recipe. It is less fatty and offers similar nutritional value.

Cooking time: 8–10 hours
Preparation time: 15 minutes
Attention: Minimal
Pot size: 3–6 quarts
Serves 8

Spicy Pot Roast

1 yellow onion
4 large white potatoes
4-pound pot roast
1 cup water
¼ cup dry white wine
¼ cup ketchup
2 teaspoons Dijon mustard
1 teaspoon Worcestershire sauce
1 package brown gravy mix
⅛ teaspoon garlic powder
¼ teaspoon ground black pepper
½ teaspoon table salt

1. Peel and chop the onion into ¼-inch pieces. Peel the potatoes and cut in half lengthwise.
2. Place all ingredients except the pot roast in the slow cooker; stir well. Add the pot roast. Cover and cook on low setting 8 to 10 hours.

Mix the liquid from the slow cooker with 2 tablespoons flour to create a luscious gravy.

Freezing Meat Dishes

When browning meat for a dish you plan to freeze, use little or no fat during the cooking process. Cooked, frozen fat can taint the flavor of the meat.

Cooking time: 4–6 hours
Preparation time: 15 minutes
Attention: Minimal
Pot size: 3–6 quarts
Serves 6

Lean, Mean Meat Loaf

2 cups cabbage, shredded
1 medium-sized white onion
1 green bell pepper
1 pound lean ground beef
½ teaspoon caraway seed
1 teaspoon table salt

1. Shred the cabbage into ¼-inch strips with a large kitchen knife. Peel and chop the onion into ¼-inch pieces. Remove the stem and seeds from the green pepper and chop the pepper into ¼-inch pieces.
2. Combine all ingredients in a mixing bowl. Shape into a round loaf. Place loaf on a meat rack or vegetable steamer in the slow cooker. Cook covered on high setting for 4 to 6 hours.

Drizzle Heinz 57 Sauce over the top of the meatloaf before serving for a spicy, tangy flavor.

Keep Meatloaf from Sticking

To keep meatloaf from sticking to the bottom of the slow cooker, place a slice of bacon on the bottom of the cooker before adding the meat mixture.

Slow-Cooked Sauerbraten

Cooking time: 5 hours

Preparation time: 15 minutes

Attention: Minimal

Pot size: 4–6 quarts

Serves 8

2 yellow onions
4-pound beef roast
½ teaspoon table salt
½ teaspoon ground black pepper
2 cups beef broth
⅓ cup brown sugar
⅓ cup cider vinegar
8 gingersnap cookies

1. Peel and chop the onions into 1-inch pieces. Sprinkle the beef roast with salt and pepper. Place the roast in the slow cooker. Add the onion, broth, brown sugar, and vinegar. Cover and cook on high setting for 5 hours.
2. Remove the roast from the slow cooker. Crumble gingersnap cookies and add to the sauce in the slow cooker. Stir slowly for about 10 minutes, or until the sauce thickens. Slice the meat and ladle the sauce over slices.

Serve with Heavy Brown Bread (page 85) for an authentic Bavarian meal.

Preventing Splatters

To keep hot fat from splattering when browning meat, sprinkle flour on the bottom of the skillet before adding the meat. You also can add water as the meat cooks.

A Dilly
of a Pot Roast

Cooking time: 8–10 hours
Preparation time: 20 minutes
Attention: Minimal
Pot size: 4–6 quarts
Serves 6

3-pound chuck roast
1 teaspoon table salt
½ teaspoon ground black pepper

2 teaspoons dried dill weed
¼ cup water
1 tablespoon vinegar

Sprinkle both sides of the meat with salt, pepper, and dill weed. Place the roast in the slow cooker. Pour water and vinegar over the top. Cover and cook on low setting for 8 to 10 hours.

This is excellent served with a sauce made of 1 cup sour cream and 2 teaspoons dill weed.

Sparkling Beef Tips

Cooking time: 8–10 hours
Preparation time: 10 minutes
Attention: Minimal
Pot size: 4–6 quarts
Serves 4

2-pound chuck roast
2 cups fresh mushrooms, sliced
1 (10¾-ounce) can cream of
  mushroom condensed soup

1 envelope dry onion soup mix
1 cup lemon-lime carbonated
  drink.

Cut the meat into 1-inch cubes, trimming off the fat as you go. Clean the mushrooms by wiping with a damp cloth; slice ⅛-inch thick. Add all ingredients to the slow cooker; mix well. Cook covered on low setting for 8 to 10 hours.

Serve with Sweet Potato and Apple Bake (page 274) for a good mix of flavors.

Cooking time: **8–10 hours**	
Preparation time: **20 minutes**	
Attention: **Minimal**	
Slow cooker size: **4–6 quarts**	
Serves **4**	

Beef Bourguignon

2-pound chuck roast
1 ½ tablespoons flour
4 large yellow onions
1 cup fresh mushrooms, sliced
1 teaspoon table salt
¼ teaspoon dried marjoram
¼ teaspoon dried thyme
¼ teaspoon ground black pepper
1 cup beef broth
1 cup burgundy wine

1. Cut the meat into 1-inch cubes, trimming off the fat as you go. Dredge the meat in flour by pressing the chunks firmly into a bowl containing the flour. Peel and slice the onions into ¼-inch rings. Wash the mushrooms by wiping with a damp cloth; slice ⅛-inch thick.
2. Add all ingredients to the slow cooker. Cover and cook on low setting for 8 to 10 hours.

Serve over wide egg noodles with a side of Cheesy Cauliflower (page 284) for a complete meal.

Cooking time: 8–10 hours

Preparation time: 20 minutes

Attention: Minimal

Pot size: 4–8 quarts

Serves 8

Hungarian Goulash

2 pounds round steak
½ teaspoon onion powder
½ teaspoon garlic powder
½ teaspoon table salt
½ teaspoon ground black pepper
1½ teaspoon paprika
2 tablespoons flour
1 (10¾-ounce) can condensed tomato soup
½ cup water
1 cup sour cream

1. Cut the steak into 1-inch cubes. Mix the meat, onion powder, garlic powder, salt, pepper, paprika, and flour together until meat is well coated. Place in the slow cooker. Pour soup and water over the top. Cover and cook on low setting for 8 to 10 hours.
2. About a half-hour before serving, stir in the sour cream. Cover and cook on low setting.

Serve over cooked elbow macaroni for an authentic look.

Low-Fat Dairy Substitutions

Substitute low-fat sour cream, cream cheese, and hard cheeses for their regular counterparts in any recipe. However, do not substitute fat-free milk products unless the recipe says you can. A certain amount of fat is needed for the milk product to melt correctly in most dishes.

| Cooking time: 8–10 hours |
| Preparation time: 20 minutes |
| Attention: Minimal |
| Pot size: 3–6 quarts |
| Serves 8 |

Beefy Spanish Rice

1 pound lean ground beef
1 medium-sized yellow onion
1 red bell pepper
1 cup tomato sauce
1 cup water
1 teaspoon chili powder
2 teaspoons Worcestershire sauce
1 cup raw white rice

1. Brown the ground beef in a medium-sized skillet on medium-high heat. Drain off fat and spread the meat on paper towels to soak up more fat. Peel the onion and chop into ¼-inch pieces. Remove the stem and seeds from the red pepper and chop into ¼-inch pieces.
2. Combine all ingredients in the slow cooker. Cover and cook on low setting for 8 to 10 hours.

Serve as a complement to Wisconsin Cheesy Beer Soup (page 40) for a hearty, flavorful meal.

Browning Meat for Recipes

The best way is to brown your meat before placing it in the slow cooker. Simply sauté it in a small amount of oil at a medium-high heat until the surface of the meat is brown. The slow cooker will do the rest.

Japanese Pepper Steak

Cooking time: 6–8 hours
Preparation time: 15 minutes
Attention: Minimal
Pot size: 3–6 quarts
Serves 4

1 pound steak
2 garlic cloves
1 green bell pepper
1 cup fresh mushrooms, sliced
1 medium-sized white onion

3 tablespoons soy sauce
*1 teaspoon ground ginger **or** 2*
*   teaspoons fresh, minced ginger*
½ teaspoon crushed, dried red
*   pepper*

1. Slice the steak about ½-inch thick. Peel the garlic and mince with a sharp kitchen knife. Remove the stem and seeds from the green pepper and slice lengthwise into ¼-inch strips. Wash the mushrooms by wiping with a damp cloth; slice paper-thin. Peel the onion and slice into ¼-inch-thick rings.
2. Combine all the ingredients in the slow cooker; stir well. Cover and cook on low setting for 6 to 8 hours.

Serve over cellophane noodles for an authentic taste.

Beef Chop Suey

Cooking time: 4–5 hours
Preparation time: 30 minutes
Attention: Minimal
Pot size: 6 quarts
Serves 6

3 pounds flank steak
½ cup chopped celery
1 cup chopped bok choy
1 small chopped onion
½ cup water

2 tablespoons dark soy sauce
1½ tablespoon dark molasses
1 teaspoon hot sauce
1 tablespoon flour
2 tablespoons water

Combine all the ingredients except the flour and 2 tablespoons water in the slow cooker; mix well. Cook on high for 4 to 5 hours. Combine the flour and water, and add mixture to the contents of the slow cooker; stir until thick.

Serve over white rice and sprinkle with sesame seeds.

Cooking time: 8–9 hours

Preparation time: 20 minutes

Attention: Minimal

Pot size: 3–6 quarts

Serves 4

Vietnamese Sweet-and-Sour Beef

2 pounds round steak

2 cups carrots, sliced

2 cups pearl onions

1 medium-sized green bell pepper

2 large ripe tomatoes

2 tablespoons oil

2 (8-ounce) cans tomato sauce

⅓ cup vinegar

½ cup light molasses

1 teaspoon paprika

¼ cup sugar

1 teaspoon table salt

1. Cut the beef into 1-inch pieces. Peel the carrots and cut into ¼-inch-thick rounds. Remove the peels from the onions. Remove the stem and seeds from the green pepper and cut lengthwise into ¼-inch strips. Cut the tomatoes into 1-inch pieces.

2. Place the oil and steak in a skillet. Cook on medium-high heat until the meat is brown, stirring occasionally. Place this and all other ingredients in the slow cooker; stir so ingredients are mingled. Cover and cook on low setting 8 to 9 hours.

Serve with sliced cabbage in a vinegar and oil dressing.

Poultry

Peachy Georgia Chicken Legs

Cooking time: 5 hours
Preparation time: 30 minutes
Attention: Minimal
Pot size: 4–6 quarts
Serves 4

4 ripe peaches
8 chicken drum sticks
1 cup dried prunes

3 tablespoons water
1 tablespoon sugar
salt and pepper to taste

Peel the peaches; cut into 1-inch pieces, removing and discarding the pits. Place chicken drum sticks in the slow cooker. Stir together the peaches, prunes, water, sugar, salt, and pepper in a small bowl; pour mixture over the chicken. Cover and cook for 5 hours on the high setting.

Serve with a fresh green salad.

Barbecued Chicken and Beans Casserole

Cooking time: 8–10 hours
Preparation time: 10 minutes
Attention: Minimal
Pot size: 3–6 quarts
Serves 4

2 cups (16 ounces) canned pork
   and beans
3-pound chicken, cut into serving
   pieces
¼ cup ketchup

2 tablespoons peach marmalade
2 teaspoons dried minced onion
¼ teaspoon soy sauce
¼ cup brown sugar

Place the beans in the slow cooker. Add the chicken pieces on top of the beans; do not stir. Mix the ketchup, marmalade, onion, soy sauce, and brown sugar in a small mixing bowl.; pour mixture over the top of the chicken. Cover and cook on low setting for 8 to 10 hours.

Serve with Orange-Glazed Vegetable Medley (page 277).

Cooking time: 6 hours

Preparation time: 45 minutes

Attention: Medium

Pot size: 4–6 quarts

Heroic Chicken Livers

Serves 4

1 pound chicken livers
¼ pound lean, thick-cut bacon
1 teaspoon whole black peppercorns
1 large leek
½ pound (1 cup) mushrooms, sliced
½ cup flour
1 teaspoon table salt
1 cup chicken broth
1 (10¾-ounce) can golden mushroom condensed soup
¼ cup dry white wine

1. Cut the chicken livers into ½- inch pieces. Cut the bacon into 1-inch pieces. Wrap the whole peppercorns in paper towels; smash the peppercorns with a hammer. Cut the top and roots off the leek, discard them, and thoroughly wash the leek; Chop coarsely. Clean the mushrooms by wiping individually with a moistened paper towel; slice the mushrooms paper-thin.

2. Fry the bacon in a large skillet on medium heat Remove the bacon from the skillet when the bacon is crispy; set the bacon aside and retain the grease in the skillet. Mix together the flour, salt, and pepper. Coat the chicken livers in the flour mixture. Cook the livers in the bacon drippings until golden brown. Remove the chicken livers from the skillet with a slotted spoon and place them in the slow cooker. Place the bacon on top of the chicken livers. Pour the chicken broth into the skillet, mixing to combine with the grease; pour mixture over the chicken livers and bacon. Add the golden mushroom soup, leeks, mushrooms, and wine. Cover and cook on low for 6 hours.

This delicate-tasting dish is best served over thick egg noodles.

Cooking time: 7–9 hours

Preparation time: 30 minutes

Attention: Minimal

Pot size: 8 quart

Serves 8

Dilled Turkey Breast

1 boneless turkey breast

1 teaspoon table salt

½ teaspoon ground pepper

2 teaspoons dill weed, plus extra for garnish

¼ cup water

1 tablespoon red wine vinegar

3 tablespoons flour

1 cup sour cream

1. Sprinkle the turkey breast with salt, pepper, and half of the dill; place in the slow cooker. Add water and vinegar. Cover and cook on low for 7 to 9 hours or until tender.

2. Remove the turkey breast. Turn the slow cooker to high. Dissolve the flour in a small amount of water and stir into the meat drippings in the cooker. Add the remaining dill. Cook on high until the sauce thickens. Turn off heat. Stir in the sour cream.

Slice the turkey breast and drizzle with the sauce before serving. Sprinkle with additional dill weed.

Leftovers Reminder

When you make a turkey or pot roast, cut the leftovers into bite-size chunks and store in the freezer for next week's slow cooker recipe.

Chicken Breast with Mushrooms and Peas

Cooking time: 6–8 hours

Preparation time: 20 minutes

Attention: Medium

Pot size: 2–6 quarts

Serves 2

1 small white onion
12 ounces fresh sliced mushrooms
2 tablespoons minced green onion
2 boneless, skinless chicken breasts
3 tablespoons flour
¼ teaspoon ground tarragon
¼ teaspoon salt
½ teaspoon pepper
1 cup milk
½ cup fresh or frozen peas

1. Peel the onion and slice ¼-inch thick. Clean the mushrooms by wiping with a damp cloth; slice paper-thin. Remove the roots and the first layer of peel from the green onions and mince the onions, including the green stems. Place the chicken breasts on the bottom of the slow cooker, then layer the onions, green onions, and mushrooms on top of the chicken breasts. Cook covered on low heat for 4 hours.
2. After the 4 hours are up, blend the flour, tarragon, salt, pepper, and milk by stirring slowly. Pour mixture over the chicken. Add the peas.
3. Cook covered on low setting 2 to 4 hours, until thick, stirring occasionally.

Serve with fresh orange and apple slices.

The Skinny on Skin

Nearly all of the fat in a chicken comes from its skin. You can buy pre-skinned chicken breasts in the grocery store but it's simple to peel the skin off yourself before cooking. (This is also cheaper!) Choose white meat over dark for the leanest meal.

Cooking time: 8–9 hours

Preparation time: 30 minutes

Attention: Minimal

Pot size: 4–6 quarts

Serves 6

Orange Chicken

3 pounds chicken breasts
2 garlic cloves
2 tablespoons diced green pepper
3 medium oranges
1 cup orange juice
⅓ cup chili sauce
2 tablespoons soy sauce
1 tablespoon molasses
1 teaspoon dry mustard
½ teaspoon table salt

1. Remove the skin from the chicken breasts. Peel the garlic and mince with a sharp kitchen knife. Remove the stem and seeds from the green pepper and chop into ¼-inch pieces. Remove the peels from the oranges and separate oranges into slices.
2. Place the chicken breasts in the bottom of the slow cooker. Combine the orange juice, chili sauce, soy sauce, molasses, dry mustard, garlic, and salt in a medium-sized bowl; mix well. Cover and cook on low setting for 8 to 9 hours.
3. Thirty minutes before serving, add the oranges and green pepper to the slow cooker; stir well. Cover and cook on low for the remaining 30 minutes.

Serve over white rice for a light-tasting meal.

To Avoid Splashing Messes

Always add the liquid ingredients last to avoid splashing. You also will have a better idea how much food your meal is going to make by seeing it in "dry" form before cooking.

Cranberry Barbecued Chicken

Cooking time: 6–8 hours
Preparation time: 10 minutes
Attention: Minimal
Pot size: 3–6 quarts
Serves 4

3 pounds chicken breasts
½ teaspoon table salt
½ teaspoon ground black pepper
2 celery ribs, chopped
1 cup barbecue sauce

1 medium-sized yellow onion, chopped
2 cups whole berry cranberry sauce

Remove the skin from the chicken breasts and place the meat in the bottom of the slow cooker. Cover with remaining ingredients. Cover slow cooker and cook on low setting for 6 to 8 hours.

Serve with Cheesy Cauliflower (page 284) for a nice mix of flavors.

Easy Italian Chicken Legs

Cooking time: 8–10 hours
Preparation time: 10 minutes
Attention: Minimal
Pot size: 3–6 quarts
Serves 4

3 pounds chicken legs
1 package dry Italian dressing mix

1 (12-ounce) can or bottle beer, a lager or pilsner is best

Remove the skin from the chicken legs and place the chicken in the slow cooker. Mix the beer with the Italian dressing mix in a medium-sized bowl; pour over the chicken legs. Cook covered on low setting 8 to 10 hours.

Remove the meat from the bones and serve on hard rolls.

Cooking time: 6–8 hours

Preparation time: 20 minutes

Attention: Minimal

Pot size: 3–6 quarts

Mandarin Chicken Breasts   Serves 4

3 pounds chicken breasts

1 medium-sized red bell pepper

1 yellow onion

½ cup chicken broth

½ cup orange juice

½ cup ketchup

2 tablespoons soy sauce

1 tablespoon light molasses

1 tablespoon prepared mustard

½ teaspoon garlic salt

1 cup fresh or frozen peas

1 (11-ounce) can mandarin
    oranges

2 teaspoons flour

1. Remove the skin from the chicken and discard. Remove the stem and seeds from red pepper and cut into ¼-inch strips. Peel the onion and cut into ¼-inch pieces.

2. Place the chicken in the slow cooker. Combine the broth, juice, ketchup, soy sauce molasses, mustard, and garlic salt in a medium-sized mixing bowl; stir until well combined. Pour mixture over the chicken. Add the onions, peas, and green peppers. Cover and cook on low setting for 6 to 8 hours.

3. Thirty minutes before serving, remove the chicken and vegetables from the slow cooker. Measure one cup of liquid from the slow cooker and place it in a saucepan. Discard the remaining liquid. Bring the liquid in the saucepan to a boil. Drain the oranges, retaining 1 tablespoon of the drained juice; mix this juice with the flour. Add mixture to the boiling liquid. Stir in the oranges.

4. Put the chicken and vegetables back into the slow cooker. Pour the orange sauce over the chicken. Cover and cook on low setting for the remaining 30 minutes.

Sprinkle with sesame seeds or chop 4 green onions into ½-inch pieces and sprinkle on top of the chicken before serving.

Cooking time: 7–9 hours

Preparation time: 10 minutes

Attention: Minimal

Pot size: 3–6 quarts

Serves 6

Tropical Chicken

3 pounds chicken breasts
¼ cup molasses
2 tablespoons Worcestershire sauce
2 teaspoons Dijon mustard
¼ teaspoon hot pepper sauce
2 tablespoons pineapple juice
¼ cup dried coconut

1. Remove the skin and bones from the chicken breasts and discard.
2. Combine the molasses, Worcestershire sauce, mustard, hot pepper sauce, and pineapple juice in a small mixing bowl.
3. Brush mixture on both sides of the chicken breasts using a pastry brush. Cover and cook on low setting for 7 to 9 hours.
4. Sprinkle with coconut before serving.

Serve with a medley of fresh tropical fruits: kiwi, papaya, banana, and guava, for example.

Money-Saving Tip
Buy a roasting or stewing chicken for the best value. They are usually bigger, older chickens so the meat is slightly tougher than a broiler-fryer. However, the slow cooking process makes the meat tender and flavorful.

Cooking time: 6–8 hours	
Preparation time: 20 minutes	
Attention: Minimal	
Pot size: 3–6 quarts	
Serves 4	

Chicken Fajitas

1 pound chicken breasts
1 medium-sized yellow onion
2 garlic cloves
1 green bell pepper
1 red bell pepper
2 tablespoons lime juice
$\frac{1}{2}$ teaspoon oregano
$\frac{1}{2}$ teaspoon ground cumin
$\frac{1}{2}$ teaspoon chili powder
$\frac{1}{2}$ teaspoon ground black pepper

1. Remove the bones and skin from the chicken breasts and cut into $\frac{1}{2}$-inch-wide strips. Peel the onion and cut into $\frac{1}{4}$-inch-thick rings; put the onion in the slow cooker. Peel the garlic and mince with a sharp kitchen knife. Remove the stems and seeds from the green and red peppers and cut into $\frac{1}{4}$-inch-wide strips.

2. Combine the garlic, lime juice, oregano, cumin, chili powder, and black pepper in a medium-sized mixing bowl. Add the chicken and toss well to coat. Pour the chicken and juice mixture over the onion. Cover and cook on low setting for 6 to 8 hours. About 30 minutes before serving, stir in the green and red pepper strips; continue cooking, covered, on low for the remaining 30 minutes.

Spoon onto warm flour tortillas and top with chopped tomato, sour cream, grated Colby cheese, and guacamole.

Chicken with Black Olives and Artichokes

Cooking time: 5–6 hours
Preparation time: 20 minutes
Attention: Minimal
Pot size: 3–6 quarts
Serves 6

6 chicken breasts
1 medium-sized white onion
6 garlic cloves
1 cup dry white wine
2 cups chicken broth
2 cups water
1 cup canned, sliced black olives, including juice
1 cup canned artichoke hearts, including juice, cut up
1 cup dry shell macaroni
1 envelop dry onion soup mix

1. Remove the bones and skin from the chicken breasts and discard. Peel the onion and slice into ¼-inch-thick rings. Peel the garlic and mince with a sharp kitchen knife.
2. Put the chicken in the slow cooker; top with onion. Combine the wine, broth, water, black olives, artichoke hearts, garlic, and macaroni in a medium-sized mixing bowl; pour mixture over the chicken and onions. Sprinkle the onion soup mix on top. Cover and cook on low setting for 5 to 6 hours.

Serve with Cheddar and Onion Bread (page 81).

Cooking with Rabbit

Rabbit is an excellent meat for slow cooked meals. It is extremely lean and tends to dry out quickly when cooked in an oven or stovetop. Substitute it for pork or chicken in virtually any recipe.

Cooking time: 8–10 hours

Preparation time: 25 minutes

Attention: Minimal

Pot size: 3–8 quarts

Serves 4

Chicken Cacciatore

3 pounds chicken
3 garlic cloves
1 cup fresh mushrooms, quartered
1 medium-sized yellow onion
1 cup sliced black olives
¼ cup flour
2 tablespoons olive oil
6 cups tomato juice
1 (12-ounce) can tomato paste
2 tablespoons dried parsley
2 tablespoons sugar
2 teaspoons table salt
1 tablespoon dried oregano
½ teaspoon dried thyme
1 bay leaf

1. Cut the chicken into serving-sized pieces. Peel the garlic and mince using a sharp kitchen knife. Clean the mushrooms by wiping with a damp cloth and slice into quarters. Peel the onion and slice into ¼-inch-thick rings. Drain the black olives.
2. Place the flour and chicken in a plastic bag and shake to coat. Heat the olive oil in a medium-sized skillet on medium-high heat and brown the chicken. Transfer the chicken to the slow cooker. Combine the remaining ingredients in a medium-sized mixing bowl and pour over the chicken. Cover and cook on low setting for 8 to 10 hours.

Serve over hot spaghetti noodles for an authentic Italian meal.

Cooking time: 6–7 hours

Preparation time: 15 minutes

Attention: Minimal

Pot size: 3–6 quarts

Chicken à la King

Serves 4

4 chicken breasts
1 medium-sized white onion
1 (10¾-ounce) can cream of chicken condensed soup
3 tablespoons flour
½ teaspoon ground black pepper
1 cup fresh or canned peas
2 tablespoons chopped pimientos
½ teaspoon paprika

1. Remove the bones and skin from the chicken breasts and discard. Cut the chicken into 1-inch cubes; place in the slow cooker. Peel the onion and chop into ¼-inch pieces
2. Combine the soup, flour, and pepper in a medium-sized mixing bowl; pour mixture over chicken. Cover and cook on low setting for 5 to 6 hours. Stir in the peas, onions, pimientos, and paprika. Cover and cook on low setting for 1 additional hour.

Cut thick slices of Heavy Brown Bread (page 85) and ladle Chicken à la King over them.

Is the Low Setting Hot Enough to Be Safe?
When set on low, the slow cooker is roughly equivalent to 200 degrees Fahrenheit. The high setting is about 350 degrees Fahrenheit. Meat cooked to 160 degrees is safe from bacteria.

Nebraskan Creamed Chicken Soup

Cooking time: 8–10 hours

Preparation time: 10 minutes

Attention: Medium

Pot size: 3–6 quarts

Serves 4

1 cup chicken, cubed
2 celery ribs
4 medium carrots
1 medium-sized white onion
1 small zucchini
½ cup (4 ounces) canned pimientos, diced
1 cup fresh peas
1 cup fresh sweet corn
½ cup uncooked rice
3 cups chicken broth
2 cups prepared Alfredo sauce

1. Chop the chicken into ½-inch pieces. Slice the celery ribs into ¼-inch pieces. Peel and slice the carrots into ¼-inch rounds. Peel and slice the onion into ¼-inch pieces. Chop the zucchini into ½-inch pieces. Dice the pimientos into ¼-inch pieces.
2. Add all ingredients except the Alfredo sauce to the slow cooker; stir gently. Cover and cook on low setting for 8 to 10 hours. A half-hour before serving, stir in the Alfredo sauce. Cover and continue cooking on low.

Serve with fresh fruit for a completely balanced meal.

Bulgur Wheat

Bulgur is a crunchy, nutty wheat grain that can be substituted for rice or pasta in most dishes. To prepare, just pour boiling water over the bulgur and let it sit until the liquid is absorbed.

Chapter 10
Pork

Salt Pork in Mustard Greens

Cooking time: 6–8 hours

Preparation time: 20 minutes

Attention: Minimal

Pot size: 3–6 quarts

Serves 4

1 pound salt pork
2 large white onions
4 garlic cloves
4 large bunches mustard greens
6 cups water
1 cup dry white wine
1 tablespoon jalapeño pepper sauce
2 tablespoons soy sauce
1 teaspoon table salt

1. Cut the salt pork into 1-inch pieces. Remove the peel and cut the onions into ¼-inch-thick slices. Peel the garlic and mince with a sharp paring knife. Wash the mustard greens and tear into 2-inch pieces.
2. Mix the water and wine in a separate bowl. Sauté the meat, onions, and garlic in ½ cup of the water and wine mixture in a large skillet on medium-high heat until the onions are limp and transparent. Put all the ingredients in the slow cooker. Cover and cook on low setting for 6 to 8 hours.

Serve with Sweet Potato and Apple Bake (page 274) for a complete meal.

Cooking with Lamb

Lamb is underused in North America yet it has a wonderful flavor. Substitute it for pork in your next slow cooker recipe for an unexpected treat.

Prosciutto, Walnut, and Olive Pasta Sauce

Cooking time: 6–8 hours
Preparation time: 25 minutes
Attention: Minimal
Pot size: 3–6 quarts
Serves 4

½ pound thin-sliced prosciutto
1 red bell pepper
3 garlic cloves
¼ cup olive oil, divided in half
1 cup chopped walnuts
½ cup chopped fresh parsley
¼ cup chopped fresh basil
½ cup chopped black olives, drained

1. Cut the prosciutto into ½-inch pieces. Remove the stem and seeds from the red pepper; cut into ¼-inch strips. Brush the pepper strips with half of the olive oil and bake in a 350-degree oven for 1 hour. Peel and mince the garlic with a sharp kitchen knife. Chop the walnuts, parsley, basil, and olives into ¼-inch pieces.
2. Put the remaining olive oil in a medium-sized skillet and sauté the garlic on medium-high heat until the garlic is brown. Remove and set aside the garlic so it doesn't burn. Add the prosciutto and sauté until crisp. Add the walnuts and sauté until they are brown. Add the cooked garlic
3. Put all ingredients in the slow cooker; stir until well mixed. Cover and cook on low setting for 6 to 8 hours.

Serve over spinach linguine noodles with a side of garlic toast.

Stale Bread

Looking for a different substitute for rice or noodles? Try serving your next dish over a slice of stale bread. Fresh bread gets mushy when it gets wet but stale bread holds up well to being the base of a meal.

Ham and Asparagus Roll-ups

Cooking time: 6–8 hours	
Preparation time: 10 minutes	
Attention: Minimal	
Pot size: 2–6 quarts	
Serves 6	

12 thin slices ham
24 fresh asparagus spears
12 slices Swiss cheese
1 teaspoon garlic salt
½ cup chicken broth

1. Lay the ham slices flat on a cutting board. Top each with two asparagus spears. Sprinkle with garlic salt. Top each with a slice of Swiss cheese. Roll up so that the asparagus spears stick out of both ends.
2. Put the chicken broth in the slow cooker. Add the ham roll-ups. Cover and cook on low setting for 6 to 8 hours, or until asparagus is soft but not mushy.

Garlic bread and pickled vegetables are the perfect complement to this dish.

The Other White Meat

Although pork is not really "the other white meat," today's pigs are not fat. In fact, pork tends to be leaner than beef. Substitute pork for beef in any recipe but remember to remove the fat from around the edges.

Ham Sandwiches

Cooking time: 8–10 hours
Preparation time: 10 minutes
Attention: Minimal
Pot size: 2–4 quarts
Serves 8

2 pounds ham, cut into slices
2 cups apple juice

1 cup brown sugar
2 teaspoons Dijon mustard

Combine the apple juice, brown sugar, and mustard. Put the ham in the bottom of the slow cooker and pour the liquid mixture over the top. Cover and cook on low setting for 8 to 10 hours. Remove the ham and discard the juice.

Make the sandwiches using Heavy Brown Bread (page 85) and Swiss cheese.

Cherry Pork Chops

Cooking time: 4–5 hours
Preparation time: 15 minutes
Attention: Minimal
Pot size: 4–6 quarts
Serves 6

6 pork chops
½ teaspoon table salt
½ teaspoon ground black pepper

1 (21-ounce) can cherry pie filling
1 chicken bouillon cube
2 teaspoons lemon juice

1. Place the pork chops in a large skillet on the stove. Brown on medium-high heat for 5 minutes. Sprinkle with salt and pepper.
2. Mix half of the can of cherry pie filling, the crushed bouillon cube, and the lemon juice in the slow cooker. Place the pork chops on top of mixture. Cover and cook on low setting for 4 to 5 hours.

Heat the remaining half of the cherry pie filling and ladle it onto the pork chops before serving.

Roast Pork with Ginger and Cashew Stuffing

Cooking time: 8–10 hours

Preparation time: 30 minutes

Attention: Minimal

Pot size: 3–6 quarts

Serves 8

¾ *cup yellow onion, diced*
1½ teaspoons fresh ginger, grated
1 cup cashews, chopped
1 teaspoon orange rind, grated
3 tablespoons parsley, chopped
2 eggs
2 tablespoons butter
4 cups corn bread crumbs
1 teaspoon table salt
1 teaspoon ground black pepper
6-pound pork roast

1. Peel and chop the onion into ¼-inch pieces. Grate the ginger finely with a vegetable grater. Chop the cashews into ¼-inch pieces. Grate the orange rind without peeling the orange. Chop the parsley into ⅛-inch pieces. Lightly beat the eggs with a fork until yolk and whites are well integrated.
2. Melt the butter in a large frying pan on the stove at medium heat. Add the onions, cashews, and ginger and cook for five minutes, stirring. Transfer to the slow cooker and add orange rind, parsley, bread crumbs, salt, pepper, and eggs. Stir well so that all the ingredients are well mixed.
3. Push the stuffing to the sides of the slow cooker and place the pork roast in the pocket. Cook covered on low setting for 8 to 10 hours.

This is a wonderful winter meal when served with Squash Medley Au Gratin (page 278).

Pork Pisole

Cooking time: 5–6 hours

Preparation time: 20 minutes

Attention: Minimal

Pot size: 3–6 quarts

Serves 4

2 pounds pork chops
1 large white onion
1 garlic clove
4 ripe, fresh tomatoes
1 15-ounce can white hominy
1 15-ounce can yellow hominy
2 teaspoons chili powder
1 teaspoon table salt
½ teaspoon thyme

1. Debone the pork chops and cut the meat into 1-inch cubes. Peel and chop the onion into ¼-inch pieces. Peel and mince the garlic using a sharp paring knife. Place the pork in a large skillet on medium-high heat and cook until brown, about 5 minutes (you may need to add a bit of oil if using very lean pork). Add the onion and garlic; turn the heat down to medium and sauté for 5 more minutes.
2. Chop the tomatoes into 1-inch pieces. Combine the pork, onion, garlic, tomatoes, hominy, and spices in the slow cooker. Cook covered on low setting for 5 to 6 hours.

To complement the flavors in this dish, serve it with a salad of field greens with a red wine vinegar dressing.

Save Time
If you don't have a lot of time for food preparation, buy boneless pork chops instead. Many grocery stores now carry pork that is cut into stir-fry strips; these are also a great substitution.

Fall Is in the Air Pork Roast

Cooking time: 8–10 hours
Preparation time: 15 minutes
Attention: Minimal
Pot size: 4–6 quarts
Serves 8

1 cup diced fresh cranberries
1 teaspoon grated orange peel
4-pound pork roast
1 teaspoon table salt

1 teaspoon ground black pepper
¼ cup honey
⅛ teaspoon ground cloves
⅛ teaspoon ground nutmeg

1. Chop the cranberries into ¼-inch pieces. Grate the orange peel while still on the orange by rubbing it over a vegetable grater.
2. Place the pork roast in the slow cooker. Sprinkle with salt and pepper. Combine the cranberries, orange peel, honey, cloves, and nutmeg; mix well. Pour mixture over the pork roast. Cover and cook on low setting for 8 to 10 hours.

Serve with fresh green beans and Dilly Mashed Potatoes (page 283).

Bavarian Pork Chops

Cooking time: 7–8 hours
Preparation time: 15 minutes
Attention: Minimal
Pot size: 3–6 quarts
Serves 6

6 pork chops
2 cups sauerkraut
¼ cup brown sugar

1 envelope dry onion soup mix
1 teaspoon caraway seeds
½ cup water

Place the pork chops in the slow cooker. Drain sauerkraut. Combine the sauerkraut, brown sugar, onion soup mix, caraway seeds, and water in a medium-sized bowl; pour mixture over the pork chops. Cover and cook on low setting for 7 to 8 hours.

Serve with Orange-Glazed Vegetable Medley (page 277).

Cooking time: 4–6 hours
Preparation time: 15 minutes
Attention: Minimal
Pot size: 3–6 quarts
Serves 6

Peachy Keen Pork Chops

6 pork chops
1 teaspoon table salt
½ teaspoon ground black pepper
1 (29-ounce) can peach halves in syrup
¼ cup syrup from peaches
¼ cup brown sugar
¼ teaspoon ground cinnamon
¼ teaspoon ground cloves
1 (8-ounce) can tomato sauce
¼ cup vinegar

1. Place the pork chops in a large skillet on the stove; sprinkle with salt and pepper. Brown for 5 minutes at medium-high heat. Drain off the fat and place the pork chops in the slow cooker. Place the drained peach halves on top of the pork chops.
2. Combine the ¼ cup of syrup from the peaches, the brown sugar, cinnamon, cloves, tomato sauce, and vinegar; pour mixture over the peaches and pork chops. Cover and cook on low setting for 4 to 6 hours.

Offset the sweet taste of this meal by serving it with pickled cauliflower and beets.

The Importance of Texture

To add variety to frequently made dishes, try experimenting with both chunky and smooth kinds of tomato sauce. The change in texture will keep the meal interesting and new.

German-Style Ham Hocks

Cooking time: 8–10 hours

Preparation time: 15 minutes

Attention: Minimal

Pot size: 3–6 quarts

Serves 4

4 smoked ham hocks

2 cans (15-ounce) sauerkraut,
   liquid retained

4 large white potatoes, peeled
   and quartered

½ teaspoon ground black pepper

Place all the ingredients in the slow cooker including the liquid from the canned sauerkraut. Cover and cook on low setting for 8 to 10 hours. Remove the ham hocks and take the meat off the bones. Discard the bones and return the meat to the slow cooker.

A traditional German meal calls for baked beans and brown beer with this dish.

Blueberry Pork Roast

Cooking time: 7–8 hours

Preparation time: 20 minutes

Attention: Minimal

Pot size: 3–6 quarts

Serves 6

3-pound pork loin

1 teaspoon grated orange peel

2 cups fresh blueberries

½ cup white grape juice

½ cup sugar

1 teaspoon table salt

Place the pork loin in the slow cooker. Grate the orange peel using a vegetable grater. Wash the blueberries and remove the stems. Combine the grape juice, sugar, orange peel, blueberries, and salt; pour mixture over the pork loin. Cover and cook on low setting for 7 to 8 hours.

Complement the sweet flavor of this dish by serving it with Garlicky Spinach and Swiss Chard (page 275).

Cooking time: 7–8 hours

Preparation time: 15 minutes

Attention: Minimal

Pot size: 3–6 quarts

Serves 6

Teriyaki Pork Tips

3-pound boneless pork loin roast
¾ cup unsweetened apple juice
2 tablespoons sugar
2 tablespoons soy sauce
1 tablespoon vinegar
1 teaspoon ground ginger
½ teaspoon garlic powder
½ teaspoon ground black pepper
2 tablespoons flour
2 tablespoons water

1. Cut the pork roast into 1-inch cubes and place in the slow cooker. Combine the apple juice, sugar, soy sauce, vinegar, ginger, garlic powder, and pepper in a medium-sized mixing bowl; pour mixture over the meat and stir well. Cover and cook on low setting for 7 to 8 hours.

2. A half-hour before serving, make a paste of the flour and water and add the mixture to the slow cooker. Stir well so that there are no lumps of flour. Cook uncovered on high setting for 20 to 30 minutes, stirring frequently.

Serve with Lemony Asparagus and Carrots (page 275).

CHAPTER 11
Wild Game

Cabbage on Pheasant

Cooking time: 6 hours

Preparation time: 30 minutes

Attention: Minimal

Pot size: 6–8 quarts

Serves 6

1 pheasant
2 pieces bacon
1 teaspoon ground black pepper
1 medium-sized yellow onion
1 carrot
1 cup hot water
1 medium head red cabbage

1. Cut the pheasant into quarters; brown the pheasant in a medium-sized saucepan with two pieces of bacon. Peel the onion and chop into ¼-inch pieces. Peel and cut the carrot into ¼-inch rounds. Place the pheasant in the slow cooker. Cover with water, onions, and carrots. Sprinkle with pepper. Cook for 5 hours on low setting.
2. Shred the cabbage into ¼-inch-wide pieces. Place the cabbage over the pheasant and cook for 1 additional hour.

Serve with Minnesota Wild Rice (page 281) as the perfect complement.

Can't Find a Pheasant?

Can't find pheasant or partridge in your grocery store and don't have a bird hunter in your family? Substitute readily available game hens. Thaw them completely before stuffing or adding to the slow cooker.

Rabbit Stuffed with Garlic Mashed Potatoes

Cooking time: 8–9 hours

Preparation time: 1 hour

Attention: Medium

Pot size: 6–8 quarts

Serves 6

4 large potatoes
6 cloves garlic
1 tablespoon vegetable oil
2 tablespoons butter
½ teaspoon ground black pepper
1 whole rabbit, cleaned

1. Clean, peel, and cut the potatoes into eighths; boil the potatoes in a medium-sized pot until tender.
2. While the potatoes are cooking, peel and chop the garlic into ¼-inch pieces. Sauté the garlic in the vegetable oil on low heat in a small skillet until lightly golden.
3. Drain the potatoes and add sautéed garlic. Mash the potatoes with the butter, salt, and pepper.
4. Fill the body of the rabbit with mashed potato stuffing. Place the rabbit in the slow cooker with legs folded under the body. Cook on low setting for 8 to 9 hours.

Serve with Lemony Asparagus and Carrots (page 275).

Slow-Baked Meat

Use a vegetable steamer in the slow cooker to "bake" meat. It will keep the meat out of the juice at the bottom of the cooker without hindering the flow of steam.

Cooking time: 9–11 hours

Preparation time: 1 hour

Attention: Medium

Pot size: 6–8 quarts

Serves 6

Wild Duck Gumbo

2 wild ducks, cleaned
1 tablespoon vegetable oil
2 tablespoons flour
1 teaspoon table salt
1 garlic clove, minced
2 cups water
2 teaspoons Worcestershire sauce

1 teaspoon hot pepper sauce
¼ cup red bell peppers, diced
⅛ cup jalapeño peppers, diced
2 medium-sized yellow onions
2 stalks celery
½ pound Polish sausage

1. In a large kettle bring 2 quarts of water to boil, then turn off heat. Add the ducks to the water. Cover and let stand for 10 minutes. Remove the ducks from the pot and place on paper towels. This process is called "parboiling"; it removes excess fat from wild poultry and other fatty meats.

2. Heat the oil on low heat in a medium-sized saucepan. Add the flour, salt, and garlic; sauté until brown. Add the two cups water, Worcestershire sauce, and hot sauce. Simmer, stirring constantly, until sauce is thick.

3. Remove the stems and seeds from the peppers; cut peppers into ¼-inch-wide lengthwise strips. Peel the onions and chop into ¼-inch pieces. Chop the celery into ¼-inch pieces. Place the vegetables on the bottom of the slow cooker. Place the ducks on top of the vegetables. Pour the prepared sauce over the ducks. Cover and cook on low setting for 8 to 10 hours. Remove and debone the ducks. Dispose of the skin and cut the meat into chunks. Cut the sausage into ¼-inch pieces. Return the duck to the slow cooker, add the sausage, and cook for 1 hour, or until the sausage is warmed through.

Serve over white rice with a side of Sweet Potato and Apple Bake (page 274).

Swiss-Style Venison Steak

Cooking time: 4–6 hours

Preparation time: 20 minutes

Attention: Minimal

Pot size: 4–6 quarts

Serves 6–8

2 pounds venison steak, approximately 2 inches thick
2 cups flour
2 large Vidalia onions
6 fresh, ripe tomatoes
½ teaspoon minced garlic
¼ cup white vinegar
½ teaspoon pepper
1 teaspoon salt
½ cup water

1. Sprinkle flour onto the steaks and pound the steaks with a meat-tenderizing mallet. Continue sprinkling flour and pounding until the meat is covered with as much flour as possible.
2. Lay the steaks in the bottom of the slow cooker. Slice the onions into ¼-inch-thick rings. Slice the tomatoes into 8 wedges each. Mince the garlic using a sharp kitchen knife. Mix together the onions, tomatoes, garlic, vinegar, pepper, salt, and water in a bowl. Add this mixture to the slow cooker. Cook covered on low setting for 4 to 6 hours.

Green Beans in Lemon Honey (page 260) and mashed potatoes are nice complements to the venison and tomato in this recipe.

Venison in Beer Barbecue Sauce

Cooking time: 8 hours

Preparation time: 10 minutes, plus some work the day before

Attention: Minimal

Pot size: 4–6 quarts

Serves 4

3 pounds roast from deer, elk, or moose
2 medium-sized yellow onions
3 cloves garlic
1 (12-ounce) can or bottle brown ale
1 teaspoon table salt
1 teaspoon ground black pepper
2 cups tomato sauce
1 teaspoon Worcestershire sauce
¼ cup brown sugar

1. Cut the meat into 1-inch cubes. Peel the onions and slice into ¼-inch-thick rings. Peel the garlic and crush it by laying a large knife over each clove and pushing until it "pops."
2. In a large bowl, combine the onions, garlic, beer, salt, and pepper. Marinate the meat in this mixture, covered in the refrigerator, for 12 to 24 hours. Turn the meat occasionally during this time.
3. Remove the meat from the marinade and place the meat in the slow cooker.
4. Mix together the tomato sauce, Worcestershire sauce, and brown sugar in a bowl; pour mixture over the meat. Cook covered on low setting for 8 hours.

Serve with a green lettuce salad and assorted cheeses to create a well-balanced meal.

Marinating Meat

Never marinate meat for longer than 24 hours. The meat begins to break down and the texture becomes mushy. The flavors should penetrate after about two hours.

Sweet-and-Sour Venison

Cooking time: 8 hours

Preparation time: 30 minutes

Attention: Frequent

Pot size: 4–6 quarts

Serves 4

2 pounds venison steak
¼ cup flour
¼ cup oil
½ cup warm water
1 teaspoon salt
1 green bell pepper
1 red bell pepper
½ cup fresh, frozen, **or** canned
   pineapple, cut into chunks

Sauce:

2½ tablespoons cornstarch
½ cup pineapple juice
¼ cup white vinegar
¼ cup white sugar
2 tablespoons soy sauce

1. Cut the venison into 1-inch cubes and roll the cubes in flour. Heat the oil in a skillet to medium and place the venison in the pan; brown the meat on all sides. Remove the meat and set it on a paper towel for a few minutes to absorb the grease. Place the meat into the slow cooker with the water and salt. Cook covered on low setting for 6 hours.

2. Remove the stems and seeds from the peppers and chop into 1-inch pieces. Cut the pineapple into 1-inch chunks. Add the peppers and pineapple to the slow cooker. Cook covered 1 more hour on low setting.

3. To make the sauce, combine the cornstarch, pineapple juice, white vinegar, white sugar, and soy sauce in a saucepan and heat on the stove on medium heat until the sauce has thickened. Add to the slow cooker and cook covered on low setting for 1 more hour.

To maintain the "wild" flavor of this dish, serve it over brown rice.

Venison Definition

Venison isn't necessarily deer meat. It also is the term used for elk or caribou meat. These meats can vary widely in taste depending on what the animal has eaten. As a result, they are best served in stews that blend many flavors.

Uncle Mike's Roast Duck

Cooking time: 8–10 hours

Preparation time: 10 minutes

Attention: Minimal

Pot size: 5–6 quarts

Serves 4

1 yellow onion
2 garlic cloves
2 celery ribs
1 3-pound duck, cleaned
1 teaspoon vegetable oil
½ teaspoon salt
½ teaspoon ground black pepper
½ teaspoon poultry seasoning

1. Peel the onion and chop into ¼-inch pieces. Crush the garlic cloves by taking a large knife and placing it on its side on top of each garlic clove; press down until the clove "pops." Chop the celery into ¼-inch pieces. Put the vegetables in slow cooker.
2. Rinse the duck cavity with cold water and swab with vegetable oil by placing the oil on a paper towel and wiping it inside the cavity. Sprinkle the cavity with the salt, black pepper, and poultry seasoning. Place the duck in the slow cooker on top of the vegetables and sprinkle with dried parsley. Cook covered on low setting for 8 to 10 hours.

Serve with German-Style Cooked Cabbage with Onions and Peppers (page 276) for a robust meal.

Oils

For a difference in taste, try using a flavored vegetable oil. You can find all kinds in specialty grocery stores.

Game Birds with Sweet Potatoes

Cooking time: 8–10 hours
Preparation time: 15 minutes
Attention: Minimal
Pot size: 5–6 quarts
Serves 4

3 medium-sized sweet potatoes
1 cup fresh sliced mushrooms
8 breasts from small game birds (pheasant, partridge, grouse, etc.)
⅔ cup flour, plus 3 tablespoons
1 teaspoon salt
1 teaspoon nutmeg
1 teaspoon cinnamon
½ teaspoon ground black pepper
½ teaspoon garlic powder
½ cup whole milk
½ cup orange juice
2 teaspoons brown sugar

1. Peel the sweet potatoes and cut into ¼-inch-thick slices; place them in the bottom of the slow cooker. Clean the mushrooms by wiping with a damp cloth, then cut into ⅛ inch-thick slices.
2. Rinse the breasts and pat dry. Combine the ⅔ cup flour, salt, nutmeg, cinnamon, pepper, and garlic powder. Thoroughly coat the breasts in this mixture. Place the breasts on top of the sweet potatoes in the slow cooker.
3. Combine the milk, mushrooms, orange juice, brown sugar, and 3 tablespoons flour; mix with a fork in a small bowl until the sugar and flour are well integrated into the liquid. Pour mixture over breasts. Cook covered on low setting for 8 to 10 hours.

For a fall harvest meal, serve the breasts over Minnesota Wild Rice (page 281).

Roasted Small Game with Onions

Cooking time: 10–12 hours

Preparation time: 15 minutes

Attention: Minimal

Pot size: 4–6 quarts

Serves 4

4–5 pounds of small game (rabbit, squirrel, etc.)
2 Vidalia onions
1 garlic clove
½ teaspoon table salt
½ teaspoon ground black pepper
1 cup water
2 tablespoons soy sauce
2 bay leaves
1 whole clove
2 tablespoons all-purpose flour
½ cup cold water

1. Cut the meat into serving-sized pieces. Peel the onions and slice into ¼-inch-thick rings. Peel the garlic and slice paper-thin. Place the onion and garlic in the bottom of the slow cooker.
2. Sprinkle the meat with salt and pepper; place in the slow cooker. Add the 1 cup water, soy sauce, bay leaves, and clove. Cook covered on low setting 10 to 12 hours.
3. Remove the rabbit and set aside. Remove the bay leaf and discard. Stir the flour into the ½ cup water until it is well blended. Pour this mixture into the slow cooker and stir until the gravy thickens.

Cut the meat off the bones and serve over mashed potatoes. Don't forget to top it with the luscious, onion-laden gravy!

Game Birds with Beer and Mushrooms

Cooking time: 6–8 hours
Preparation time: 20 minutes, plus
2–4 hours of marinating time
Attention: Medium
Pot size: 4–6 quarts
Serves 4

3 pounds of small game bird breasts (pheasant, grouse, partridge, etc.)
¾ cup teriyaki sauce
½ cup flour
2 teaspoons garlic salt
1 teaspoon ground black pepper
⅓ cup olive oil
1 large yellow onion, sliced
¾ cup fresh mushrooms, sliced
12-ounce can or bottle dark beer

1. Debone the bird and cut the meat into 1-inch cubes. Marinate the meat in teriyaki sauce in the refrigerator for 2 to 4 hours.
2. Combine the flour, garlic salt, and pepper; coat the meat in this mixture. Place the olive oil in a medium-sized skillet. Add the flour-covered meat and cook on medium heat, stirring constantly until the meat is slightly browned. Add the onion and sauté for 3 minutes, stirring constantly. Remove the meat and onions and place in slow cooker. Clean the mushrooms by wiping with a damp cloth; slice paper-thin. Add the beer and mushrooms to the slow cooker. Cook covered on low setting 6 to 8 hours.

For a more delicate-tasting meal, substitute white wine for the beer.

How Much Marinade?

Allow about ½ cup of marinade for each two pounds of meat, fish or vegetables. Always marinate in the refrigerator to avoid bacteria growth. Discard the marinade or cook it to boiling before adding to a recipe.

Holiday Goose with Cranberries

Cooking time: 8–10 hours
Preparation time: 10 minutes
Attention: Minimal
Pot size: 6 quart oval
Serves 4

1 wild goose, gutted and skinned (note that domestic goose is much greasier and should not be substituted)
½ teaspoon table salt
½ teaspoon ground black pepper
1 (15-ounce) can whole berry cranberry sauce
1 envelope dry onion soup mix
½ cup orange juice

Wash the goose cavity with cold water and sprinkle with salt and pepper. Place the goose in the slow cooker. Combine the cranberry sauce, dry onion soup mix, and orange juice; pour mixture over the goose. Cook covered on low setting 8 to 10 hours.

Garnish with fresh orange slices, baked sweet potatoes, and parsley to create a festive-looking meal.

What If I Get Home Late?
Because the slow cooker cooks using steam and a low temperature, most dishes will stay moist and tasty for several hours after the recommended cooking time.

Freshwater Fish and Seafood

Cooking time: 5½ –7½ hours

Preparation time: 30 minutes

Attention: Medium

Pot size: 4–6 quarts

Cream of Shrimp Soup

Serves 8

1 pound potatoes

1 white onion

1 celery rib

2 carrots

2 cups water

½ cup vegetable broth

2 tablespoons white wine

¼ teaspoon dried thyme

½ pound baby shrimp (**or** large precooked shrimp cut into
   ½-inch pieces)

2 cups shredded Swiss cheese

1 cup whole milk

½ teaspoon ground black pepper

1. Peel the potatoes and cut into ½-inch cubes. Peel the onions and chop into ¼-inch pieces. Chop the celery into ¼-inch pieces. Peel the carrots and shred using a vegetable grater. Place the potatoes, onions, celery, carrots, water, vegetable broth, white wine, and thyme into the slow cooker. Cook covered on high heat 4 to 6 hours.

2. Use a hand-held mixer to purée the vegetables in the slow cooker; the resulting mixture should be the consistency of baby food. Add the shrimp and cook covered for 30 minutes on low setting. Shred the cheese using a vegetable grater. Add the cheese, milk, and pepper to the soup. Cook covered on low setting for about 1 hour, stirring every 15 minutes, until the cheese is melted.

Garnish with fresh sprigs of cilantro.

Cooking time: 2–3 hours

Preparation time: 20 minutes

Attention: Medium High

Pot size: 4–6 quarts

Serves 4

Salmon in White Wine with Dried Peaches

1½ pounds salmon fillets

¼ cup all-purpose flour

2 tablespoons extra-virgin olive oil

1 cup dry white wine

½ cup vegetable stock

1 cup dried peaches, quartered

½ teaspoon freshly ground black pepper

1. Pat the salmon dry with paper towels. Coat with a light layer of flour. Heat the olive oil in a frying pan at medium heat. Add the salmon and brown on all sides. Discard the oil and place the salmon fillets on paper towels to soak up additional oil.

2. Add the wine and vegetable stock to the slow cooker and cook on high setting until it bubbles. Turn the slow cooker to the low setting. Place the salmon fillets in the bottom of the slow cooker. Place the quartered dried peaches on top. Sprinkle with pepper. Cook covered on low setting for 2 to 3 hours.

Serve with fresh steamed broccoli drizzled with fresh-squeezed lime juice.

Minnesota Mock Lobster

Cooking time: 2–4 hours

Preparation time: 15 minutes

Attention: Minimal

Pot size: 4–6 quarts

Serves 6

3 stalks celery
1 medium onion
½ cup water
½ cup lemon juice
*2 tablespoons butter **or** margarine*
3 pounds frozen torsk fillets
1 teaspoon salt
1 teaspoon paprika
6 lemon wedges
½ cup melted butter

1. Chop the celery into 1-inch pieces. Peel and quarter the onion.
2. Add the celery, onion, water, lemon juice, and butter to the slow cooker. Cook uncovered on high setting until the butter is melted. Stir mixture and turn the slow cooker to low setting. Lay the torsk fillets on the bottom of the slow cooker. Sprinkle salt and paprika over the fillets. Cook covered on low setting for 2 to 4 hours. Serve with melted butter and lemon wedges.

Add color to this main dish by serving it with Lemony Asparagus and Carrots (page 275).

Too Salty?
If the dish tastes too salty, add a teaspoon each of cider vinegar and sugar to the recipe. They will neutralize the salt without adding additional flavor.

Brown Rice Curry with Vegetables and Scallops

Cooking time: 7–9 hours

Preparation time: 30 minutes

Attention: Medium

Pot size: 4–6 quarts

Serves 6

1 large yellow onion
3 cloves garlic
1 tablespoon olive oil
1 pound baby scallops
1½ cups water
1 tablespoon curry powder
½ teaspoon cinnamon
½ teaspoon table salt
2 large potatoes
1 large zucchini
2 large carrots
1 (16-ounce) can tomatoes, liquid retained

1. Peel and chop the onions into ¼-inch pieces. Peel and slice the garlic paper-thin with a sharp kitchen knife. Heat the olive oil in medium-sized skillet; sauté the scallops, onions, and garlic on medium-high heat until the onions are translucent and limp. The scallops should be slightly brown. Drain off the oil and place the scallops, onions, and garlic in the slow cooker.
2. Add the water, curry powder, cinnamon, and salt to the slow cooker; stir well. Cook covered on high setting for 1 hour.
3. Peel and cut the potatoes into 1-inch cubes. Slice the zucchini into ¼-inch-thick pieces. Peel and slice the carrots into ¼-inch pieces. Slice the tomatoes into 1-inch pieces, retaining the juice. Add the potatoes, zucchini, and tomatoes to the slow cooker. Cook covered on low setting for 6 to 8 hours.

Serve with a dry white wine and Italian Beets (page 285).

Cooking time: 6–9 hours

Preparation time: 20 minutes

Attention: Minimal

Pot size: 3 to 6 quarts

Serves 4

Shrimp Marinara

4 large red tomatoes
1 garlic clove
2 tablespoons fresh parsley, minced
½ teaspoon dried basil
1 teaspoon table salt
¼ teaspoon ground black pepper
1 teaspoon dried oregano
1 (6-ounce) can tomato paste
½ pound small- to medium-sized fresh shrimp

1. Chop the tomatoes into 1-inch pieces. Peel and mince the garlic with a sharp paring knife. Mince the parsley by chopping it into very small pieces. Add the tomatoes, garlic, parsley, basil, salt, pepper, oregano, and tomato paste to the slow cooker. Cook covered on low setting for 6 to 8 hours.

2. Cook the shrimp by boiling it in a large kettle for 10 minutes. Rinse with cold water. Remove the shells and tails. Devein by using the tine of a fork to remove the blackish membrane along the back of each shrimp. Add the shrimp to the slow cooker and stir well. Turn the setting to high. Cook covered for 15 minutes.

Serve over linguine noodles. Top with Parmesan cheese and dried parsley flakes.

Preparing Fresh Shrimp

When using fresh shrimp, boil them for 3 minutes. Run under cold water. Remove all of the shell, although you can keep the tail on if you like. Take a small fork and run it along the back of the shrimp to remove the black vein.

Cooking time: 4–6 hours

Preparation time: 20 minutes

Attention: Minimal

Pot size: 3–6 quarts

Freshwater Fish Stew

Serves 4

1½ pounds freshwater fish (walleye, northern, trout, bass, etc.),
cleaned, skinned, and deboned
¾ cup fresh mushrooms, sliced
1 clove garlic
1 large white onion
1 green bell pepper
2 small zucchini
4 large ripe tomatoes
2 tablespoons olive oil
½ teaspoon dried basil
½ teaspoon dried oregano
1 teaspoon table salt
¼ teaspoon ground black pepper
¼ cup dry white wine

1. Cut the fish into 1-inch cubes. Clean the mushrooms by wiping with a damp cloth. Remove the stems and slice the mushroom heads paper-thin. Peel and mince the garlic. Peel the onion and slice into ¼-inch-thick rings. Remove the seeds and stem from the green pepper and chop into 1-inch pieces. Cut the tomatoes into 1-inch pieces.
2. Combine all ingredients in the slow cooker. Stir gently because the fish will break up if stirred too quickly. Cover and cook on low setting 4 to 6 hours.

Use shark, sea bass, or other mild saltwater fish to give a lighter flavor to this dish.

Lobster in Havarti and Cognac Cream Sauce

Cooking time: 1–2 hours

Preparation time: 30 minutes

Pot size: 3–6 quarts

Attention: Frequent

Serves 4

1 pound fresh lobster meat (approximately 3 whole lobsters)
4 garlic cloves
1 teaspoon fresh tarragon, chopped
2 cups Havarti cheese, grated
1 cup light cream
¼ cup cognac
1 tablespoon ground black pepper
½ teaspoon table salt
1 egg

1. Cook lobster by immersing them in boiling water head first. Cover and boil about 20 minutes.
2. Remove the meat from the lobster tails and claws and cut into 1-inch cubes. Peel and chop the garlic cloves into paper-thin slices. Chop the tarragon into ¼-inch lengths.
3. Combine the cheese, cream, cognac, garlic, pepper, salt, and tarragon in the slow cooker on low temperature setting; stir constantly with a wooden spoon until all the cheese has melted.
4. Pour the sauce into a blender and add the egg. Purée for 2 minutes on medium speed. Return the sauce to the slow cooker. Add the lobster meat. Cook covered on low setting for 30 to 60 minutes.

Ladle over cooked spinach linguine noodles.

Cooking time: 1½ hours

Preparation time: 15 minutes

Attention: Minimal

Pot size: 3–6 quarts

Citrus Fish Fillets

Serves 6

1 fresh orange
1 fresh lemon
1 white onion
5 tablespoons fresh chopped parsley
¼ teaspoon butter
2 pounds fresh fish fillets, skinned and deboned
½ teaspoon table salt
¼ teaspoon ground black pepper
4 teaspoons vegetable oil

1. Before peeling, run the orange and lemon over the smallest teeth on a vegetable grater to yield 2 teaspoons of grated rind from each. Peel the remaining rind from the orange and lemon, discard, and slice the fruit into ¼-inch-thick pieces. Peel and chop the onion into ¼-inch pieces. Wash the parsley under cold water and chop into ¼-inch lengths.
2. Rub the butter on the bottom of the slow cooker. Add the fish fillets. Sprinkle salt and pepper over the fillets. Put the onion, parsley, and grated rinds on top of fish. Drizzle with vegetable oil. Cover and cook on low setting for 1½ hours. Ten minutes before serving, add the orange and lemon slices on top.

Serve with a vegetable medley of broccoli, cauliflower, and carrots slices about ¼-inch thick, steamed and drizzled with lemon juice.

Cooking time: 7–9 hours	
Preparation time: 20 minutes	
Attention: Minimal	
Pot size: 2–6 quarts	
Serves 4	

Shrimp Creole

1 pound fresh shrimp
1¼ cup yellow onion, chopped
1 medium-sized green bell pepper
1½ cups celery, chopped
6 large ripe tomatoes
1 (8-ounce) can tomato sauce
1 teaspoon garlic salt
¼ teaspoon ground black pepper
½ teaspoon Tabasco or other hot pepper sauce

1. Cook the shrimp by boiling it for 20 minutes. Immerse in cold water until cool. Remove the shells and tails. Devein by using a fork tine to remove the blackish membrane on the back of each shrimp.
2. Peel and chop the onion into ¼-inch pieces. Remove the stem and seeds from the green pepper and chop the pepper into ¼-inch pieces. Cut the celery into ¼-inch pieces. Cut the tomatoes into 1-inch cubes. Add the celery, onion, green pepper, fresh tomatoes, tomato sauce, garlic salt, black pepper, and hot pepper sauce to the slow cooker. Cover and cook on low setting 6 to 8 hours. Add the shrimp, stir well, cover and cook an additional 1 hour.

Serve over long-grain brown rice. Top with fresh chopped chives.

Slow Cooking with Shellfish

To keep shellfish from getting rubbery in a slow cooked meal, add them during the last two hours of the cooking process. Always use fresh shellfish, if possible, as freezing can cause the flesh to toughen.

Vegetable Seafood Chowder

Cooking time: 8–10 hours

Preparation time: 20 minutes

Attention: Minimal

Pot size: 2–6 quarts

Serves 4

3 large potatoes
1 medium-sized white onion
1 cup fresh carrots, chopped
½ cup celery, chopped
1 cup fresh broccoli, chopped
1 cup frozen or fresh peas
1 cup fresh haddock, cubed
2 cups vegetable stock
1 teaspoon table salt
½ teaspoon ground black pepper

1. Peel the potatoes and chop into 1-inch cubes. Peel and chop the onion in ¼-inch pieces. Cut the carrots, celery, and broccoli into ¼-inch pieces.
2. Add all the ingredients except fresh peas and fish to the slow cooker. Cover and cook on low setting for 7 to 8 hours. Add peas and fish, cook for 1 to 2 hours more.

Add 1 additional cup vegetable stock and 1 cup assorted other fresh seafood such as scallops, oysters, shrimp, and shark meat to make this a diverse, surprising treat.

Manhattan Clam Chowder

Cooking time: 8–10 hours

Preparation time: 20 minutes

Attention: Minimal

Pot size: 2–6 quarts

Serves 4

¼ pound bacon

1 large Vidalia onion

2 medium carrots

1 celery rib

8 medium-sized ripe tomatoes

3 medium potatoes

1 tablespoon dried parsley

3 cups fresh or canned clams

½ teaspoon table salt

½ teaspoon ground black pepper

1 teaspoon dried thyme

4 cups water

1. Brown the bacon in a medium-sized skillet on medium-high heat until crisp. Drain the grease. Lay the bacon on paper towels to cool. Crumble the bacon and add it to the slow cooker. Peel the onion and cut into ¼-inch pieces. Peel and slice the carrots into ¼-inch rounds. Cut the celery into ¼-inch pieces. Cut the tomatoes into ½-inch cubes. Peel the potatoes and cut into ½-inch cubes.
2. Add all ingredients to the slow cooker. Cover and cook on low setting for 8 to 10 hours.

Serve with Sweet Corn Pudding (page 285) for a nice blend of flavors.

Cooking time: 7–8 hours

Preparation time: 20 minutes

Attention: Minimal

Pot size: 4–8 quarts

Serves 8

Cioppino

12 mussels

12 clams

12 large shrimp

1 pound cod

1 large yellow onion

1 medium-sized green bell pepper

2 medium-sized ripe tomatoes

2 garlic cloves

2 tablespoons fresh minced parsley

3 tablespoons olive oil

2 cups clam juice

½ cup dry white wine

1 bay leaf

1 teaspoon table salt

1 teaspoon ground black pepper

4 soft-shell crabs

1. Leave the mussels and clams in their shells. Remove the shells from the shrimp and devein the shrimp by running a fork tine along the back of each shrimp. Cut the cod into 1-inch cubes. Peel the onion and chop into ¼-inch pieces. Remove the stem and seeds from the green pepper; chop into ¼-inch pieces. Chop the tomatoes into ½-inch pieces. Peel the garlic and mince with a sharp kitchen knife. Mince the parsley with a sharp kitchen knife.

2. Heat the olive oil in a large skillet on medium heat. Add the onions, green pepper, and garlic and sauté for about 5 minutes, or until the onions are translucent; pour into the slow cooker. Stir in the tomatoes, parsley, clam juice, wine, and bay leaf. Cover and cook on low setting for 6 to 7 hours.

3. Remove the bay leaf. Add the salt, pepper, mussels, clams, shrimp, fish, and crab; stir gently. Cover and cook on low setting for 1 hour. Discard any mussels or clams that remain closed.

Serve with Slightly Seedy White Bread (page 84) for sopping up the wonderful juice.

Cooking time: 8–10 hours
Preparation time: 20 minutes
Attention: Minimal
Pot size: 2–6 quarts
Serves 4

Tuna Tomato Bake

1 medium-sized green bell pepper
1 small yellow onion
1 celery rib
2 cups (16 ounces) water-packed tuna, drained
2 cups (16 ounces) tomato juice
2 tablespoons Worcestershire sauce
3 tablespoons vinegar
2 tablespoons sugar
1 tablespoon Dijon mustard
¼ teaspoon chili powder
½ teaspoon cinnamon
¼ teaspoon hot pepper sauce

1. Remove the seeds and stem from the green pepper and chop the pepper into ¼-inch pieces. Peel the onion and chop into ¼-inch pieces. Cut the celery stalk into ¼-inch pieces.
2. Combine all ingredients; mix gently. Cover and cook on low setting for 8 to 10 hours.

Serve as a sandwich spread with Heavy Brown Bread (page 85).

Slow-Baked Fish

To bake fish in a slow cooker, use a vegetable steamer or other rack that keeps it out of the juices. Sprinkle it with lemon or lime juice and cook on low for only a couple hours. The fish is done when it flakes when separated by a fork.

Cooking time: 3–4 hours

Preparation time: 15 minutes

Attention: Minimal

Pot size: 3–6 quarts

Salmon Casserole

Serves 4

8 ounces (1 cup) fresh mushrooms, quartered
1 small yellow onion
1 cup shredded Cheddar cheese
2 eggs
2 cups (16 ounces) canned salmon with liquid
1½ cups bread crumbs
1 tablespoon lemon juice

1. Clean the mushrooms by wiping with a damp cloth; cut into quarters. Peel the onion and chop into ¼-inch pieces. Shred the Cheddar cheese with a vegetable grater. Beat the eggs by stirring quickly with a fork.
2. Put the fish in a medium-sized mixing bowl and flake with a fork, removing any bones. Mix together all the ingredients; pour into the slow cooker. Cover and cook on low setting for 3 to 4 hours.

Serve with Cheesy Cauliflower (page 284) for a nice blend of flavors.

Peppery Salmon Chowder

Cooking time: 6–7 hours
Preparation time: 20 minutes
Attention: Minimal
Pot size: 4–6 quarts
Serves 6

1 pound fresh salmon
1 medium-sized red bell pepper
1 medium-sized green bell pepper
1 medium-sized yellow bell pepper
4 medium potatoes
3 medium carrots
1 celery rib
2 medium-sized white onions
2 cups sweet corn
3 cups vegetable broth
1 teaspoon whole black peppercorns

1. Remove the skin and bones from the salmon and cut the meat into 1-inch cubes. Remove the stems and seeds from the bell peppers and chop the peppers into ½-inch pieces. Leave the peels on the potatoes and cut the potatoes into ½-inch cubes. Peel and chop the carrots and celery into ¼-inch pieces. Peel the onions and chop into ¼-inch pieces.

2. Combine all ingredients in the slow cooker. Cover and cook on low for 6 to 7 hours.

Serve with fresh Zucchini Bread (page 79) for a nice complement to the spicy vegetables in this chowder.

CHAPTER 13
Kids' Favorites

Cooking time: 2–3 hours

Preparation time: 20 minutes

Attention: Minimal

Pot size: 4–6 quarts

Serves 12

Sloppy Joes

1 medium-sized yellow onion

2 celery ribs

2 pounds extra-lean hamburger

2 cups tomato sauce

½ cup can tomato paste

¼ cup white vinegar

3 teaspoons Worcestershire sauce

2 tablespoons brown sugar

1 teaspoon garlic salt

½ teaspoon pepper

1. Peel the onion and chop into ¼-inch pieces. Chop the celery into ¼-inch pieces. Put the onion, celery, and hamburger in a medium-sized skillet on medium-high heat. Cook until the hamburger is brown and no pink remains. Drain off the grease.
2. Combine all ingredients in the slow cooker. Cook covered on low setting for 2 to 3 hours.

Add potato chips and carrot sticks to the plate and you have a true all-American lunch that is perfect for chilly outings or teen get-togethers.

Mini-Bakery

Use the slow cooker as a mini-bakery for young children. Let them mix up a batch of chocolate chip cookies and watch through the glass lid as one or two cookies at a time bake right before their eyes.

Cooking time: 2 hours

Preparation time: 30 minutes

Attention: Minimal

Pot size: 5–6 quarts

Serves 6–8

Pizza Meatballs

Meatballs:

½ pound (1 cup) shredded
   Swiss cheese
1 medium-sized yellow onion
½ of a medium-sized green bell
   pepper
2 pounds extra-lean hamburger
2¾ cups bread crumbs
1 teaspoon salt
¼ teaspoon basil
¼ teaspoon pepper
1 cup canned condensed vegetable soup
¼ cup skim milk

Sauce:

1 garlic clove
1 medium-sized yellow onion
6 large ripe tomatoes
1 cup beef broth
½ cup (4 ounces) tomato paste
1 teaspoon salt
1 teaspoon oregano

1. To make the meatballs, cut the cheese into ¼-inch cubes. Peel and chop the onion into ¼-inch pieces. Remove the stem and seeds from the green pepper and chop the pepper into ¼-inch pieces. Mix all the meatball ingredients together well and form into firm balls no larger than 2 inches in diameter. Lay the meatballs in the bottom of the slow cooker.

2. To make the sauce, peel the garlic and slice thinly with a paring knife. Peel and chop the onions into ½-inch pieces. Peel the tomatoes with a sharp paring knife, gently lifting the skin off, quarter them, and mix in a blender on low speed for 2 minutes. Combine all sauce ingredients and pour over the meatballs.

3. Cook covered on low setting for 2 hours.

Make these ahead of time and freeze them. They can be thawed in the microwave for those last-minute lunch demands or as an after-school snack.

Cooking time: 1½ hours

Preparation time: 15 minutes

Attention: Constant

Pot size: 6 quarts

Serves 12

Party Snack Mix

½ teaspoon vegetable oil

4 tablespoons butter (or margarine)

1 teaspoon garlic salt

½ teaspoon onion salt

4 teaspoons Worcestershire sauce

3 cups Corn Chex cereal

3 cups Wheat Chex cereal

3 cups Rice Chex cereal

1 cup shelled, skinless peanuts

2 cups mini pretzel sticks

½ cup Parmesan cheese, grated

1. Put the vegetable oil on a paper towel and spread the oil over the bottom and insides of the slow cooker. Combine the butter (or margarine), garlic salt, onion salt, and Worcestershire sauce in the slow cooker. Heat on high setting until the butter is melted. Mix well and add the Corn Chex, Wheat Chex, Rice Chex, peanuts, and pretzel sticks. Cook uncovered on high setting for 1 hour, stirring every 15 minutes. Reduce to low setting and cook uncovered for 30 minutes, stirring every 15 minutes.

2. Spread the mixture on paper towels. Lightly sprinkle with Parmesan cheese. Let cool before serving.

This nutritious, low-fat treat keeps for weeks in airtight containers, making it the ideal after-school snack.

Caramel Corn with Peanuts

Cooking time: 1½ hours
Preparation time: 15 minutes
Attention: Constant
Pot size: 6 quarts
Serves 12

¼ cup maple-flavored syrup
¼ cup packed brown sugar
1 teaspoon vanilla
3 tablespoons butter (or margarine)
10 cups unsalted, dry popped popcorn
2 cups skin-on Spanish peanuts

1. Combine the maple-flavored syrup, brown sugar, vanilla, and butter or margarine in the slow cooker. Cook uncovered on high setting until the butter (or margarine) melts and the brown sugar is dissolved; stir well. Add the popcorn and peanuts. Cook covered on high setting for 1 hour, stirring every 15 minutes. Cook uncovered on low setting an additional 30 minutes, stirring every 15 minutes.
2. Spread the mixture on lightly greased cookie sheets to cool before serving.

Add almonds or coconut instead of the peanuts.

A Sweeter Treat
For an even yummier snack, experiment with adding chocolate chips or small candy pieces to the caramel corn mixture.

Real Baked Beans and Franks

Cooking time: 7–9 hours

Preparation time: 15 minutes

Attention: Minimal

Pot size: 5–6 quarts

Serves 6

3 cups dried navy beans
6 cups water
1 medium-sized yellow onion
1 large tomato
½ cup brown sugar
½ cup maple-flavored syrup

1 cup ketchup
2 teaspoons dried mustard
2 teaspoons vinegar
1 cup water
12 all-beef hotdogs, cut into
    ½-inch round slices

1. Wash the beans then soak them in 6 cups of water for 12 hours before cooking. Drain and wash the beans again.
2. Peel the onion and cut into ⅛-inch pieces. Chop the tomato. Combine the brown sugar, maple-flavored syrup, ketchup, mustard, vinegar, tomato, and onion in the slow cooker. Cook uncovered on high setting until the brown sugar has dissolved; stir well. Add 1 cup water, beans, and hotdogs. Stir to cover the beans and hot dogs with sauce. Cook covered on low setting for 7 to 9 hours. One hour before serving, remove the cover and continue cooking on low setting.

To add interest to the meal, serve with apple slices sprinkled with cinnamon.

Cracked Crockery

Slow cookers are simple devices that can take a lot of abuse. However, the crockery pot can crack if dropped. It's also heavy and could easily break a toe. If you do inadvertently drop the slow cooker, check it for cracks and make sure it is heating correctly before you use it again.

Cooking time: 8 hours

Preparation time: 20 minutes

Attention: Minimal

Pot size: 3–6 quarts

Serves 8

Halftime Chili

2 pounds lean ground beef

1 medium-sized yellow onion

3 medium tomatoes

2 cups (16 ounces) canned or frozen corn

4 cups (32 ounces) precooked or canned red kidney beans

1 cup water

2 tablespoons chili powder

2 teaspoons table salt

1 teaspoon ground black pepper

¼ teaspoon dried red pepper flakes

1. Brown the meat in a large skillet on the stove. Continue browning at medium heat until no pink remains in the meat. Drain off the fat and lay the meat on paper towels to absorb remaining fat.

2. Peel and dice the onion into ¼-inch pieces. Dice the tomatoes into ¼-inch pieces. Drain and rinse the kidney beans. Combine the onion, tomatoes, corn, kidney beans, water, chili powder, salt, black pepper, and dried red peppers; stir to combine. Cook covered on low setting for 8 hours.

Place small bowls of shredded Cheddar cheese, diced jalapeño peppers, sour cream, and diced green onion tops on the table and let kids top their own chili.

Macaroni and Cheese with Hamburger

Cooking time: 3 hours

Preparation time: 20 minutes

Attention: Minimal

Pot size: 4–6 quarts

Serves 8

1 pound lean hamburger
6 cups elbow macaroni
2 cups whole milk
2 cups shredded Cheddar cheese
2 teaspoons dry mustard
¼ teaspoon garlic salt
¼ teaspoon ground black pepper

1. Brown the hamburger in a skillet on medium-high heat on the stove. Drain off the fat and spread the hamburger on paper towels to absorb remaining grease. Cook the macaroni in boiling water until soft.
2. Combine the milk, Cheddar cheese, dry mustard, garlic salt, and black pepper in the slow cooker. Cook uncovered on high setting until the cheese has melted completely. Add the cooked macaroni and hamburger; stir well. Cook uncovered on low setting for 3 hours.

Try different pastas such as rotini or alphabet shapes. Substitute hot dog or sausage slices for the hamburger

Using Skim Milk

If a recipe calls for whole milk, half and half, or cream, you can easily substitute skim milk. You will get all the nutrition and most of the creamy taste with much less fat.

Mom's Cure for a Winter Cold: Easy Chicken Noodle Soup

Cooking time: 8–10 hours

Preparation time: 30 minutes

Attention: Medium

Pot size: 4–6 quarts

Serves 10

1 chicken, cleaned, with skin and bones
1 medium-sized yellow onion
8 carrots
4 celery ribs
6 cups water
2 chicken bouillon cubes
1 teaspoon table salt
½ teaspoon ground black pepper
8 ounces dried egg noodles

1. Cut the chicken into serving portions—legs, wings, thighs, breasts. Peel and dice the onions and carrots into about ¼-inch pieces. Slice the celery ribs into ¼-inch pieces.
2. Combine the water, bouillon cubes, salt, pepper, and chicken pieces in the slow cooker. Cook covered on high for 4 to 5 hours. Remove the chicken and discard the bones and skin. Place the meat back in the slow cooker. Add the noodles, carrots, celery, and onions in the slow cooker. Cook covered on high setting for 4 to 5 additional hours.

Spicy dill pickles, Cheddar cheese, and saltine crackers are the perfect complement to chicken noodle soup.

Minty Hot Chocolate . . .

Cooking time:	30 minutes
Preparation time:	5 minutes
Attention:	Constant
Pot size:	2–6 quarts
Serves 12	

12 cups whole milk
1 cup chocolate syrup
1 teaspoon peppermint extract

Combine the milk, syrup, and peppermint extract in the slow cooker. Cook uncovered on high setting for 30 minutes, stirring every 5 minutes until the chocolate syrup is dissolved.

Use a soup ladle to let kids serve themselves right from the slow cooker.

. . . And Ooey, Gooey S'mores

Cooking time:	10 minutes
Preparation time:	5 minutes
Attention:	Minimal
Pot size:	2–6 quarts
Serves 4	

8 graham cracker squares
2 Hershey's chocolate bars without almonds
4 large marshmallows

Preheat the slow cooker on high setting for 10 minutes. Place 4 graham cracker squares on the bottom of the slow cooker. Top each with half of a chocolate bar. Top this with one marshmallow each. Cook covered on high setting for 10 minutes. Add 4 graham cracker squares to the tops to make 4 sandwiches. Press down until the chocolate and marshmallow begin to ooze out of the sandwich.

For a different yet still scrumptious treat, use half of a chocolate bar with almonds or half of a Mounds bar instead of the half all-chocolate candy.

Barbecued Chicken Drummies

Cooking time: 5 hours

Preparation time: 15 minutes

Attention: Minimal

Pot size: 3–6 quarts

Serves 12

1 teaspoon yellow onion, grated

2 garlic cloves

1 cup water

¼ cup honey

2 teaspoons soy sauce

2 tablespoons vinegar

1 cup bottled barbecue sauce

2 tablespoons hot pepper sauce (optional)

½ teaspoon table salt

½ teaspoon ground black pepper

1 teaspoon cayenne pepper (optional)

36 chicken drummies (the fleshy part of the wing that attaches to the breast)

Peel and grate the onion using a vegetable grater. Peel the garlic cloves and slice paper thin. Combine the onion, garlic, water, honey, soy sauce, vinegar, barbecue sauce, hot pepper sauce (if using), salt, black pepper, and cayenne (if using) in the slow cooker. Cook on high setting about 15 minutes, until all ingredients are well combined. Stir well and add the chicken drummies. Cook covered on low setting for 5 hours.

This is a perfect appetizer for slumber parties or teen get-togethers. Add the optional ingredients for older teens to get the flavor of Buffalo wings. Remember to serve them with celery sticks and blue cheese dressing!

Sicilian Potatoes

Cooking time: 4–5 hours

Preparation time: 20 minutes

Attention: Medium

Pot size: 4–6 quarts

Serves 4

1 small yellow onion
4 garlic cloves
4 ripe tomatoes
¼ teaspoon oregano
2 teaspoons salt
3 tablespoons olive oil
14 small new potatoes
6 links Italian sausage

1. Peel and chop the onions and garlic into ¼-inch pieces. Chop the tomatoes into ½-inch pieces. Turn the slow cooker on high setting. Add the olive oil, garlic, and onions. Cook for 10 minutes. Add the tomatoes, oregano, and salt. Reduce heat to low, cover, and cook for 15 minutes.
2. Peel and wash the potatoes. Cut each Italian sausage link into 4 equal pieces. Place the potatoes and sausage in the slow cooker. Cook on low setting for 4 hours, or until the potatoes are tender.

Low-Fat Substitutions

If you want to make these potatoes healthier and lower in fat, use Italian-spiced turkey or chicken sausages instead.

I Did It Myself Ham and Vegetable Soup

Cooking time: 2–3 hours

Preparation time: 10 minutes

Attention: Minimal

Pot size: 2–6 quarts

Serves 8

4 cups water
1 can sliced carrots
1 can corn
1 can peas
1 can sliced potatoes
1 can green beans
1 ham soup bone
A dash of ground black pepper

1. Add the water to the slow cooker and turn on low setting.
2. Empty all ingredients into the slow cooker, including the juices from the canned vegetables; stir well. Cook covered on low setting for 2 to 3 hours.
3. Remove the soup bone and take off all of the meat that hasn't already fallen off. Tear the meat into bite-sized pieces if necessary. Return the meat to the slow cooker and discard the bone.

Even a preschooler will be proud to make this tasty soup—all Mom or Dad did was open the cans! Serve it with cheese sandwiches and olives for a complete do-it-yourself meal.

Cooking time: 8–10 hours
Preparation time: 30 minutes
Attention: Minimal
Pot size: 3–6 quarts
Serves 8

Vegetarian Stone Soup

1 large white onion
1 cup rutabaga, chopped
1 turnip
2 large potatoes
1 cup baby carrots
2 celery ribs
1 cup broccoli, chopped

1 small zucchini
1 stone, about the size of an egg
4 cups water
1 cup fresh or frozen green beans
1 teaspoon table salt
½ teaspoon ground black pepper

1. Peel and chop the onion, rutabaga, turnip, and potatoes into 1-inch pieces. Slice the carrots in half. Chop the celery into ¼-inch pieces. Chop the broccoli and zucchini into ½-inch pieces. Clean the stone well—it's best to run it through the dishwasher!

2. Put the stone and water in the slow cooker. Add one ingredient at a time to the slow cooker, stirring as each ingredient is added. Cook covered on low setting for 8 to 10 hours. Remove the stone before serving.

This is a fun party recipe for preschoolers or kindergarteners. Have each child bring one or two ingredients and let them stir their own ingredients into the soup! Serve with crackers and American cheese for a healthy lunch.

Replacing Broccoli

If you don't have fresh broccoli handy, substitute green beans. They hold up well while slow cooking and offer similar nutritional value as broccoli.

Cooking time: 1–2 hours

Preparation time: 10 minutes

Attention: Constant

Pot size: 2–6 quarts

Serves 50 as snacks

Chocolate-Covered Cherries

5 pounds confectioners' sugar
½ pound (1 cup) butter
¼ teaspoon vanilla
1 (12-ounce) can sweetened condensed milk
¾ pound edible paraffin
3 (12-ounce) packages semisweet chocolate chips
1 large jar maraschino cherries (about 200)
Round toothpicks

1. Using your hands, mix together the confectioners sugar, butter, vanilla, and condensed milk. Cover and set aside. Shave the paraffin with a vegetable grater. Place the chocolate chips and paraffin in the slow cooker. Heat on high setting uncovered, stirring periodically, until melted.
2. In the meantime, drain and discard the juice from the cherries. Mold the sugar mixture over the cherries and spear with a toothpick. When the chocolate is melted, dip each of the cherries into the chocolate, then place them on wax paper to harden.

Substitute peppermint flavoring for the vanilla.

Slow-Cooked Candy
Use the slow cooker instead of a saucepan for making basic candies such as caramel apples and candy-coated pretzels. It will melt the ingredients without scorching. It's also safer than a hot stove.

	Cooking time: 1 hour
	Preparation time: 15 minutes
	Attention: Minimal
	Pot size: 1–3 quarts
Peanut Butter Crunch	Serves 8

½ cup chocolate-covered toffee
1 (16-ounce) jar crunchy peanut butter
½ cup miniature semisweet chocolate chips

Break the chocolate-covered toffee into small pieces using a wood mallet or cleaver. Place the toffee, peanut butter, and miniature chocolate chips into the slow cooker; mix well. Cook covered on low setting for 1 hour.

Use as a dip for graham crackers or vanilla wafers.

Doubling a Recipe

When doubling or tripling a recipe in the slow cooker, be sure you have a large enough slow cooker. Add enough water for the single recipe then add more later in the cycle if needed.

CHAPTER 14

Hot and Spicy

South o' the Border Chicken Casserole

Cooking time: 4–5 hours

Preparation time: 15 minutes

Attention: Minimal

Pot size: 3–6 quarts

Serves 4

4 boneless, skinless chicken breasts
1 small yellow onion
1½ cups grated Cheddar cheese
12 flour tortillas
1 (10¾-ounce) can cream of mushroom condensed soup
1 (10¾-ounce) can cream of chicken condensed soup
1 cup sour cream
½ cup (4 ounces) canned chopped jalapeño peppers
1 cup salsa

1. Cut the chicken into 1-inch cubes. Peel the onion and grate using the fine side of a vegetable grater. Grate the cheese using the larger side of the vegetable grater. Tear the tortillas into eighths.

2. Combine the onion, cheese, soups, sour cream, and jalapeño peppers in a medium-sized bowl. Make layers in the slow cooker using a third of the torn tortillas, soup mixture, chicken, then salsa. Repeat twice more. Cover and cook on low setting for 4 to 5 hours. Gently stir before serving.

Serve over a bed of lettuce and baked tortilla chips.

Onion Varieties

Onions vary in sweetness. Vidalia tend to be the sweetest, followed by red then yellow. White onions are the least sweet and are better in meat dishes than in soups.

Cooking time: 6–8 hours

Preparation time: 15 minutes

Attention: Minimal

Pot size: 3–6 quarts

Serves 6

Mexican Beef

2 pounds round steak
1 yellow onion
4 fresh tomatoes
1 beef bouillon cube
1 (16-ounce) can kidney beans
¼ teaspoon ground black pepper
½ teaspoon garlic salt
1 tablespoon chili powder
1 tablespoon prepared mustard
½ cup (4 ounces) canned chopped jalapeño peppers

1. Cut the beef into 1-inch cubes. Peel and chop the onion into ¼-inch pieces. Cut the tomatoes into quarters. Crush the bouillon cube. Drain the kidney beans.
2. Mix meat, pepper, garlic salt, chili powder, and mustard in slow cooker. Cover with onion, crushed bouillon cube, tomatoes, jalapeño peppers and beans; mix well. Cover and cook on low setting 6 to 8 hours. Mix well before serving.

Serve over white rice with fresh-sliced oranges.

Tomato Types

All tomatoes are not alike. Substitute plum tomatoes for a more robust flavor. Choose golden tomatoes for a more mellow taste. Reserve pricier hot-house tomatoes for recipes in which tomatoes are the main ingredient.

Mexican Chicken Chowder

Cooking time: 7–8 hours

Preparation time: 20 minutes

Attention: Medium

Pot size: 3–6 quarts

Serves 4

1½ pounds boneless, skinless chicken breasts

2 medium-sized white onions

2 garlic cloves

2 celery ribs

½ cup (4 ounces) canned or fresh green chilies, chopped

1 cup (8 ounces) Velveeta cheese, cubed

1 tablespoon olive oil

4 cups chicken broth

1 package dry chicken gravy mix

2 cups milk

2 cups salsa

1 (32-ounce) bag frozen hash brown potatoes

1. Cut the chicken into ½-inch cubes. Peel the onion and cut into ¼-inch pieces. Peel the garlic and mince with a sharp kitchen knife. Cut the celery into ¼-inch pieces. Cut the chilies into ⅛-inch pieces. Cut the cheese into ½-inch cubes.

2. Combine the chicken, onions, garlic, celery, oil, and broth in the slow cooker. Cover and cook on low for 3 to 4 hours.

3. Dissolve the gravy mix in the milk in a medium-sized mixing bowl. Stir into chicken mixture. Add the salsa, potatoes, chilies, and cheese; mix well. Cover and cook on low for 4 hours.

Serve with Corn Bread in the Round (page 76) for an authentic Mexican meal.

Cooking time: 6½ –8½ hours

Preparation time: 30 minutes, plus 1 hour soaking time

Attention: Medium

Pot size: 4–6 quarts

Chicken Creole

Serves 8

4 large chicken breasts (about four cups of meat)
4 tablespoons dehydrated onion
1 tablespoon dehydrated green onion
1 tablespoon dehydrated parsley flakes
1 teaspoon garlic powder
2 cups warm water
2 cups chicken or vegetable stock (or water)
1 cup dry white wine
3 tablespoons steak sauce
2 teaspoons hot sauce
4 cups (32 ounces) canned, peeled tomatoes
½ cup (4 ounces) canned, chopped jalapeño peppers

1. Boil the chicken for 20 minutes in water in a large pot on the stove. Cut the meat off the bones.
2. Mix the dehydrated onions, green onions, parsley, and garlic powder in 2 cups of water and set aside; let this soak for about 1 hour. Combine the water, wine, steak sauce, hot sauce, tomatoes, and jalapeño peppers in the slow cooker. Cook uncovered on high for 30 minutes. Add the soaked dehydrated ingredients to the slow cooker; stir well. Add the chicken and mint to the seasoned water and stir well. Cover and cook on low setting for 6 to 8 hours.

Serve over white rice.

Cooking time: 8–10 hours	
Preparation time: 20 minutes	
Attention: Minimal	
Pot size: 3–6 quarts	
Serves 6	

Southwestern Beef Roast with Peppers

4 garlic cloves
3 medium-sized yellow onions
1 green bell pepper
1 red bell pepper
1 yellow bell pepper
2 tablespoons jalapeño pepper, minced

5 large ripe tomatoes
1 tablespoon olive oil
3-pound chuck roast
2 cups hot salsa

1. Remove the peel and mince the garlic with a sharp kitchen knife. Remove the peels from the onions and slice into ¼-inch-thick rings. Remove the stems and seeds from the peppers and slice lengthwise into ¼-inch-wide strips. Mince the jalapeño pepper with a paring knife. Chop the tomatoes into ½-inch pieces.

2. Place the olive oil, garlic, onions, bell and jalapeño peppers, and roast in a large skillet on the stove. Cook on medium-high heat until the roast is browned. Flip it so both sides are browned. Scoop the mixture into the slow cooker. Do not drain the oil. Pour the salsa over the ingredients in the slow cooker. Add the tomatoes on top. Cover and cook on low setting for 8 to 10 hours.

Serve with Lemony Asparagus and Carrots (page 275) for a wonderful mix of flavors.

No Time for Browning?

If you don't want to brown meat in a skillet before adding it to the slow cooker, plan to make a thick gravy to serve with it. This will hide the grayish color of the meat.

Tex-Mex Pork and Potatoes

Cooking time: 4–5 hours

Preparation time: 20 minutes

Attention: Medium

Pot size: 3–8 quarts

Serves 6

3-pound pork roast
3 large white onions
4 garlic cloves
10 assorted whole chili peppers
5 medium-sized new potatoes
10 whole cloves
1 cinnamon stick
10 black peppercorns
1 teaspoon whole cumin seeds
2 tablespoons white vinegar

1. Trim the fat from the pork roast. Peel the onions and cut into quarters. Peel the garlic and mince with a sharp kitchen knife. Remove the stems from the chili peppers; cut in half lengthwise. Peel the potatoes and cut in half.
2. Place the pork in the slow cooker. Cover with onions, garlic, chili peppers, cloves, cinnamon, peppercorns, and cumin. Add just enough water to cover ingredients. Cover and cook on low setting for 3 hours.
3. Stir mixture. Add the potatoes. Cover and cook for 1 to 2 hours, or until the potatoes are soft. Ten minutes before serving, remove the spices and add vinegar.

Serve with Cheddar and Onion Bread (page 81).

Mushy Potatoes

Have your raw potatoes gone mushy? They're still good if you use them right away. Remove the peels and slice the potatoes thickly. Put them into a soup or stew and no one will know they were past their prime.

Mexican Pork Carnitas

Cooking time: 4–6 hours

Preparation time: 15 minutes

Attention: Minimal

Pot size: 3–6 quarts

Serves 4

4 garlic cloves
2–4-pound pork butt roast
1 bunch fresh cilantro
1 fresh jalapeño pepper, seeded and chopped
1 (12-ounce) can or bottle lager beer

1. Peel and slice the garlic cloves about ⅛-inch thick. Using a sharp paring knife, cut slices into the butt roast and insert the garlic cloves, one slice in each opening. Place the butt roast in the slow cooker.
2. Chop the cilantro into ¼-inch lengths. Place the cilantro and jalapeño pepper on top of the butt roast. Pour the beer over the top and cook on high setting for 4 to 6 hours. Remove the meat and shred it. Discard the jalapeño pepper and cilantro.

Steam corn tortillas by placing them in the microwave with a cup of water and cooking on high for 20 seconds. Ladle the meat into the tortillas and top with chopped tomatoes and onions.

Quick Marinade

An easy marinade for any meat is half Heinz 57 sauce and half Italian salad dressing. Cut the meat into bite-size pieces and place in a container in the refrigerator for a couple hours before using.

Cooking time: 1–3 hours

Preparation time: 20 minutes

Attention: Minimal

Pot size: 4–6 quarts

Spicy Chicken Chili Stew

Serves 4

4 chicken breasts

1 large white onion

2 stalks celery

2 (4-ounce) cans of tomato paste

2 (12-ounce) cans of tomato sauce

2 (15-ounce) cans of red chili beans, with juice

6 tablespoons chili powder

2 tablespoons cumin

3 teaspoons dried hot red peppers

4 tablespoons hot red pepper sauce

4 bay leaves

8 cups cooked rice

1. Remove the skin from the chicken and boil the chicken for about 15 minutes in water on the stove. Remove the bone and shred the chicken meat, using 2 forks.
2. Peel and chop the onion into ⅛-inch pieces. Chop the celery into ⅛-inch pieces. Place all ingredients in the slow cooker and stir well. Cook on low setting for 1 to 3 hours. Remove the bay leaves.
3. Prepare the rice as per package directions to yield 8 cups cooked. Add the rice to the slow cooker and mix together all the ingredients well.

Instead of adding rice, create a wonderful chicken chili stew by mixing 2 tablespoons of flour with 2 cups of water until well blended; then add the mixture to the ingredients in the slow cooker about 20 minutes before serving.

Freezing Cooked Rice

Cooked rice can be frozen up to six months. The next time you make some for a meal, make twice what you need and freeze the rest in an airtight container. It needs virtually no thawing before being added to a slow cooker recipe.

Cooking time: 4–6 hours

Preparation time: 20 minutes

Attention: Minimal

Pot size: 4–6 quarts

Serves 6

Hot as a Devil Green Chili

1 large yellow onion
4 garlic cloves
4 large potatoes
1 cup (8 ounces) fresh or canned green chilies, diced
1 pound lean ground beef
½ pound ground pork
1½ cups whole kernel corn
3 cups chicken broth
1 teaspoon ground black pepper
1 teaspoon crushed dried oregano
½ teaspoon ground cumin
1 teaspoon table salt
2 teaspoons red pepper sauce

1. Remove the peel from the onion and cut into ¼-inch pieces. Remove the peel from the garlic cloves and mince with a sharp paring knife. Peel the potatoes and cut into ½-inch cubes. Dice the green chilies with a sharp paring knife.
2. Put the meat, onion, and garlic in a large skillet and cook on medium-high heat until the meat is well browned; drain off grease. Put all ingredients in the slow cooker; stir well. Cover and cook on low setting for 4 to 6 hours.

Let people make their own chili tacos by serving this with warm flour tortillas, fresh chopped lettuce, grated Colby cheese, and sour cream.

Cooking time: 10 hours	
Preparation time: 10 minutes	
Attention: Minimal	
Pot size: 3–6 quarts	
Serves 8	

Super Taco Filling

1 medium-sized yellow onion
1½ cups fresh or canned green chilies, minced
4-pound beef chuck roast
1 envelope dry taco seasoning
1 tablespoon white vinegar
2 teaspoons red pepper sauce
½ teaspoon garlic salt

1. Peel the onion and chop into ¼-inch pieces. Mince the green chilies with a sharp paring knife. Add all ingredients to the slow cooker. Cover and cook on low setting for 9 hours.
2. Remove the meat and shred with a fork. Return the meat to the slow cooker and stir into the other ingredients. Cover and cook on low setting for 1 additional hour.

Let people make their own tacos by serving this with warm flour tortillas, grated cheese, refried beans, shredded lettuce, chopped tomatoes, and sour cream.

Tex-Mex Necessities

Always have plenty of guacamole, salsa, limes, shredded cheese, sour cream, and hot sauce handy whenever you're serving a Tex-Mex inspired meal.

Cooking time:	7–8 hours
Preparation time:	20 minutes
Attention:	Minimal
Pot size:	4–6 quarts
Serves 4	

Szechuan Chicken

4 chicken breasts
3 green onions
2 garlic cloves
1 tablespoon peanut oil
¼ cup sesame paste
3 tablespoons strong-brewed green tea
2 tablespoons wine vinegar
2½ tablespoons soy sauce
1½ tablespoons rice wine
2 teaspoons crushed red pepper
1 teaspoon dried ginger
½ teaspoon cayenne pepper

1. Remove the skin and bones from the chicken and slice the meat into ¼-inch strips. Remove the roots and first layer of green onion and chop the onion into ¼-inch pieces, including the stems. Peel the garlic and chop into eighths.
2. Place the peanut oil in a medium-sized skillet on medium heat. Add the chicken, sauté until browned and set aside. Add the garlic and onions; sauté until the onions are limp and translucent. Pour into the slow cooker. Add the remaining ingredients; stir well. Cover and cook on low setting for 6 to 7 hours, add chicken and cook for another hour.

Serve over white rice and sprinkle with chopped peanuts.

Barbecueless Chicken

Cooking time: 8 hours
Preparation time: 30 minutes
Attention: Minimal
Pot size: 6–8 quarts
Serves 4

1 whole chicken
½ cup onion, chopped
4 garlic cloves
1 can tomato sauce
¼ cup vinegar
¼ cup dark brown sugar
2 tablespoons Bourbon
1 tablespoon Worcestershire sauce
½ teaspoon table salt
2 tablespoons hot sauce

1. Cut the chicken into serving portions (legs, thighs, wings, breasts).
2. Peel and chop the onion into ¼-inch pieces. Peel the garlic and smash each clove with the broad side of a large knife. Combine the onion, garlic, tomato sauce, vinegar, dark brown sugar, Bourbon, Worcestershire sauce, salt, and hot sauce in a small mixing bowl.
3. Place the chicken in the slow cooker. Pour the prepared barbecue sauce over the chicken. Cover and cook on low setting for 8 hours.

Serve with Corn Bread in the Round (page 76).

Cooking Meat

The smaller the cut of meat the less time it has to cook. If you overcook a bite-size piece of beef, for example, it will fall apart and mix with the other ingredients in the slow cooker. If you're in doubt, add the meat half-way through the cooking process.

CHAPTER 15
Ethnic Cuisine

Cooking time: 7–9 hours

Preparation time: 20 minutes

Attention: Minimal

Pot size: 3–8 quarts

Serves 8

Congo Stew

2-pound pork roast

1 large white onion

1 green bell pepper

2 garlic cloves

2 plum tomatoes

½ teaspoon curry powder

½ teaspoon ground coriander

½ teaspoon ground cumin

½ teaspoon ground black pepper

1 teaspoon crushed red pepper
  flakes

½ teaspoon ground ginger

¼ teaspoon cinnamon

1 bay leaf

1 teaspoon table salt

2 cups chicken broth

1 tablespoon tomato paste

½ cup chunky peanut butter

1. Cut the pork into 1-inch cubes. Peel and chop the onion into ¼-inch pieces. Remove the stems and seeds from the green pepper and chop into ¼-inch pieces. Peel and mince the garlic using a sharp kitchen knife. Chop the plum tomatoes into ¼-inch pieces.

2. Brown the pork in a large skillet at medium-high heat. Add the onions, garlic, curry powder, coriander, cumin, black pepper, and crushed red pepper; stir well and cook for 1 minute. Transfer the mixture to the slow cooker. Add the ginger, cinnamon, salt, bay leaf, chicken broth, and tomato paste. Cover and cook on low setting for 6 to 8 hours.

3. Add the peanut butter and stir well to blend. Stir in the chopped tomato and bell pepper. Cover and cook on low setting for 1 hour.

Add no-salt, skinless peanuts to the top of the bowl before serving.

Mexican Green Chili Burros

Cooking time: 8–10 hours
Preparation time: 15 minutes
Attention: Minimal
Pot size: 3–6 quarts
Serves 4

2-pound beef rump roast
1 cup chopped yellow onions
1 (10-ounce) can diced green chilies
1 (16-ounce) can tomato sauce
1 package taco seasoning mix
1 tablespoon oregano
1 teaspoon garlic powder
8 flour tortillas
½ cup sour cream
1 large green onion, diced
¼ cup chopped black olives

1. Add the meat to the slow cooker. Peel and chop the onions into ¼-inch pieces. Add all ingredients on top of the meat. Cook on low setting for 7 hours. Remove the meat and shred it using 2 forks. Return the meat to the slow cooker and stir together all the ingredients. Cook on low setting for an addition 1 to 3 hours.
2. Serve on flour tortillas that have been warmed in a 250-degree oven for 10 minutes. Top with sour cream, diced green onions, and olives.

Serve on flour tortillas that have been warmed in a 250-degree oven for 10 minutes. Top with sour cream and diced avocado.

Avocados

Avocados are one of the only vegetables high in fat. Substitute cucumber for avocado for a fresh flavor with none of the fat grams. Choose a seedless cucumber and remove the skin before dicing it.

Cooking time: 5–6 hours

Preparation time: 20 minutes

Attention: Minimal

Pot size: 3–6 quarts

Serves 6

Egyptian Chicken

12 chicken legs
2 medium-sized yellow onions
1 red bell pepper
1 green bell pepper
2 celery ribs
2 cups chicken broth
½ cup crunchy peanut butter
1 teaspoon crushed red chili pepper

1. Remove the skin from the chicken legs. Peel and slice the onion into ¼-inch-thick rings. Remove the stems and seeds from the peppers and slice into ¼-inch-thick rings. Slice the celery into ¼-inch pieces.
2. Combine the onions, peppers, celery, and chicken broth in the slow cooker. Spread the peanut putter over the chicken legs and sprinkle with chili pepper. Place on top of the onions and peppers; do not stir. Cover and cook on low setting for 5 to 6 hours.

Serve with Roasted Garlic (page 12) and Slightly Seedy White Bread (page 84).

Bouillon Cubes

Bouillon cubes will work in place of broth when necessary. When using them instead of homemade broth, be sure to add a little extra of the aromatic vegetables such as onion, celery, and carrots.

Chicken from the French Countryside

Cooking time: 7–9 hours

Preparation time: 45 minutes

Attention: Minimal

Pot size: 6 quarts

Serves 4

1 *whole chicken*
2 *teaspoons table salt*
¼ *teaspoon coarsely ground*
   pepper
4 *carrots*
1 *large Bermuda onion*
2 *cups fresh green beans*

½ *cup fresh mushrooms, sliced*
8 *garlic cloves*
2 *bay leaves*
6 *ripe tomatoes*
⅓ *cup brown rice*
½ *cup water*

1. Cut the chicken into serving portions (legs, thighs, wings, breasts), then rinse off the pieces and dry them. Peel and dice the carrots and onions. Wash the green beans and cut into 2-inch pieces. Clean the mushrooms by wiping individually with a moistened paper towel; slice the mushrooms. Smash, peel, and dice the garlic. Wash, core, and chop the tomatoes into ¼-inch pieces.
2. Place the chicken in the slow cooker. Add the carrots, onions, green beans, mushrooms, garlic, tomatoes, salt, pepper, and bay leaves to the slow cooker. Cover and cook on low for 4 to 5 hours.
3. Stir in the rice and water. Cover and cook on low for 3 to 4 more hours.

Serve on a platter with a dry white wine.

Replacing Fresh Tomatoes
You can substitute one 28-ounce can of peeled whole tomatoes for three fresh tomatoes in any slow cooker recipe. Be sure to include the juice from the can when adding it to the recipe.

Savory Chinese Beef

Cooking time: 6–7 hours

Preparation time: 30 minutes

Attention: Minimal

Pot size: 3–6 quarts

Serves 6

1½ pounds sirloin tip

1 bunch (approximately 8)
    green onions **or** 1 large leek

8 ounces (1 cup) bean sprouts

8 ounces (1 cup) Chinese
    pea pods

1 cup low-fat beef broth

¼ cup low-sodium soy sauce

2 tablespoons cornstarch

2 tablespoons lukewarm water

¼ teaspoon ground ginger **or**
    ½ teaspoon fresh minced ginger

½ teaspoon hot sauce (optional)

1 small can water chestnuts, drained

1 small can bamboo shoots, drained

1. Thinly slice the sirloin tip (slicing is easier if the meat is frozen and then cut when partially thawed). Wash all the fresh vegetables. Cut off the roots at the ends of the green onions (or leek); finely chop the onions (or leek).
2. Place the sliced sirloin in the slow cooker with the beef broth, soy sauce, ginger, and chopped green onions (or leeks). Cover and cook on low for 6 to 7 hours.
3. Uncover and turn setting to high. Mix the cornstarch with the water in a small measuring cup. Stir the cornstarch mixture and the hot sauce into the slow cooker. Cook on high for 15 minutes, or until thickened; stir periodically. During the last 5 minutes of cooking add the remaining canned and fresh vegetables.

For an adventurous audience, serve in individual bowls over Chinese noodles with chopsticks.

Fruit Compote

Nearly any combination of fresh fruits makes a wonderful fruit compote in the slow cooker. Add one cup of sugar for every eight cups of fruit and cook on low until the sauce is thick.

Native American Pudding

Cooking time: 4–5 hours

Preparation time: 45 minutes

Attention: Medium

Pot size: 3–6 quarts

Serves 4

2 tablespoons butter, plus ¼ tablespoon for greasing

3 cups 1 percent milk

½ cup cornmeal

½ teaspoon salt

3 large eggs, beaten

¼ cup packed light brown sugar

⅓ cup molasses

½ teaspoon cinnamon

¼ teaspoon allspice

½ teaspoon ginger

Lightly grease the slow cooker with ¼ tablespoon butter by putting butter on a paper towel and rubbing it along the inside of the slow cooker. Preheat the slow cooker on high for 15 minutes. In a medium-sized saucepan bring the milk, cornmeal, and salt to boil. Boil, stirring constantly, for 5 minutes. Cover and simmer on low for 10 minutes. In a large bowl, combine the remaining ingredients. Gradually whisk the cornmeal mixture into the combined ingredients until thoroughly mixed and smooth. Pour into slow cooker. Cook covered on medium for 4 to 5 hours.

Serve in small bowls with a dollop of low-fat whipping cream.

Cooking time: 8–9 hours

Preparation time: 45 minutes

Attention: Minimal

Pot size: 4–6 quarts

Serves 8

Brazilian Paella

½ pound medium-spicy pork sausage

2–3-pound chicken

2 large yellow onions

1 pound (16 ounces) canned tomatoes

½ teaspoon table salt

½ teaspoon ground black pepper

1½ cups uncooked long-grain brown rice

3 chicken bouillon cubes

2 cups hot water

1. Form the sausage into balls about the size of large marbles. Clean and cut the chicken into serving size pieces. Peel and chop the onions into ¼-inch pieces. Drain the tomatoes, retaining the liquid, and cut into 1-inch pieces.

2. Using a large skillet on medium-high heat, fry the sausage balls until they are well browned and crisp. Place them on paper towels to absorb the grease. Sprinkle the chicken with salt and pepper. Without emptying the grease from the skillet, fry the chicken pieces for about 10 minutes. Place the chicken on paper towels to absorb the grease.

3. Drain all but 3 tablespoons of grease from the skillet. Sauté the onions on medium heat in the skillet until translucent. Add the rice to the skillet and continue to sauté, stirring constantly for 10 minutes.

4. Place the sausage balls, chicken, the onion and rice mixture, tomato juice, and tomatoes in the slow cooker. Mix the bouillon in 2 cups of hot water; add to the slow cooker. Cover and cook on low setting for 8 to 9 hours.

Serve with fresh-sliced oranges and bananas sprinkled with coconut to achieve a true Brazilian flavor.

Mongolian Mixed Meat Stew

Cooking time: 8–9 hours
Preparation time: 20 minutes
Attention: Minimal
Pot size: 3–6 quarts
Serves 8

¼ cup A-1 Steak Sauce
2 chicken bouillon cubes
1 teaspoon table salt
½ teaspoon ground black pepper
1 teaspoon sugar
½ cup hot water
3 pounds chicken thighs

1 pound lean stewing beef
1 medium-sized yellow onion
2 medium potatoes
8 ounces (1 cup) baby carrots
1 (16-ounce) can stewed tomatoes, liquid retained
¼ cup flour

1. Combine steak sauce, bouillon cubes, salt, pepper, sugar, and hot water in the slow cooker; stir well. Remove the skin from the chicken thighs and discard. Cut the chicken meat into 1-inch cubes. Cut the stewing beef into 1-inch cubes. Peel and chop the onions into ¼-inch pieces. Peel the potatoes and cut into ½-inch cubes.

2. Add the chicken, beef, onion, potatoes, carrots, and tomatoes, including juice, to the slow cooker. Cover and cook on low setting for 8 to 9 hours. Before serving, mix the ¼ cup flour with enough water to make a paste; stir mixture into the stew. Cook on high setting uncovered until thick, about 15 to 30 minutes.

Cheddar and Onion Bread (page 81) goes well with this meal.

Freshly Ground Pepper

If possible, use freshly ground black peppercorns when pepper is called for in a recipe. These retain their flavor better than pre-ground pepper and you'll need less of it to get the same flavor.

Portuguese Sweet Bread

Cooking time: 2–3 hours
Preparation time: 10 minutes
Attention: Medium
Pot size: 3–8 quarts
Serves 8

Bread:

½ cup milk
1 package active dry yeast
⅛ cup warm water
¾ cup sugar
½ teaspoon salt
3 eggs
¼ cup butter, softened
3 cups flour

Glaze:

1 egg
1 teaspoon sugar

1. To make the bread, put the milk in a small saucepan on the stove and heat on high until the milk is slightly yellowed. Let the milk cool to room temperature. Dissolve the yeast in warm water in large bowl. Stir in the milk, sugar, salt, eggs, and butter. Beat with an electric mixer until smooth and creamy. Stir in flour. Place the dough onto a lightly floured surface and knead until smooth and elastic, about 5 minutes. Place the dough in a greased bowl; cover and let rise in a warm place for about 2 hours. Shape a round, slightly flat loaf.
2. Grease the slow cooker by putting a small amount of shortening on a paper towel and rubbing it along the inside of the slow cooker. Place the loaf of bread in the slow cooker. To make the glaze, beat the egg until the yellow and white are well mixed brush over the loaf. Sprinkle with sugar.
3. Cover and cook on high setting for 2 to 3 hours. The loaf should be golden.

This is excellent served with Egyptian Chicken (page 202).

Cooking time: 8–10 hours

Preparation time: 20 minutes

Attention: Minimal

Pot size: 3–6 quarts

Serves 8

Russian Vegetable Beef Borscht

1 pound leftover beef roast

½ head cabbage

3 medium potatoes

4 carrots

1 large white onion

1 cup fresh tomatoes, chopped

1 cup green beans

1 cup diced beets

1 cup fresh sweet corn

2 cups beef broth

2 cups tomato juice

¼ teaspoon garlic powder

¼ teaspoon dill seed

2 teaspoons salt

½ teaspoon pepper

1. Cut the beef roast into 1-inch cubes. Slice the cabbage into ¼-inch strips. Peel the potatoes and dice into ½-inch cubes. Peel and slice the carrots into ¼-inch pieces. Remove the skin from the onion and chop into ¼-inch pieces. Chop the tomatoes into ½-inch pieces. Remove the stems from the green beans. Precook the beets by slicing the tops and roots off. Boil in water for ½ hour. Set beets in cool water and use a sharp paring knife to remove the skins. Cut into ½-inch pieces.

2. Add all ingredients to the slow cooker. Add enough water so that the slow cooker is ¾ full. Cook covered on low setting for 8 to 10 hours.

Add a dollop of sour cream to the top of each bowl right before serving.

Polish Sauerkraut Soup

Cooking time: 8–10 hours

Preparation time: 10 minutes

Attention: Minimal

Pot size: 4–6 quarts

Serves 8

1 pound smoked Polish sausage
5 medium potatoes
2 large yellow onions
3 medium carrots
6 cups chicken broth
4 cups (32 ounces) canned or bagged sauerkraut
1 (6-ounce) can tomato paste

1. Slice the Polish sausage into ½-inch-thick pieces. Do not remove the peel from the potatoes; slice into ½-inch cubes. Remove the peel from the onions and chop into ¼-inch pieces. Peel and slice the carrots ¼-inch thick.
2. Add all ingredients to the slow cooker. Cover and cook on low setting for 8 to 10 hours.

Serve with Heavy Brown Bread (page 85)

Pepperoni Rigatoni

Cooking time: 4–5 hours

Preparation time: 15 minutes

Attention: Minimal

Pot size: 4–8 quarts

Serves 8

12 ounces rigatoni
1 cup fresh mushrooms, sliced
1 large yellow onion
4 garlic cloves
1 medium-sized green bell pepper
2 pounds pepperoni slices
1 (28-ounce) jar spaghetti sauce
3 cups shredded mozzarella cheese

1. Cook the rigatoni in boiling water until soft but not mushy. Clean the mushrooms by wiping with a damp cloth; slice ⅛-inch thick. Remove the peel from the onion and cut into ¼-inch pieces. Remove the peel from the garlic and mince with a sharp paring knife. Remove the stem and seeds from the green pepper; cut into ¼-inch pieces.
2. Add all the ingredients to the slow cooker; stir well. Cover and cook on low setting for 4 to 5 hours.

Serve with a fresh green salad with Italian dressing.

Mushroom Varieties

Different mushrooms have very different tastes. Don't hesitate to substitute exotic dried mushrooms such as wood ear, enoci, and porcini even if the recipe calls for fresh mushrooms.

East Indian Green Curried Chicken

Cooking time: 6½ –7½ hours

Preparation time: 20 minutes

Attention: Medium

Pot size: 4–6 quarts

Serves 6

6 chicken breasts

2 fresh green chili peppers

¼ cup fresh mint leaves, chopped

1½ cups unsweetened coconut milk, divided

1½ tablespoons green curry paste

1 cup sliced, canned bamboo shoots

¼ cup fish sauce

1 tablespoon sugar

1. Remove the skin and bones from chicken breast. Remove the stems and seeds from the chili peppers and chop into ⅛-inch pieces. Chop the mint leaves into ¼-inch pieces.
2. Heat ½ cup of the coconut milk and the green curry paste in a medium-sized skillet on medium heat; stir until well blended. Add the chicken and sauté for 10 minutes. Put the chicken breasts into the slow cooker. Stir in the remaining coconut milk, bamboo shoots, fish sauce, and sugar. Cover and cook on low setting for 6 to 7 hours. Stir in the mint and chili peppers. Cover and cook an additional 30 minutes.

Serve with long-grain brown rice.

Stocking Up on Ethnic Staples

If your local grocery store doesn't carry certain ethnic spices or ingredients, you may be able to find them on the Internet or at specialty shops. Just make sure to stock up on shelf-stable necessities so you can make these dishes whenever you like.

Mediterranean Couscous with Vegetables

Cooking time: 6½ –7½ hours

Preparation time: 30 minutes

Attention: Medium

Pot size: 3–8 quarts

Serves 8

2 medium zucchini
6 plum tomatoes
½ pound (1 cup) fresh
   mushrooms
4 garlic cloves
2 medium-sized white onions
2 celery ribs
1 large red bell pepper
2 medium carrots
½ cup black olives, pitted
   and diced

¼ cup minced fresh basil
2 tablespoons olive oil1
½ teaspoons dried oregano
   leaves
1 teaspoon salt
¼ teaspoon cinnamon
¼ teaspoon ground black pepper
3 tablespoons balsamic vinegar
1½ cups whole-wheat couscous

1. Cut the zucchini into 1-inch pieces. Chop the tomatoes into ¼-inch pieces. Clean the mushrooms by wiping with a damp cloth; cut in half. Peel the garlic and mince with a sharp kitchen knife. Peel the onions and chop into ¼-inch pieces. Chop the celery into ¼-inch pieces. Remove the stem and seeds from the bell pepper and slice into ¼-inch strips. Peel and slice the carrots into ¼-inch rounds. Chop the black olives into ¼-inch pieces. Chop the basil into ¼-inch pieces.

2. Heat the olive oil in a large skillet at medium-high heat. Add the garlic, onion, and red pepper. Sauté until the onion is limp and translucent. Add the celery, carrots, mushrooms, zucchini, tomatoes, olives, and half the basil; sauté for 5 minutes. Transfer to slow cooker. Add half the remaining basil, oregano, salt, cinnamon, and black pepper. Cover and cook on low setting for 6 to 7 hours.

3. Stir in the vinegar and couscous. Cover and cook on low setting for an additional 30 minutes.

Serve with pocket bread and hummus for an authentic meal.

Thai Shrimp and Scallop Soup

Cooking time: 8–9 hours
Preparation time: 20 minutes
Attention: Minimal
Pot size: 3–8 quarts
Serves 8

1 small white onion
8 ounces (1 cup) fresh mushrooms, sliced
2 garlic cloves
6 green onions
1/3 cup fresh parsley, chopped
1/2 pound precooked popcorn shrimp
1/2 pound baby scallops
6 cups water
1/2 teaspoon thyme
1 teaspoon table salt
1/4 teaspoon ground black pepper
2 teaspoons ground coriander
1 1/2 teaspoons chili powder
1 teaspoon red pepper sauce
1 tablespoon soy sauce
2 cups uncooked white rice

1. Peel the onion and chop into 1/4-inch pieces. Clean the mushrooms by wiping with a damp cloth; cut into paper-thin slices with a sharp kitchen knife. Peel the garlic and mince with a sharp kitchen knife. Remove the roots and first layer of skin from the green onions and chop into 1/4-inch pieces. Chop the parsley into 1/2-inch pieces.
2. Combine all ingredients except the parsley, green onions, precooked shrimp, and baby scallops in the slow cooker. Cover and cook on low setting for 7 to 8 hours. Add shrimp and scallops and cook for 1 to 2 hours. Stir in the parsley and green onions right before serving.

Serve with Slightly Seedy White Bread (page 84).

Cooking time: 8–9 hours

Preparation time: 30 minutes

Attention: Minimal

Pot size: 3–6 quarts

Serves 6

Turkish Pork Chops

½ teaspoon salt

½ teaspoon pepper

2 tablespoons paprika

½ cup flour

6 lean pork chops

4 medium onions

2 garlic cloves

4 tablespoons butter

1 cup chicken stock

1. Combine salt, pepper, paprika, and flour. Dredge the pork chops by smashing them into the flour. Peel the onions and chop into ¼-inch pieces. Peel the garlic and chop into eighths.
2. Heat the butter in large skillet at medium-high heat. Brown the pork chops. Remove the pork chops and put into the slow cooker. Add the onions and garlic to skillet and sauté until the onions are limp and translucent. Drain off the grease and place the onions and garlic on top of the pork chops. Add chicken stock. Cover and cook on low setting for 8 to 9 hours.

Make a sauce by combining 1 cup sour cream with 1 tablespoon dill. Add dollops of the sauce to the top of each pork chop.

Greek Lamb Chops with Lentils

Cooking time: 7–9 hours
Preparation time: 30 minutes
Attention: Minimal
Pot size: 3–6 quarts
Serves 6

6 medium lamb chops
1 medium-sized yellow onion
4 garlic cloves
3 medium carrots
2 medium-sized ripe tomatoes
1 cup black olives, chopped
1 cup lentils

3 cups water
½ cup vodka
2 tablespoons olive oil
1 teaspoon table salt
½ teaspoon ground black pepper

1. Trim the fat from the lamb chops. Peel and chop the onion into ¼-inch pieces. Peel the garlic and mince with a sharp kitchen knife. Peel and slice the carrots into ¼-inch rounds. Chop the tomatoes into ¼-inch pieces. Chop the olives into ¼-inch pieces.
2. Put the lentils in the slow cooker with the water and vodka. Add the carrots, onions, and tomatoes. Begin cooking on low setting. In the meantime, heat the olive oil in a large skillet at medium heat. Sprinkle the lamb chops with the salt and pepper and place in the skillet. Add the garlic. Cook until the lamb chops are browned on both sides. Transfer to the slow cooker. Sprinkle the black olives on top. Cover and cook on low setting for 7 to 9 hours.

Serve with a fresh green salad with Greek dressing.

If You Substitute Lamb or Veal . . .

Since lamb and veal are inherently tender meats, they need less cooking time than their grown-up counterparts. Decrease the time by half and add the meat later in the cooking cycle.

California Cuisine

Cooking time: 6–7 hours	
Preparation time: 30 minutes	
Attention: Minimal	
Pot size: 4–6 quarts	
Serves 4	

Citrus Chicken Breasts

4 pounds chicken breasts
4 medium potatoes
2 tablespoons cider vinegar
¼ teaspoon ground nutmeg
1 teaspoon dry basil
2 tablespoons brown sugar
1 cup orange juice
4 fresh peaches
2 fresh oranges
fresh strawberries, for garnish

1. Remove the skin and bones from the chicken breasts and discard. Peel and slice the potatoes ¼-inch thick. Put the potatoes on the bottom of the slow cooker. Place the chicken breasts on top.
2. Mix the vinegar, nutmeg, basil, brown sugar, and orange juice in a small mixing bowl; Pour mixture over the chicken. Cover and cook on low setting for 6 to 7 hours.
3. Using a slotted spoon, remove the chicken and potatoes from the slow cooker and place in a 250-degree oven to keep warm. Peel the peaches and slice ½-inch thick. Peel the oranges and break into slices. Place the peaches and oranges into the slow cooker. Cook uncovered on high setting for 20 minutes. Pour over the chicken and potatoes before serving.

Garnish with fresh sliced strawberries before serving.

Adding Fruit

Cut fruit right before putting it in the slow cooker. Exposure to air can cause the fruit to discolor while mixing it with sugar or other fruits can draw out the juices.

Cooking time: 5–6 hours

Preparation time: 30 minutes

Attention: Medium

Pot size: 4–6 quarts

Spinach Feta Chicken

Serves 6

1 bunch fresh spinach
4 garlic cloves
1 tablespoon extra-virgin olive oil
4 boneless, skinless chicken breasts
½ teaspoon table salt
¼ teaspoon coarsely ground black pepper
¼ cup dry white wine
⅓ cup feta cheese

1. Thoroughly wash and dry the spinach; cut off the stems from the leaves. Peel and finely chop the garlic.
2. Heat a large skillet on medium-high; add the olive oil. Add the chicken and lightly sprinkle with salt and pepper. Sauté until golden brown. Remove the chicken with a slotted spoon or tongs and place the chicken in the slow cooker. Add the wine to the skillet and mix with the drippings; pour mixture over the chicken. Cover and cook on low setting for 5 to 6 hours, or until the chicken is tender and no longer pink in the middle.
3. Add the spinach, cover, and cook for 1 hour on low setting. Transfer the contents of the slow cooker to a serving platter. Crumble the feta cheese on top.

Serve with a side of garlic-buttered penne pasta.

Turkey for Chicken

For a lean alternative in your next chicken recipe, substitute turkey. It has much less fat and much more protein than chicken while often being a better per-pound buy at the grocery store.

Cooking time: 6–7 hours	
Preparation time: 45 minutes	
Attention: Minimal	
Pot size: 6 quarts	
Serves 6	

Portobello Mushroom Pork Tenderloin

1 pound (2 cups) portobello mushrooms, sliced
2-pound pork tenderloin
½ cup red wine
1 teaspoon table salt
¼ teaspoon pepper

1. Wash and dry the portobello mushrooms; slice into pieces.
2. Broil the tenderloin on high until the top and bottom are golden brown. Place the tenderloin in the slow cooker. Add the wine, salt, pepper, and mushrooms. Cover and cook on low setting for 6 to 7 hours.
3. Remove the tenderloin from the slow cooker and place on a platter. Slice the tenderloin into 1-inch pieces. Pour the mushroom-wine sauce over the tenderloin.

Serve with new potatoes coated in butter and chopped chives.

Slow-Roasting Meats

Rub salt into the surface of a roast before cooking it to enhance the flavor without overdrying the meat. As an alternative, use garlic or onion salt.

Cooking time: 3 hours

Preparation time: 30 minutes

Attention: Medium

Pot size: 3–6 quarts

Halibut with Almonds

Serves 4

4 halibut fillets
2 tablespoons chopped parsley
½ cup butter, divided in half
¼ cup slivered almonds
1 lemon
¼ teaspoon Worcestershire sauce

1. Wash and dry the halibut fillets. Wash and dry the parsley; chop coarsely.
2. Turn the slow cooker on high. Melt half of the butter in the slow cooker and stir in the Worcestershire sauce. Place the halibut fillets on top of the butter. Place a dollop of butter on each fillet. Sprinkle almonds on top of each fillet. Cover and cook on low setting for 2 hours. Sprinkle parsley on top of the fillets and cook covered for 1 more hour on low setting. Cut lemons into fourths and squeeze one quarter onto each fillet right before serving.

Serve with Brussels Sprouts à la Orange (page 259).

Fatty Oils

All oils are 100 percent fat, including butter and margarine. For a healthy diet, use them sparingly and substitute unsaturated vegetable oil or extra virgin olive oil whenever possible.

Salmon with Asparagus

Cooking time: 4 hours
Preparation time: 30 minutes
Attention: Medium
Pot size: 3–6 quarts
Serves 4

1½ pounds asparagus
¼ cup butter, divided
4 salmon steaks
1 teaspoon dried marjoram
1 teaspoon table salt
½ teaspoon ground black pepper

1. Wash and dry the asparagus; cut off the bottom 1 inch (the light pinkish-green part) of the asparagus.
2. Turn the slow cooker on high. Melt half of the butter in the slow cooker. Place the salmon steaks on top of the butter. Sprinkle the spices over the salmon. Place a dollop of butter on each steak. Cover and cook on low for 3 hours. Add the asparagus. Cover and cook on low for an additional hour, or until salmon flakes.

Serve with Hot Fruit Medley (page 302) over vanilla yogurt for dessert.

Add a Little Zest
Citrus goes great with seafood of all kinds. Try squeezing some lemon or lime on any of your favorite fish recipes.

Cooking time: 2 hours	
Preparation time: 20 minutes, plus some work the day before	
Attention: Medium	
Pot size: 3–6 quarts	
Serves 4	

Kiwi Shrimp

1½ pounds raw tiger shrimp, shelled and deveined
¼ cup parsley, chopped
¼ cup lemon juice
2 kiwi fruit
3 cloves garlic
2 tablespoons butter

1. Coarsely chop the parsley. Mix the lemon juice with the parsley; combine mixture with the shrimp, making sure all the shrimp is well covered. Refrigerate overnight.
2. Peel the kiwi and cut into ¼- inch slices. Peel and mince the garlic. Turn the slow cooker onto high. Melt the butter, then add the garlic. Cover and cook for 15 minutes. After the garlic is tender, add the shrimp. Cover and cook on low for 1½ hours, or until the shrimp begins to turn pink. Add the kiwi. Cover and cook for 15 more minutes. Transfer the shrimp and kiwi to a platter.

Serve with Green Beans in Lemon Honey (page 260).

Provincial Zucchini and Tomatoes

Cooking time: 1 hour
Preparation time: 30 minutes
Attention: Minimal
Pot size: 3–6 quarts
Serves 4

2 small zucchini
12 cherry tomatoes
2 garlic cloves
2 tablespoons olive oil
½ teaspoon dried thyme
½ teaspoon table salt
¼ teaspoon ground pepper

1. Wash the zucchini and tomatoes. Trim the ends from the zucchini and cut lengthwise into ½-inch-thick slices. Peel and dice the garlic.
2. Turn on the slow cooker to high setting; add the olive oil and garlic. Cover and cook for 15 minutes. After the garlic is tender, add the zucchini. Reduce heat to low, cover, and cook for 1 hour. Add tomatoes and cook until they are warmed through. Add the thyme, salt, and pepper just prior to serving.

This is a nice complement to Citrus Chicken Breasts (page 218).

Summertime Specialty

Add yellow summer squash to any recipe with zucchini. Those two vegetables work really well together.

Cooking time: 1 hour

Preparation time: 30 minutes

Attention: Minimal

Pot size: 3–6 quarts

Serves 4

Red Cabbage with Apples

1 small head red cabbage
1 medium leek
1 tart apple
2 tablespoons light vegetable oil
¼ cup cider vinegar
2 tablespoons brown sugar
½ teaspoon table salt
¼ teaspoon ground black pepper

1. Core and shred the cabbage into ¼-inch-wide pieces. Cut the end off the leek and cut the leek into slices about ¼-inch thick. Core, peel, and cut the apple into ¼-inch slices.
2. Turn on the slow cooker to high setting. Add the oil and leek. Cover and cook for 15 minutes, or until the leek is tender. Add the vinegar, sugar, salt, and pepper; mix thoroughly. Add the cabbage and apple; reduce temperature to low setting. Cover and cook for 45 minutes, or until the cabbage is slightly tender.

This is a wonderful complement to Portobello Mushroom Pork Tenderloin (page 220).

Minted Green Peas with Lettuce

Cooking time: 1 hour
Preparation time: 20 minutes
Attention: Medium
Pot size: 2–4 quarts
Serves 4

2 cups fresh peas (1 package frozen peas can be substituted)
2 cups red leaf lettuce, shredded
1 teaspoon chopped fresh mint leaves
2 tablespoons butter
½ teaspoon table salt
½ teaspoon sugar
Mint sprigs for garnish

1. Shuck and wash the peas. Wash and tear the lettuce into small pieces, about the size of a quarter. Finely chop the mint leaves.
2. Turn on the slow cooker to low setting. Melt the butter in the slow cooker. Add peas, cover, reduce heat to low, and cook until the peas arc tender (approximately 45 minutes). Add the lettuce and chopped mint. Cook uncovered until the lettuce wilts. Add the salt and sugar. Serve in medium-sized serving bowl with mint sprigs for a garnish.

Serve as a complement to Halibut with Almonds (page 221).

Fresh vs. Dry

If you don't have fresh herbs, you can always use dry ones. Just make sure to experiment with the proper amount; some dry herbs have a more concentrated flavor while others have a weaker one.

East Asian Green Beans with Sesame Seeds

Cooking time: 1 hour

Preparation time: 30 minutes

Attention: Medium

Pot size: 2–4 quarts

Serves 4

2 pounds (4 cups) fresh green beans
1 tablespoon soy sauce
2 teaspoons fresh minced ginger
1 tablespoon vinegar
1 tablespoon butter
2 tablespoons water
2 tablespoons sesame seed

1. Wash the green beans, then cut off the stems. Mix the soy sauce, ginger, and vinegar in a small bowl.
2. Turn on the slow cooker to high setting. Melt the butter in the slow cooker. Add the water and green beans; reduce heat to low. Cover and cook for 45 minutes, or until the beans are tender. Add soy sauce, ginger, and vinegar mixture; mix so that the beans are well covered. Sprinkle with sesame seeds.

This is a perfect complement to Spicy Pot Roast (page 106).

Korean Chicken Breasts with Snow Pea Pods

Cooking time: 6 hours
Preparation time: 30 minutes
Attention: Medium
Pot size: 4–6 quarts
Serves 4

4 chicken breasts
6 garlic cloves
1 pound (2 cups) snow pea pods
1 cup soy sauce
¼ cup red wine vinegar
2 teaspoons crushed red pepper flakes
¼ cup sugar
2 tablespoons vegetable oil

1. Remove the bone and skin from the chicken breasts. Peel and mince the garlic. Wash the snow pea pods and the remove stems. Combine the soy sauce, vinegar, red pepper flakes, and sugar in a small bowl.
2. Turn on the slow cooker to high setting. Add the oil and garlic. Cover and cook for 15 minutes. After the garlic is tender, add the chicken and soy sauce mixture. Reduce the heat to low setting. Cover and cook for 5 hours. Add the snow pea pods. Cover and cook on low setting for 1 more hour.

Serve over a bed of Minnesota Wild Rice (page 281).

Curried Chicken Thighs

Cooking time: 6 hours
Preparation time: 20 minutes
Attention: Medium
Pot size: 4–6 quarts
Serves 4

1 pound chicken thighs
2 garlic cloves
2 tablespoons virgin olive oil
1 tablespoon dry mustard

3 tablespoons curry powder
1 tablespoon ground ginger
1 cup fresh peas

Remove the skin and bones from the chicken. Peel and mince the garlic. Turn on the slow cooker to high setting. Add the oil, garlic, mustard, curry powder, and ginger. Cook for 5 minutes. Reduce heat to low. Add the chicken. Cover and cook for 5 hours. Add the peas and mix thoroughly with the chicken. Cook covered for 1 hour on low setting.

Serve with Minted Green Peas with Lettuce (page 226) for a nice mix of flavors.

Sole with Red Grapes

Cooking time: 4 hours
Preparation time: 20 minutes
Attention: Minimal
Pot size: 4–6 quarts
Serves 4

¼ cup butter
¼ cup lemon juice
¼ cup minced parsley

1¼ pounds sole fillets
1 cup seedless red grapes

Turn on the slow cooker to high setting. Melt the butter in the slow cooker, then mix in the lemon juice and parsley. Add the sole fillets. Cover and cook on low setting for 3 hours. Add the grapes. Cover and cook 1 hour on low setting.

Keep the flavor of this meal light by serving it with Red Cabbage and Apples (page 225).

CHAPTER 17
Potluck Favorites

Squishy, Squashy Succotash

Cooking time: 8–10 hours	
Preparation time: 30 minutes	
Attention: Minimal	
Pot size: 3–6 quarts	
Serves 6	

1½ pounds acorn squash
4 garlic cloves
2 medium-sized yellow onions
2 jalapeño peppers
1 medium-sized yellow bell
    pepper
¼ fresh minced cilantro
2 cups fresh corn kernels

1 tablespoon olive oil
1 teaspoon cumin seeds
1 teaspoon red pepper flakes
1 teaspoon table salt
1 cup water
2 tablespoons tomato paste
1 teaspoon table salt
2 cups precooked lima beans

1. Peel the acorn squash and cut into 1-inch pieces. Peel the garlic cloves and mince with a sharp kitchen knife. Peel the onions and chop into ¼-inch pieces. Remove the stems from the jalapeño peppers and cut the peppers into ¼-inch pieces. Remove the stem and seeds from the yellow bell pepper and cut into ¼-inch pieces. Mince the cilantro with a sharp kitchen knife.
2. Add all the ingredients except the lima beans and cilantro to the slow cooker. Cover and cook on low setting for 7 to 9 hours. Add the cilantro and lima beans; stir gently. Cook uncovered on low setting for 1 additional hour.

Serve with an assortment of pickled vegetables.

Check for Damage

Check for cracks and deep scratches in the crockery food container and cover before using the slow cooker. Because the stoneware is porous, cracks and scratches can harbor dangerous bacteria.

Almondy Rice Pilaf

Cooking time: 6–8 hours
Preparation time: 15 minutes
Attention: Minimal
Pot size: 3–8 quarts
Serves 4

1 medium-sized yellow onion
8 ounces (1 cup) fresh
  mushrooms
2 cups vegetable broth

1 cup raw converted rice
1 cup canned or frozen peas
2 tablespoons butter
½ cup almond slivers

Peel the onion and mince. Clean the mushrooms by wiping with a damp cloth; slice paper-thin. Add all ingredients to the slow cooker. Cover and cook on low setting for 6 to 8 hours.

This makes an excellent side dish to hot sandwiches.

Emma's Seven-Layer Bars

Cooking time: 2–3 hours
Preparation time: 10 minutes
Attention: Minimal
Pot size: 3–6 quarts
Serves 12

¼ cup melted butter
½ cup graham cracker crumbs
½ cup chocolate chips
½ cup butterscotch chips

½ cup flaked coconut
½ cup chopped walnuts
½ cup sweetened condensed milk

Grease the inside of a 2-pound coffee can by putting shortening on a paper towel and rubbing it along the inside of the can. Place the ingredients in the coffee can in the order listed; do not mix. Cover and cook on high setting for 2 to 3 hours. Let cool before removing from the coffee can.

Use pecans instead of walnuts.

Cook's Surprise Meatballs

Cooking time: 4 hours

Preparation time: 45 minutes

Attention: Medium

Pot size: 4–6 quarts

Serves 4

1 large yellow onion
1 green bell pepper
1 red bell pepper
2 garlic cloves
½ cup crushed saltine crackers
1 egg
1 pound ground turkey
1 pound ground beef

1 pound ground pork
1 (6-ounce) can tomato paste
1 teaspoon oregano
½ teaspoon basil
1 teaspoon salt
1 teaspoon ground black pepper
2 tablespoons vegetable oil

1. Peel the onion and chop into ¼-inch pieces. Remove the stems and seeds from the bell peppers and chop the peppers into ¼-inch pieces. Crush the garlic by laying a large knife on its side over the top of each garlic clove; push down until the garlic clove "pops." Crush the crackers using a spoon in a small bowl. Beat the egg with a fork in a small bowl until the egg yolk and white are thoroughly mixed.
2. In a medium-sized bowl, use your hands to mix the meat, egg, tomato paste, onion, red pepper, green pepper, oregano, basil, garlic, salt, black pepper, and crushed crackers. Form into firm balls about the size of golf balls. Place the meatballs on a cookie sheet and bake in a 350-degree conventional oven for about 10 minutes.
3. Put the vegetable oil in the slow cooker. Transfer all the meatballs to the slow cooker and cook covered on low setting for 4 hours.

Serve the meatballs over fresh egg noodles and peas for a complete meal.

Hold the Salt

Resist the urge to salt. Salt draws flavors and juices out of meat and vegetables. Let the flavors release on their own time for the best result. Guests can salt their own dishes if they prefer. They'll also use less than if you add it while cooking.

Cooking time: 6–8 hours

Preparation time: 30 minutes

Attention: Minimal

Pot size: 3–6 quarts

Serves 6

Barbecued Green Beans

1 pound bacon
¼ cup white onions, chopped
2 garlic cloves
2 large tomatoes
½ cup white vinegar
½ cup brown sugar
3 teaspoons Worcestershire sauce
¾ teaspoon salt
4 cups fresh green beans

1. Brown the bacon in a large skillet on medium-high heat until it is crisp. Transfer the bacon to paper towels to cool. Crumble the bacon by placing it between two layers of paper towel and twisting it. Discard all but 2 tablespoons of the bacon drippings.
2. Peel and chop the onions into ¼-inch pieces. Peel and slice the garlic paper-thin with a sharp paring knife. Sauté the onions and garlic in the retained bacon drippings for about 5 minutes, until the onions are translucent. Remove the skillet from the stove.
3. Skin and mash the tomatoes with a large wooden spoon. Remove skin from tomatoes with a sharp paring knife, gently lifting the skin and peeling it off. Add the tomatoes, vinegar, brown sugar, Worcestershire sauce, and salt to the onions and garlic in the skillet; stir well.
4. Clean the green beans in cold water; snap off and discard the ends. Place the green beans in the slow cooker. Pour the mixture from the skillet on top. Stir 2 or 3 times with a wooden spoon. Cook covered on low setting 6 to 8 hours.

This makes an excellent complement to ham or beef pot roasts.

Hot Dog Lentil Soup

Cooking time: 7–9 hours

Preparation time: 30 minutes

Attention: Minimal

Pot size: 3–8 quarts

Serves 8

1 pound all-beef hot dogs
2 medium-sized yellow onions
3 garlic cloves
2 medium carrots
2 ribs celery
2 tablespoons olive oil
8 cups water
2 cups lentils, rinsed and drained
1 bay leaf
1 teaspoon salt
½ teaspoon ground black pepper
2 tablespoons cider vinegar.

1. Cut the hot dogs into 1-inch pieces. Peel and chop the onion into ¼-inch pieces. Peel and mince the garlic with a sharp kitchen knife. Peel the carrots, then chop carrots and celery into ¼-inch pieces.
2. Heat the olive oil in a medium-sized skillet on medium heat. Add the onions, garlic, carrots, and celery; sauté until the onions are limp and translucent. Drain off the grease and put the vegetables in the slow cooker. Add the water, lentils, bay leaf, salt, pepper, cider vinegar, and hot dog pieces. Cover and cook on low setting for 7 to 9 hours.

Substitute Polish sausage or kielbasa for a more robust flavor.

Italian Beef Sandwiches

Cooking time: 8–10 hours
Preparation time: 10 minutes
Attention: Minimal
Pot size: 6 quarts
Serves 6

1 teaspoon salt
1 teaspoon pepper
1 teaspoon oregano
1 teaspoon onion salt
1 teaspoon garlic salt
1 teaspoon basil
1 cup Italian salad dressing
2 cups water
5-pound beef pot roast

Mix the spices with the salad dressing and water in the slow cooker. Place the beef roast in the slow cooker. Cover and cook on low setting for 8 to 10 hours. Thirty minutes before serving, remove the beef and shred it using 2 forks and pulling the meat apart. Return the meat to the broth and stir well. Cook covered on low setting for the remaining 30 minutes.

Cut loaves of French bread into 6-inch-long pieces, then cut each piece down the middle and ladle the meat inside. Add a slice of mozzarella cheese on top of the meat.

Using Fresh Herbs

Add fresh herbs during the last 60 minutes of cooking to ensure they retain their flavor. Dried herbs can be added at the beginning of the process.

Texas Barbecued Beef Sandwiches

Cooking time: 9 hours

Preparation time: 15 minutes

Attention: Minimal

Pot size: 5–6 quarts

Serves 8

4-pound chuck roast
½ cup water
2 cups ketchup
10 ounces cola
¼ cup Worcestershire sauce
2 tablespoons prepared mustard
2 tablespoons liquid smoke
¼ teaspoon Tabasco or other hot pepper sauce
8 hamburger buns

1. Cover and cook the roast with the water in the slow cooker on high setting for 8 hours, or until tender.
2. Remove the roast. Shred the meat, trimming off the fat and discarding it in the process. Place the shredded meat in the slow cooker along with ketchup, cola, Worcestershire sauce, mustard, liquid smoke, and hot sauce. Cook covered on high setting for 1 hour. Ladle over buns to serve.

Potato chips and baked beans make this meal an authentic American potluck event!

Meat Grades

The higher the grade of meat, the more marbling (fat) contained in the cut. For a healthy alternative, use a lower grade of meat and cook it in the slow cooker to tenderize it. Select is the least fatty grade.

Cooking time: 1–2 hours

Preparation time: 15 minutes

Attention: Minimal

Pot size: 4–6 quarts

Serves 8

Ham Barbecue

2 pounds chopped ham
1 bottle chili sauce
½ cup ketchup
½ cup water
¼ cup white corn syrup
8 whole wheat bulky rolls

1. Mix together all the ingredients in the slow cooker. Cook covered on low setting 1 to 2 hours, stirring occasionally.
2. Serve on whole wheat rolls.

Leftover Ham

Ham slices are the perfect "don't know what to make" ingredient. Cube it and add the meat to beans to make soup or cut it into quarters and cook it with potatoes, carrots and onions to create a "mock" ham roast.

Holiday Punch

Cooking time: 1 hour

Preparation time: 15 minutes

Attention: Minimal

Pot size: 3–6 quarts

Serves 4

½ medium-sized orange
1 quart apple juice
1 quart cranberry juice cocktail
1 cup brown sugar
4 cinnamon sticks
4 whole cloves

Peel and cut the orange into ¼-inch-thick slices. Add the apple juice, cranberry juice, and brown sugar to the slow cooker. Cook on low setting, stirring occasionally, until the brown sugar is dissolved. Add the cinnamon sticks and cloves. Cook covered for 1 hour on low setting. Right before guests arrive, add the orange slices.

Use a soup ladle to let guests serve the punch themselves.

Slow Cooker vs. Crock-Pot®?

A slow cooker is any cooking appliance that is designed to cook at a low temperature for several hours. A Crock-Pot® is a trade-marked slow cooker that is manufactured by Rival.

Cooking time: 8–9 hours

Preparation time: 30 minutes

Attention: Minimal

Pot size: 3–6 quarts

Serves 12

Cabbage Rolls

12 large cabbage leaves
1 pound lean ground beef
½ cup cooked white rice
½ teaspoon salt
⅛ teaspoon ground black pepper
¼ teaspoon thyme
¼ teaspoon nutmeg
¼ teaspoon cinnamon
1 (6-ounce) can tomato paste
¾ cup water

1. Wash the cabbage leaves. Boil four cups of water in a saucepan on the stove. Turn off the heat and soak the leaves in the water for 5 minutes. Remove the leaves, drain, and cool.
2. Combine the ground beef, rice, salt, pepper, thyme, nutmeg, and cinnamon. Place 2 tablespoons of the meat mixture on each leaf and roll firmly. Stack the cabbage rolls in the slow cooker. Combine the tomato paste and water; pour over the stuffed cabbage rolls. Cook covered on low setting 8 to 9 hours.

Serve with a selection of pickled vegetables and hard cheeses.

Award-Winning Tuna Noodle Casserole

Cooking time: 6–8 hours

Preparation time: 15 minutes

Attention: Minimal

Pot size: 3–6 quarts

Serves 8

2 cups (16 ounces) water-packed tuna
3 hard-boiled eggs
1 (10¾-ounce) can cream of mushroom condensed soup
1 (10¾-ounce) can cream of celery condensed soup
3 hard-boiled eggs
2 celery ribs
1 medium-sized yellow onion
1 cup frozen mixed vegetables
2 cups cooked egg noodles
1½ cups crushed potato chips

1. Drain the tuna. Chop the hard-boiled eggs into ¼-inch pieces. Chop the celery into ¼-inch pieces. Peel the onion and chop into ¼-inch pieces. Thaw the frozen vegetables overnight in the refrigerator, or thaw them in the microwave. Precook the egg noodles in boiling water. Crush the potato chips while still in the bag.
2. Combine all ingredients except ½ cup potato chips. Put mixture into the slow cooker. Cover with remaining potato chips. Cover and cook on low setting for 6 to 8 hours.

Serve with Slightly Seedy White Bread (page 84).

Hearty Appetites

Southern-Style Barbecued Pork Ribs

Cooking time: 6–9 hours
Preparation time: 20 minutes
Attention: Medium
Pot size: 4–8 quarts
Serves 4

2 pounds pork ribs
1 medium-sized yellow onion
¼ cup fresh green pepper, chopped
1 cup brewed coffee
1 cup ketchup
½ cup sugar
½ cup Worcestershire sauce
¼ cup white vinegar
¼ teaspoon ground black pepper
¼ teaspoon garlic salt

1. Cut the ribs into pieces that will easily fit into the slow cooker. Cover and cook the ribs on low setting for 4 to 5 hours.
2. Cut the onion and green pepper into dime-sized pieces. Combine the coffee, ketchup, sugar, Worcestershire sauce, vinegar, black pepper, garlic salt, onion, and green pepper. Stir until all ingredients are well mixed; pour mixture over the ribs and continue to cook covered on low setting for another 2 to 4 hours.

Corn Bread in the Round (page 76) makes an excellent complement to this dish.

Ribs per Person

Spare ribs are the least meaty of any red meat. The rule of thumb is to buy one pound for each serving. If you're buying country style ribs, you can buy about ¾ pound per person.

Cooking time: day 1, 6 hours;
day 2, 8 hours

Preparation time: 30 minutes

Attention: Minimal

Pot size: 6–8 quart

Serves 6

Sauerkraut-Stuffed Roast Duck

1 domestic duck
1 cup vinegar
¼ teaspoon salt
Dash of pepper
2 apples
1 medium yellow onion
1 quart (4 cups) sauerkraut
1 pound pork spareribs

1. Clean and wash the duck, then place it in a large kettle. Cover with water and add the vinegar. Soak for 3 hours. Remove the duck from liquid, dry it off, and season with salt and pepper, cover and place in the refrigerator overnight.
2. While the duck is being soaked, core and chop the apples and chop the onion into ½-inch chunks. Combine the apple, onion, sauerkraut, and spareribs in the slow cooker. Cook for 6 hours, or until the meat from the ribs falls from the bones. Discard the bones and refrigerate the slow-cooker mixture. The next day stuff the sparerib-sauerkraut mixture into the duck. Place the stuffed duck into the slow cooker and cook on medium for 8 hours, or until golden and tender.

Serve with Minnesota Wild Rice (page 281).

High-Altitude Slow Cooking
Since water boils at a higher temperature in high altitudes, you may want to cook most of your dishes on the high setting to ensure they're getting hot enough. You also can easily test the slow cooker by heating water in it and determining the temperature with a thermometer.

Cooking time: 6–8 hours

Preparation time: 15 minutes

Attention: Minimal

Pot size: 3–6 quarts

Ham Hocks and Beans

Serves 4

2 cups dried pinto beans, rinsed

3 smoked ham hocks

4 cups water

1 bay leaf

½ teaspoon ground black pepper

Place all the ingredients in the slow cooker. Cover and cook on high setting for 6 to 8 hours. Remove the ham hocks and take the meat off the bones. Discard the bones and return the meat to the slow cooker; stir well. Remove the bay leaf before serving.

Smoked ham hocks are quite salty, so resist the urge to salt this dish before serving.

A Word on Canned Beans

Remember that canned beans have been precooked. If substituting them in a recipe calling for dry beans, decrease the water by four cups per cup of beans. You also can reduce the cooking time by half.

Cooking time: 10–11 hours
Preparation time: 30 minutes
Attention: Minimal
Pot size: 4–6 quarts
Serves 6

Sweet and Saucy Beef Roast

3-pound chuck roast
1 teaspoon vegetable oil
1 large white onion
1 (10¾-ounce) can cream of mushroom condensed soup
½ cup water
¼ cup sugar
¼ cup vinegar
2 teaspoons table salt
1 teaspoon prepared yellow mustard
1 teaspoon Worcestershire sauce

1. Place the beef roast and oil in a skillet on the stove and cook on medium-high heat until the roast is brown; flip the roast so it browns on both sides. Transfer the roast to the slow cooker.
2. Chop the onion into ¼-inch pieces. Combine the onions and the remaining ingredients in a medium-sized bowl, stirring so they are well mingled; pour mixture over the beef roast. Cover and cook on low setting for 10 to 11 hours.

Serve with Heavy Brown Bread (page 85).

Meat Safety

To prevent bacteria growth, thaw and brown large cuts of meat before putting them in the slow cooker. This gets them into the hot, bacteria-killing temperature zone quicker.

Cooking time: 8–9 hours	
Preparation time: 15 minutes	
Attention: Medium	
Pot size: 3–6 quarts	

Beef Dumpling Soup

Serves 6

1 pound lean steak
1 package dry onion soup mix
6 cups hot water
2 carrots
1 celery rib
1 tomato
1 tablespoon fresh chopped parsley
1 cup packaged biscuit mix
6 tablespoons milk

1. Cut the steak into 1-inch pieces. Sprinkle with the dry onion soup mix. Place in the bottom of the slow cooker and add the hot water. Peel the carrots with a potato peeler, then shred the carrots using a vegetable grater. Chop the celery. Peel and chop the tomato into ¼-inch pieces. Add the vegetables to the slow cooker. Cover and cook on high setting for 8 to 9 hours.

2. Finely chop the parsley. In a small bowl, combine the biscuit mix with the parsley. Add the milk and stir until the biscuit mix is moistened. About 30 minutes before serving, drop the batter by heaping teaspoonfuls onto the top of the soup. Cover and cook on high for remaining 30 minutes.

Serve with Cheery Cherry Crispy (page 266) for a wonderful fall meal.

Cooking time: 4–6 hours

Preparation time: 20 minutes

Attention: Minimal

Pot size: 3–6 quarts

Serves 4

Barbecued Pork and Beans

2 tablespoons yellow onion, chopped
1 pound canned or fresh baked beans
4 lean pork chops
½ cup prepared mustard
½ cup prepared ketchup
¼ cup lemon juice
¼ cup sugar

1. Chop the onion with a medium-sized knife into pieces about the size of a dime. Mix with the beans and place in the bottom of the slow cooker.
2. Using a butter knife, spread the mustard and ketchup over both sides of the pork chops. Sprinkle both sides with lemon juice and sugar. Lay the pork chops on top of the beans. If possible, do not layer them. Cook on low heat for 4 to 6 hours.

Serve with steamed broccoli and baked potatoes for a complete meal.

Cooking Dried Beans

Instead of soaking beans overnight, cook them on low in the slow cooker overnight. Add some onion, garlic, salt, and pepper and you have a ready-to-eat-anytime treat. You also can freeze the cooked beans for later use in recipes.

Sausage, Red Beans, and Rice

Cooking time: 6–8 hours
Preparation time: 30 minutes
Attention: Medium
Pot size: 3–6 quarts
Serves 8

1 pound dry red kidney beans
6 cups water
1 meaty ham bone
2 large yellow onions
1 green bell pepper
2 ribs celery
¼ cup chopped fresh parsley
2 cloves garlic
1 teaspoon table salt
½ teaspoon ground black pepper
¼ teaspoon sugar
1 bay leaf
2 pound smoked sausage, cut up
8 cups prepared long-grain white rice

1. Soak the beans overnight in the water. Drain and rinse the beans. Trim the fat from the ham bone. Peel and chop the onions into ¼-inch pieces. Seed and chop the green bell pepper into ¼-inch pieces. Chop the celery into ¼-inch pieces. Chop the parsley into ¼-inch lengths. Peel and slice the garlic paper-thin with a sharp kitchen knife.
2. Put the beans, ham bone, onions, green pepper, celery, garlic, salt, pepper, sugar, and bay leaf in the slow cooker. Cook covered on low setting for 3 to 4 hours.
3. Slice the sausage into ½-inch pieces. Brown the sausage in a medium-sized skillet on medium-high heat on the stove; cook until the sausage is crisp. Drain off the grease and place the sausage pieces on paper towels to soak up remaining grease. Add the sausage to the slow cooker. Cook covered on low setting for 3 to 4 additional hours.
4. Just before serving, remove the bay leaf and add the parsley. Serve over rice.

| Cooking time: 6 hours |
| Preparation time: 20 minutes |
| Attention: Medium |
| Pot size: 3–6 quarts |
| Serves 4 |

Easy Steak Stroganoff

2 pounds round steak
1 garlic clove
¼ cup flour
½ teaspoon ground black pepper
½ teaspoon table salt
1 small yellow onion
½ pound (1 cup) fresh mushrooms, sliced
3 tablespoons butter
1 tablespoon soy sauce
½ cup whole milk
1 cup water
2 beef bouillon cubes
1 (8-ounce) package cream cheese

1. Cut the steak into 1-inch cubes. Peel and mince the garlic using a sharp paring knife. Mix the steak with the flour, pepper, salt, and garlic. Peel and chop the onion into ¼-inch pieces. Clean the mushrooms by wiping with a damp cloth; slice paper-thin.

2. Add all ingredients except the cream cheese to the slow cooker. Cover and cook on low setting for 6 hours, stirring occasionally. Approximately a half-hour before serving, cut the cream cheese into 1-inch cubes and stir into the slow cooker. Continue stirring until melted.

This is excellent served over wide egg noodles. Sprinkle with parsley and eat with a heavy red wine.

Hamburger Rice Skillet

Cooking time: 6–8 hours

Preparation time:

Attention: Minimal

Pot size: 3–6 quarts

Serves 4

1 medium-sized yellow onion
1 medium-sized green bell pepper
1 clove garlic
4 medium-sized tomatoes
1 pound lean ground beef
1 cup medium-grain dry rice
1 (8-ounce) can tomato sauce
1 teaspoon Worcestershire sauce
½ teaspoon dry crushed basil
1½ cups water
1 teaspoon table salt

1. Peel and slice the onion into rings. Remove the stem and seeds from the green pepper and chop the pepper into ¼-inch pieces. Peel and the mince garlic using a sharp paring knife. Cut the tomatoes into quarters.

2. Combine the beef, onion, pepper, and garlic in a skillet on the stove. Cook on medium-high heat, stirring constantly, until the meat is browned. Drain off the grease and put the meat and vegetables into the slow cooker. Add the rice, tomatoes, tomato sauce, Worcestershire sauce, basil, water, and salt; stir well. Cover and cook on low setting 6 to 8 hours.

Serve with a vegetable medley of broccoli, cauliflower, and carrots drizzled with honey.

Northwestern Baked Beans

Cooking time: 6–8 hours

Preparation time: 20 minutes

Attention: Minimal

Pot size: 3–6 quarts

Serves 8

1 pound ground beef
¾ pound bacon
1 large white onion
1 cup ketchup
¼ cup brown sugar
½ teaspoon ground black pepper
1 teaspoon hickory smoke flavoring
1 (16 ounce) can pork and beans
1 (16 ounce) can lima beans
1 (16 ounce) can butter beans
1 (16 ounce) can kidney beans

Brown the ground beef in a medium-sized skillet on medium-high heat. Drain off the grease and place the meat in the slow cooker. Fry the bacon in medium-sized skillet on medium-high heat. Drain off the grease and lay the bacon on paper towels to cool. Crumble the bacon and add it to the slow cooker. Remove the skin from the onion and chop into ¼-inch pieces. Add the onion, ketchup, brown sugar, pepper, hickory flavoring, and all the beans, including their liquid, to the slow cooker; stir well. Cook covered on low setting for 6 to 8 hours.

Serve with Heavy Brown Bread (page 85) for sopping up all that wonderful juice.

Aunt Mary's Easy Lasagna

Cooking time: 5 hours

Preparation time: 20 minutes

Attention: Minimal

Pot size: 3–6 quarts

Serves 8

1 pound lean ground beef

1 teaspoon Italian seasoning

1 cup fresh mushrooms, sliced

1 tablespoon shortening, for greasing

8 lasagna noodles, uncooked

1 (28-ounce) jar spaghetti sauce

⅓ cup water

2 cups ricotta cheese

2 cups mozzarella cheese, shredded

1. Brown the ground beef in a medium-sized skillet on medium-high heat until no pink remains. Stir in the Italian seasoning. Drain off the grease. Wash the mushrooms by wiping with a damp cloth; slice ⅛-inch thick.
2. Grease the slow cooker by putting the shortening on a paper towel and rubbing it around the inside of the slow cooker. Break the noodles and place half of them in the bottom of the slow cooker. Spread half of the ground beef over the top. Layer half of the sauce, water, mushrooms, ricotta cheese, and mozzarella cheese over the beef. Repeat layers.
3. Cover and cook on low setting for 5 hours.

Serve with a fresh green salad and Italian dressing.

| Cooking time: 2–3 hours |
| Preparation time: 10 minutes |
| Attention: Minimal |
| Pot size: 1–3 quarts |
| Serves 8 |

Beefy Cheese Spread

3 green onions
3 ounces dried beef
8 ounces cream cheese
½ cup whole milk
1 teaspoon dry mustard

1. Remove the roots and first layer of skin from the green onions; chop the onions into ¼-inch pieces, including the stems. Chop the dried beef into ¼-inch pieces. Cut the cream cheese into ½-inch cubes.
2. Put the cream cheese and milk in the slow cooker. Cover and cook on low setting for 1 to 2 hours, until the cheese is fully melted. Add the mustard, onion, and dried beef; stir thoroughly. Cover and cook on low setting for 1 more hour.

Serve as a spread for sandwiches or as a dip with sourdough bread.

Keep It On!

Never leave food in the slow cooker when it isn't turned on. Any temperature below the low setting on the slow cooker will allow dangerous bacteria to grow.

Summer Tantalizers

Cooking time: 8–9 hours	
Preparation time: 20 minutes	
Attention: Medium	
Pot size: 3–6 quarts	
Serves 8	

Risotto with Fresh Summer Vegetables

1 tablespoon butter
1 large white onion
1 cup fresh zucchini, chopped
⅓ cup fresh parsley, chopped
1 cup uncooked white rice
4 cups chicken broth
1 cup fresh or frozen green beans
1 cup fresh or frozen snow peas
½ teaspoon table salt
¼ teaspoon ground black pepper

1. Melt the butter in small skillet on medium-high heat on the stove. Peel and chop the onions into ¼-inch pieces. Sauté the onions in the butter for 3 to 5 minutes, until the onions are translucent; drain.
2. Chop the zucchini into 1-inch pieces. Chop the parsley into ¼-inch lengths. Place the onions, zucchini, uncooked white rice, chicken broth, green beans, salt, and pepper in the slow cooker; mix well. Cook covered on low setting 7 to 8 hours, or until the rice is soft. Add the peas and cook 1 to 2 hours more.
3. Add the parsley; stir well. Cook uncovered 15 to 30 minutes.

Serve with assorted gourmet crackers and cheeses.

Brussels Sprouts à la Orange

Cooking time: 2 hours
Preparation time: 15 minutes
Attention: Medium
Pot size: 2–4 quarts
Serves 4

1 ¼ cup fresh-squeezed orange juice
4 cups fresh Brussels sprouts
½ teaspoon cornstarch
¼ teaspoon ground cinnamon

Squeeze 6 to 8 oranges to make 1¼ cup orange juice; ripe oranges produce the most juice. In the slow cooker, combine the Brussels sprouts, juice, cornstarch, and cinnamon. Cover and cook on low for 1 hour. Uncover and cook on low for 1 additional hour until the sauce has thickened and the Brussels sprouts are tender.

This is the perfect complement to Sparkling Beef Tips (page 109).

Using Frozen Veggies

If using frozen vegetables, thaw them overnight in the refrigerator or for a few minutes in the microwave before adding them to the slow cooker. This will prevent bacteria growth as the food is heating up.

Green Beans in Lemon Honey

Cooking time: 1 hour
Preparation time: 25 minutes
Attention: Minimal
Pot size: 3–6 quarts
Serves 4–6

½ lemon
2 tablespoons butter
3 tablespoons honey
1 teaspoon cider vinegar
½ teaspoon salt
1 tart apple
1 teaspoon cornstarch
1 tablespoon water
3 cups fresh green beans
1 medium yellow onion

1. Slice the lemon into wedges no thicker than ⅛ inch. Combine the butter, honey, vinegar, salt, and lemon slices. Bring to a boil, stirring constantly, for 5 minutes.
2. Core and dice the apple into pieces about ¼ inch square; do not remove the peel. Add to the lemon mixture and cook on medium heat for about 5 minutes.
3. Stir together the cornstarch and water until you have a light paste. Stir this into the apple-lemon mixture. Bring to a boil, then cook on low heat for about 3 minutes.
4. Snap the ends off the green beans and discard. Wash the green beans thoroughly in cold water. Peel and slice onion into ¼-inch rings. Place the green beans and onions in the slow cooker and pour the apple-lemon mixture over them. Cook on low heat for 1 hour.

Even vegetable haters will love this combination of sweet and tart flavors! Use this recipe to complement a grilled steak or pork chops.

Czech Garlic and Bean Soup

Cooking time: 8–10 hours

Preparation time: 10 minutes

Attention: Minimal

Pot size: 3–6 quarts

Serves 8

6 garlic cloves
4 tablespoons chopped fresh parsley
3 tablespoons olive oil
1 pound (2 cups) dry white beans
1 quart (4 cups) beef broth
1 quart (4 cups) water
2 teaspoons table salt
1 teaspoon ground white pepper

1. Remove the skins from the garlic and mince with a sharp paring knife. Finely chop the parsley. Sauté the garlic and parsley in olive oil in a medium-sized skillet on medium-high heat. The garlic should be slightly brown but not hard. Do not drain the oil.
2. Add all the ingredients to the slow cooker. Cover and cook on low setting for 8 to 10 hours.

Serve with Grandma Margaret's Summer Dill Bread (page 83).

Cooking Beans

Any bean recipe gives you two options. Cook it longer and let the beans dissolve for a creamy texture. Serve it earlier in the cooking process, as soon as the beans are completely soft, for more distinct flavors in every bite.

Lemony Chicken and Okra Soup

Cooking time: 7–9 hours

Preparation time: 30 minutes

Attention: Minimal

Pot size: 3–8 quarts

Serves 8

6 chicken breasts

2 tablespoons lemon juice

1 large yellow onion

3 medium tomatoes

2 cups fresh okra, sliced

⅓ cup uncooked long-grain rice

6 cups chicken broth

½ cup (4 ounces) tomato paste

2 teaspoons table salt

¼ ground black pepper

½ teaspoon cayenne pepper

1 teaspoon ground turmeric

1. Remove the bones and skin from the chicken breasts. Rub the chicken with lemon juice, then cut into 1-inch cubes. Peel and chop the onion into ¼-inch pieces. Peel and chop the tomatoes into ½-inch pieces. Wash and slice the okra into ¼-inch rounds.
2. Put all the ingredients in the slow cooker. Cover and cook on low setting for 7 to 9 hours.

Serve with spicy dill pickles and assorted cheeses.

Wild Rice Stuffed Zucchini

2 small zucchini
1 cup wild rice
1 small yellow onion
½ cup chopped fresh chives
½ teaspoon ground black pepper
½ teaspoon table salt
½ cup shelled, salted, and roasted sunflower seeds

1. Cut the zucchini in half lengthwise and scrape out the inside, leaving about ¾-inch around the sides; discard the insides.
2. Precook the wild rice according to the package directions. Peel and chop the onion into ¼-inch pieces. Chop the chives into ¼-inch lengths. Combine the wild rice, onion, black pepper, salt, and chives in a medium-sized mixing bowl. Use the mixture to stuff the zucchini boats. Sprinkle with sunflower seeds. Place the stuffed zucchini in the slow cooker. Cover and cook on low setting for 8 to 9 hours.

This is a wonderful complement to a grilled steak or pork chops.

Wild Wild Rice

In many states wild rice is a protected crop that can only be raised and harvested by Native Americans. Look for unbroken, dark brown rice for the best flavor and consistency.

Mushroom Vegetable Barley Soup

Cooking time: 3–4 hours

Preparation time: 45 minutes

Attention: Minimal

Pot size: 3–6 quarts

Serves 6

1 pound (2 cups) fresh mushrooms, sliced
4 celery stalks
5 medium carrots
1 cup fresh chopped broccoli
2 cups chopped yellow onion
1½ tablespoons minced garlic
3 tablespoons olive oil
½ teaspoon ground thyme
1 bay leaf
½ cup dry barley
8 cups chicken broth
1 teaspoon salt
½ teaspoon pepper

1. Clean the mushrooms by rubbing with a damp towel, then slice into quarters. Wash the celery, carrots, and broccoli thoroughly in cold water, then cut into ½-inch pieces. Peel the onions and chop into ¼-inch pieces. Peel and mince the garlic.
2. Place the olive oil in the slow cooker. Add the onions and cook on high for about 10 minutes. Add the garlic, thyme, bay leaf, and mushrooms. Cook for about 20 minutes on low heat, stirring occasionally.
3. Add the barley, celery, broccoli, carrots, and broth. Stir in the salt and pepper. Cook covered on low heat for 3 to 4 hours. Remove the bay leaf before serving.

Serve with Zucchini Bread (page 79) for a fun taste combination.

Cooking time: 6–8 hours

Preparation time: 20 minutes

Attention: Minimal

Pot size: 3–8 quarts

Harvest Vegetable Soup

Serves 8

3 cups fresh tomatoes, chopped

2 cups fresh carrots, sliced

2 cups fresh zucchini, sliced

2 cups fresh green beans

1 large onion

⅛ cup diced fresh red bell pepper

1 cup fresh, canned or frozen whole kernel corn

1 cup fresh or frozen peas

1 bay leaf

½ teaspoon thyme (optional)

½ teaspoon marjoram (optional)

½ teaspoon table salt

3 cups water

1. Cut the tomatoes, carrots, and zucchini into 1-inch pieces. Snap the ends off the green beans and discard; cut the green beans into 1-inch lengths. Peel the onion and chop into ¼-inch pieces. Remove the stem and seeds from the red pepper and chop into ¼-inch pieces. Combine all the ingredients except the peas in the slow cooker. Stir with a wooden spoon until the ingredients are evenly distributed and covered with liquid. Cover and cook on low heat for 5 to 7 hours. Add the peas and cook 1 to 2 hours more.

2. Remove cover 15 minutes before serving; stir well. Remove and discard the bay leaf.

Because this soup has almost no fat, it makes an excellent first course to a heavier meal such as Southwestern Beef Roast with Peppers (page 190).

Caution When Freezing Soups

When freezing soups, remember that water expands when frozen. Fill the container to within one inch of the top and cover tightly.

Cooking time: 3–4 hours

Preparation time: 10 minutes

Attention: Minimal

Pot size: 3–6 quarts

Serves 8

Cheery Cherry Crispy

⅓ cup softened butter (or margarine), divided
2 pounds fresh cherries
⅓ cup water
2/3 cup packed brown sugar
½ cup quick-cooking oats
½ cup flour
1 teaspoon cinnamon

1. Lightly grease the slow cooker with ½ teaspoon of the butter or margarine. Remove the stems and pits from the cherries and put the cherries in slow cooker. Add water.

2. In a bowl, mix the brown sugar, oats, flour, and cinnamon. Cut in the remaining butter (or margarine) by using a fork and slicing the butter into small pieces; continue doing this until the mixture is crumbly. Sprinkle the crumbs over the cherries. Cook uncovered on low setting for 3 to 4 hours.

This dish works equally well with blueberries or raspberries.

Using Cannned Fruit

If substituting canned fruit for fresh in a dessert recipe, choose fruit in a water base, not syrup. The syrup bases tend to draw the sugar out of the fruit while in the can.

Cooking time:	2–3 hours
Preparation time:	30 minutes
Attention:	Minimal
Pot size:	3–5 quarts
Serves 6	

Pistachio-Buttered Vegetable Medley

1 cup fresh asparagus tips
3 medium-sized fresh carrots
1 cup fresh green beans
½ cup chopped pistachio nuts
½ cup butter (or margarine), melted
1 tablespoon fresh lemon juice
½ teaspoon dry marjoram

Clean the vegetables and slice into ½-inch pieces. Shell and finely chop the pistachio nuts with a sharp paring knife. Mix the vegetables and nuts together and place in the slow cooker. Add the butter, lemon juice, and marjoram. Cook covered for 2 to 3 hours on low setting. Place the mixture in a serving bowl and top with pistachio nuts if desired.

This is an excellent complement to grilled chicken breasts.

Add Some Tartness

Use lemon juice when cooking vegetables in the slow cooker. Sprinkle a little juice on top and the vegetables will retain their color better. The lemon juice also adds a tang that is a nice substitute for fatty butter.

Cooking time: 4 hours

Preparation time: 30 minutes

Attention: Minimal

Pot size: 3–5 quarts

Romanian Sauerkraut

Serves 6

6 cups sauerkraut
6 ripe tomatoes
1 large yellow onion
1 green bell pepper
2 garlic cloves
1½ pounds kielbasa

1. Drain and rinse the sauerkraut. Chop the tomatoes into ½-inch pieces. Peel the onion and chop into ¼-inch pieces. Remove the stem and seeds from the green pepper and chop into ¼-inch pieces. Peel the garlic and mince with a sharp kitchen knife. Chop the kielbasa into 1-inch pieces.
2. Mix all the ingredients in the slow cooker. Cook covered on low setting for 4 hours.

Serve with an assortment of fresh summer fruits.

Cooking time: 5–6 hours

Preparation time: 30 minutes

Attention: Minimal

Pot size: 2–4 quarts

Serves 6

German-Style Hot Potato Salad

4 slices bacon
½ cup onion, chopped
½ cup celery, sliced
¼ cup diced green pepper
2 potatoes
¼ cup chopped fresh parsley
1 teaspoon sugar
½ teaspoon salt
½ teaspoon ground black pepper
¼ cup white vinegar
¼ cup vegetable oil

1. Fry the bacon in frying pan or cook in the microwave until crisp, then crumble by placing the bacon in a paper towel and wringing it with your hands. Peel and chop the onions into ¼-inch pieces. Chop the celery into ¼-inch pieces. Remove the stem and seeds from the green pepper and chop into ¼-inch pieces. Wash and scrub the potatoes thoroughly; do not peel. Slice about ¼-inch thick. Roughly chop the parsley.
2. Combine all the ingredients except the parsley and bacon; stir well. Cook covered on low setting 5 to 6 hours. Stir in the bacon and parsley before serving.

Use as a side dish when grilling steaks or pork chops.

Discolored Potates

To prevent discoloration, add potatoes to the slow cooker right before turning it on. If you must prepare the slow cooker the night before, layer the potatoes on the bottom of the cooking container so the least amount of air reaches them.

Fresh Zucchini Casserole

Cooking time: 6–7 hours

Preparation time: 20 minutes

Attention: Minimal

Pot size: 3–6 quarts

Serves 8

2 cups zucchini, diced
2 cups yellow summer squash, diced
1 large yellow onion
2 cups fresh mushrooms, sliced
2 cups cubed Cheddar cheese
1 package onion soup mix
1 quart (4 cups) fresh or canned spaghetti sauce

1. Clean but do not peel the zucchini and summer squash; chop into bite-size pieces. Peel and chop the onion into ½-inch pieces. Clean the mushrooms by wiping with a damp cloth; slice paper-thin with a sharp paring knife. Cut the cheese into ½-inch cubes.
2. Combine all the ingredients in the slow cooker; mix well. Cook uncovered on low setting 5 to 6 hours. Remove the cover, stir well, and cook 1 hour uncovered on low setting.

Use as a complement to beef or pork roasts.

Cooking time: 8 hours

Preparation time: 30 minutes

Attention: Minimal

Pot size: 4–6 quarts

Serves 4

Lemony Chicken

4 chicken breasts
½ teaspoon table salt
¼ teaspoon ground black pepper
2 tablespoons butter
¼ cup sherry
4 cloves garlic, minced
1 teaspoon crumbled dry oregano
¼ cup lemon juice
1 teaspoon grated lemon peel

Wash the chicken breasts; do not remove the bone or skin. Sprinkle the chicken with salt and pepper. Heat the butter in medium-sized skillet. Sauté the chicken until brown. Using a slotted spoon or tongs, transfer the chicken to the slow cooker. Add the sherry to the skillet and stir to loosen the brown bits on the bottom of the skillet (deglaze). Pour the sherry mixture over the chicken. Sprinkle the chicken with the oregano and garlic. Cover and cook on low for 7 hours. Cut the lemon peel into ⅛-inch squares. Add the lemon juice and bits of lemon peel. Cook covered on low for 1 additional hour.

Serve over long-grain brown rice and complement with a variety of pickled vegetables.

Slow Cooking Rice and Pasta
You can cook rice and pasta in the slow cooker although it tends to get mushy over a long cooking cycle. Instead, add precooked rice or pasta during the last half hour of the cooking process.

Pizza-Stuffed Potato Boats

Cooking time: 5–6 hours

Preparation time: 30 minutes

Attention: Minimal

Pot size: 4–8 quarts

Serves 8

4 large potatoes
½ pound (1 cup) pepperoni, diced
1 medium-sized yellow onion
1 cup shredded mozzarella cheese
1 cup spaghetti sauce
¼ cup grated Parmesan cheese

1. Bake the potatoes in the microwave or conventional oven; slice in half lengthwise. Scoop out the insides (do not discard), leaving about ¾-inch of potato all around.

2. Cut the pepperoni into ¼-inch pieces. Peel the onion and chop into ¼-inch pieces. Shred the cheese with a vegetable grater. Mix the left-over potato insides, onion, pepperoni, cheese, and spaghetti sauce in a medium-sized mixing bowl. Put into the potato boats, stuffing firmly. Sprinkle with Parmesan cheese. Place potato boats in the slow cooker. You may have to stack them. Cover and cook on low setting for 5 to 6 hours.

Serve with a fresh green salad and Italian dressing for a completely balanced meal.

Cleaning Roots!

Clean root vegetables thoroughly by scrubbing them with a nail brush or scouring pad designated for that purpose. Because they grow in fertilized soil, they can harbor bacteria on their skins.

CHAPTER 20
Vegetables

Sweet Potato and Apple Bake

Cooking time: 6–8 hours

Preparation time: 30 minutes

Attention: Minimal

Pot size: 3–6 quarts

Serves 8

4 medium-sized sweet potatoes
6 medium-sized apples
2 teaspoons cinnamon
1 teaspoon nutmeg
¼ teaspoon salt
¼ teaspoon vegetable oil
½ cup apple cider

1. Peel the sweet potatoes and cut into ¼-inch slices. Peel and core the apples, then cut into ¼-inch slices.
2. Combine the cinnamon, nutmeg, and salt; mix well.
3. Lightly spread oil over bottom of slow cooker. Add the apple cider to the slow cooker. Layer the sweet potatoes and apples in the slow cooker, alternating the layers: begin with a layer of sweet potatoes, then sprinkle the cinnamon mixture lightly over each layer of sweet potatoes and apples. Cook covered on low setting for 6 to 8 hours.

This is an excellent sweet potato variation for a Thanksgiving feast.

Veggie Water

Next time you are boiling or steaming vegetables, reserve the liquid in a large container in the refrigerator. Use it instead of water in slow cooker recipes to add extra, subtle flavors.

Lemony Asparagus and Carrots

Cooking time: 2–4 hours
Preparation time: 10 minutes
Attention: Minimal
Pot size: 2–6 quarts
Serves 6

2 bunches fresh asparagus
½ pound (1 cup) precleaned
  baby carrots

2 tablespoons lemon juice
1 teaspoon lemon pepper

Clean the asparagus by running under cold water; cut off the bottoms so that no red or white part of the stem remains. Layer the asparagus in the bottom of the slow cooker. Add the baby carrots on top of the asparagus layers. Drizzle the lemon juice on top, then sprinkle with lemon pepper. Cook covered on low setting for 2 to 4 hours.

The beautiful color combination and slightly exotic flavor make this an excellent dish for entertaining.

Garlicky Spinach and Swiss Chard

Cooking time: 4–6 hours
Preparation time: 20 minutes
Attention: Minimal
Pot size: 3–6 quarts
Serves 6–8

1 bunch fresh spinach
1 bunch fresh Swiss chard
3 cloves garlic

½ teaspoon olive oil
¼ cup water

Prepare the spinach and Swiss chard by washing in cold water and removing the stems so that only the tender leaves remain. Peel and slice the garlic paper-thin. Sauté the garlic in the olive oil in small skillet on medium high-heat for 2 to 3 minutes; drain. Add all the ingredients to the slow cooker. Cook covered on low setting 4 to 6 hours.

Press the mixture firmly into small ramekins, discarding the juice that rises to the top. Tip the ramekin over onto a plate and remove the ramekin to create a small "mound of greens."

German-Style Cooked Cabbage with Onions and Peppers

Cooking time: 4–6 hours

Preparation time: 20 minutes

Attention: Minimal

Pot size: 3–6 quarts

Serves 8

1 large cabbage
1 cup celery, sliced
1 green bell pepper
½ red bell pepper
1 yellow onion
¼ cup white vinegar
½ teaspoon table salt
½ teaspoon ground black pepper
1 teaspoon celery seeds
1 teaspoon caraway seeds

1. Cut the cabbage into 12 to 16 pieces with a heavy knife on a firm surface. Slice the celery into ¼-inch pieces. Remove the seeds from the green pepper and red pepper; chop the peppers into ¼-inch pieces. Peel and chop the onion into ¼-inch pieces.
2. Place ingredients in the slow cooker in the following order:
    1. Vinegar
    2. Cabbage
    3. Onion
    4. Red and green peppers
    5. Celery
3. Sprinkle salt, black pepper, caraway seeds, and celery seeds on top. Cook covered on low setting 4 to 6 hours, or until the cabbage is tender and translucent.

The tangy flavors in this dish are a perfect complement to beef or pork roasts.

Cooking time: 4–5 hours

Preparation time: 20 minutes

Attention: Medium

Pot size: 3–6 quarts

Serves 8

Orange-Glazed Vegetable Medley

1 medium parsnip
4 medium carrots
1 medium turnip
1 cup fresh cauliflower pieces
1 cup fresh broccoli pieces
½ cup packed brown sugar
½ cup orange juice
3 tablespoons butter (or margarine)
¾ teaspoon cinnamon
2 tablespoons cornstarch
¼ cup water

1. Peel and chop the parsnip into ½-inch pieces. Peel and slice the carrots into ¼-inch rounds. Peel and slice the turnip into ½-inch pieces. Break the cauliflower and broccoli florets into pieces about the size of a marble.
2. Combine all the vegetables with the brown sugar, orange juice, butter, and cinnamon in the slow cooker. Cover and cook on low setting 4–5 hours. Remove the vegetables and put in a serving dish.
3. Pour the juice from the slow cooker into a saucepan and place on the stove; bring to a boil. Mix the cornstarch and water in a small bowl until well blended. Add to the juices. Boil 2 to 3 minutes, stirring constantly. Pour over the vegetables.

The sweet taste of these vegetables makes this dish a natural complement to lamb or pork.

Squash Medley Au Gratin

Cooking time: 6–8 hours
Preparation time: 30 minutes
Attention: Minimal
Pot size: 4–6 quarts
Serves 8

1 medium to large zucchini
1 medium to large acorn squash
4 large ripe tomatoes
2 medium yellow onions
1 cup shredded mozzarella cheese
½ teaspoon salt
1 teaspoon dried basil

1. Prepare the zucchini by peeling and slicing into ¼-inch-thick rounds. Prepare the acorn squash by cutting into quarters, removing the seeds and "strings," and cutting the "meat" from the rind; cut the meat of the squash into 1-inch cubes. Peel and mash the tomatoes with a wooden spoon. Peel and slice the onions into ¼-inch-thick rings.
2. Layer the ingredients in slow cooker in the following order:

   1. Zucchini   4. Tomatoes
   2. Onions   5. Cheese
   3. Acorn squash

3. Sprinkle with salt and basil. Cook covered on low setting 6–8 hours.

This dish can be a meal in itself. It makes a nice fall luncheon.

Grandma Dorothy's Peas and Rice

Cooking time: 3–4 hours

Preparation time: 10 minutes

Attention: Minimal

Pot size: 3–6 quarts

Serves 8

1 medium-sized yellow onion
1½ cups uncooked white rice
3 cups chicken broth
1 teaspoon Italian seasoning
½ teaspoon garlic salt
½ teaspoon ground black pepper
1 cup fresh or frozen baby peas

1. Peel and chop the onion into ¼-inch pieces. Put the rice and onions in the slow cooker.
2. Mix the chicken broth, Italian seasoning, garlic salt, and pepper in a medium-sized saucepan on the stove; bring to a boil. Pour over the rice and onions mix well. Cook covered on low setting for 3 hours, or until all the liquid is absorbed. Stir in the peas. Cook an additional 30 minutes.

Use broccoli instead of peas and garnish with grated Cheddar cheese.

Refrain from Using Canned Veggies

Whenever possible, don't use canned vegetables in a slow cooker recipe. They are precooked and will get very mushy. Carrots and peas will lose their color and can even disintegrate over a long cooking process.

Curried Vegetables and Garbanzo Beans

Cooking time: 9–10 hours

Preparation time: 20 minutes

Attention: Minimal

Pot size: 5–6 quarts

Serves 8

3 medium potatoes
1 pound (2 cups) fresh green beans
1 green bell pepper
½ red bell pepper
1 large yellow onion
2 cloves garlic
4 large ripe tomatoes
2 cups (16 ounces) precleaned baby carrots
2 cups (16 ounces) precooked garbanzo beans
3 tablespoons quick-cooking tapioca
3 teaspoons curry powder
2 teaspoons table salt
2 chicken bouillon cubes
1¾ cups boiling water

1. Peel the potatoes and cut into 1-inch cubes. Slice off the ends of the green beans and cut into approximately 2-inch lengths. Remove the stems and seeds from the red and green bell peppers and chop into ¼-inch pieces. Peel and chop the onion into ¼-inch pieces. Peel the garlic cloves and mince using a sharp, medium-sized knife. Peel the tomatoes and mash in a bowl using a wooden spoon.

2. Combine potatoes, green beans, green pepper, red pepper, onions, garlic, tomatoes, carrots, and garbanzo beans in a large bowl. Stir in the tapioca, curry powder, and salt; mix well, then place mixture in the slow cooker.

3. Dissolve the bouillon in the boiling water; pour over the vegetable mixture. Cook covered on low setting 9 to 10 hours.

Serve this with a pork roast or ham sandwiches for the perfect mix of flavors.

Minnesota Wild Rice

Cooking time: 3–4 hours

Preparation time: 15 minutes

Attention: Minimal

Pot size: 3–6 quarts

Serves 6

½ cup sliced fresh mushrooms

½ cup chopped onion

1 clove garlic

½ cup chopped green bell pepper

1 cup unbroken wild rice

4 cups chicken broth

½ teaspoon salt

½ teaspoon ground black pepper

1. Prepare the mushrooms by wiping with a damp cloth and slicing paper-thin. Peel the onion and chop in ¼-inch pieces. Peel and mince the garlic using a sharp medium-sized knife. Remove the seeds from the green pepper and chop into ¼-inch pieces.
2. Layer the dry ingredients in the slow cooker with the rice on the bottom. Pour the chicken broth over the top. Sprinkle salt and pepper on top. Cover and cook on high setting 3 to 4 hours, or until the liquid is absorbed and the rice is soft and fluffed open.

Unlike its cultivated cousins, wild rice is a very heavy and filling dish. Use this recipe to stuff squash or chicken breasts for a hearty meal.

Power Outage Info

If food is completely cooked and removed from the heat source, such as during a power outage, it will remain safe for up to two hours at room temperature.

Stuffed Acorn Squash with Pecans

Cooking time: 8–10 hours	
Preparation time: 15 minutes	
Attention: Minimal	
Pot size: 2–6 quarts	
Serves 2	

2 cups cooked wild rice
1 medium-sized yellow onion
1 celery stalk
2 medium acorn squash
½ cup fresh pecan halves, chopped

1. Cook the wild rice as per the package directions to yield 2 cups cooked. Peel and chop the onion into ¼-inch pieces. Chop the celery into ¼-inch pieces. Chop the pecans into ⅛-inch pieces. Slice the tops off the squash and remove the seeds by scraping the inside with a spoon.
2. Combine the wild rice, celery, onion, and pecans; mix well. Scoop the mixture into the cavities of the squash. Place the squash in the slow cooker and cook covered on low setting 8 to 10 hours.

This makes an excellent lunch all by itself. Or serve it with steak for a heavier meal in the fall.

When Preparing Ahead

If you're preparing the food the evening before you will be cooking it, do not add rice or pasta until right before you'll begin cooking. They could absorb juices from the meats and vegetables.

Dilly Mashed Potatoes

Cooking time: 7 hours
Preparation time: 20 minutes
Attention: Medium
Pot size: 3–6 quarts
Serves 6

6 large white potatoes
2 cloves garlic
1 medium-sized yellow onion
6 cups water
1 teaspoon table salt
½ cup skim milk
1 tablespoon butter
2 teaspoons dill weed

1. Wash, peel, and cut the potatoes into 1-inch cubes. Peel and mince the garlic using a sharp paring knife. Peel and chop the onion into ¼-inch pieces. Place the potatoes, onions, and garlic in the slow cooker and cover with the water. Add the salt; stir lightly. Cook covered on high setting for 6 hours, or until the potatoes are tender.
2. Transfer the potatoes from the slow cooker to a large bowl. Drain and discard the liquid in the slow cooker. Add the milk, butter, and dill weed to the potatoes and mash together until there are no lumps. Return the mashed potatoes to the slow cooker and cook covered on low setting for 1 hour.

This makes an excellent complement to a beef or pork roast. The potatoes are excellent without gravy, but the complementary flavors also don't fight with even the richest gravy.

Cheesy Cauliflower

Cooking time: 3–4 hours

Preparation time: 30 minutes

Attention: Medium

Pot size: 3–6 quarts

Serves 8

1 medium head cauliflower
1 small white onion
1 (8-ounce) package of cream cheese
5 ounces processed cheese
¼ pound dried beef, shredded
½ cup dehydrated potatoes

1. Remove the leaves and cut the cauliflower into 1-inch pieces. Place in a pot on the stove and cover with water; bring to a boil. Turn off the heat and let the cauliflower sit (do not discard the water). Peel the onion and chop into ¼-inch pieces. Cut the cheeses into ½-inch cubes. Shred the beef into ⅛-inch-thick pieces.

2. In the slow cooker, combine the cream cheese, processed cheese, cauliflower, and 2 cups of the water the cauliflower was boiled in. Cook on low setting, stirring until the cheese is dissolved and the cauliflower pieces are covered with cheese. Add the dried beef, onions, and dehydrated potatoes; mix well. Cover and cook on low setting for 3 hours.

This is an excellent complement to Lemony Chicken (page 271).

Keep Food Warm

Use your slow cooker as a warming device to keep beverages, rolls, and other food items moist and warm. If breads will be in the slow cooker for a long time, place a cup with an inch of water in the bottom in the slow cooker along with the food.

Sweet Corn Pudding

Cooking time: 2–3 hours

Preparation time: 10 minutes

Attention: Minimal

Pot size: 3–6 quarts

Serves 8

2 (10-ounce) cans whole kernel
  corn with juice

3 (10-ounce) cans creamed corn

2 cups corn muffin mix

¼ pound margarine, softened

8 ounces (1 cup) sour cream

Mix together all the ingredients in a medium-sized mixing bowl. Pour into the slow cooker. Cover and heat on low setting for 2 to 3 hours

Serve to complement Swiss-Style Venison Steak (page 145).

Italian Beets

Cooking time: 9–10 hours

Preparation time: 15 minutes

Attention: Minimal

Pot size: 3–6 quarts

Serves 8

4 medium beets

3 cups water

1 cup Italian salad dressing

¼ cup balsamic vinegar

Remove the tops and stems from the beets. Peel the beets and slice into ¼-inch-thick rounds. Mix together the water, dressing, and vinegar in the slow cooker. Add the beets to the mixture. Cover and cook on low setting for 9 to 10 hours.

This is the perfect complement to Slow-Cooked Sauerbraten (page 108).

Spinach and Brown Rice Hot Dish

Cooking time: 3–5 hours

Preparation time: 15 minutes

Attention: Minimal

Pot size: 3–6 quarts

Serves 6

1 cup frozen or canned chopped spinach
1 small yellow onion
3 cups precooked brown rice
1 cup sharp Cheddar cheese, shredded
3 eggs
1½ cups evaporated milk

1. Thaw the spinach, if necessary. Peel and chop the onion into ¼-inch pieces. Cook the rice according to the package directions. Shred the cheese using a vegetable grater.
2. Combine the eggs and milk in a medium-sized mixing bowl; whisk quickly until well blended and slightly frothy. Add the onion, spinach, rice, and cheese; mix well. Pour into the slow cooker. Cover and cook on low setting for 3 to 5 hours.

Serve as a complement to Peachy Georgia Chicken Legs (page 116).

CHAPTER 21
Romance with a Slow Cooker

Cooking time: 6–8 hours	
Preparation time: 30 minutes	
Attention: Minimal	
Pot size: 3–5	
Serves 6	

French Onion Soup

3 cups yellow onion, sliced
1 tablespoon sugar
1 quart (4 cups) beef bouillon
¼ cup butter
1 teaspoon salt
2 tablespoons flour
¼ cup Cognac

1. Peel and slice the onions about ¼-inch thick. Place in a medium skillet with butter and cook on medium heat for 15 minutes. When the onions are limp, add the sugar and cook for 5 more minutes.
2. Add all the ingredients to the slow cooker. Cover and cook on low setting for 6 to 8 hours.

Place garlic toast slices covered with Romano and Mozzarella cheese on top of soup. Heat in an oven until the cheese is melted and slightly brown.

Two Slow Cookers are Better Than One

Use two at once. Make your meat dish in one slow cooker while you make the vegetables or even the bread in another. You'll come home to a fully cooked meal with no hassles.

Cooking time: 1 hour

Preparation time: 30 minutes

Attention: Minimal

Pot size: 3–8 quarts

Serves 8

Blue Cheese Soup

½ pound Stilton cheese
½ pound Cheddar cheese
1 medium-sized white onion
2 celery ribs
2 medium carrots
2 garlic cloves
2 tablespoons butter
⅓ cup flour
2 teaspoons cornstarch

3 cups chicken stock
1 cup heavy whipping cream
⅓ cup dry white wine
⅛ teaspoon baking soda
½ teaspoon table salt
½ teaspoon ground white pepper
⅛ teaspoon cayenne pepper
1 bay leaf.

1. Crumble the cheeses into pieces the size of small marbles. Peel and chop the onion into ¼-inch pieces. Clean and chop the carrots and celery into ¼-inch pieces. Peel the garlic and mince with a sharp kitchen knife.

2. Preheat the slow cooker at low setting. Melt the butter in a large skillet on medium heat. Add the onion, celery, carrots, and garlic; sauté until the onion is tender and translucent. Pour into the preheated slow cooker. Stir in the flour and cornstarch until no lumps remain.

3. Add the stock, cream, wine, baking soda, and both cheeses; stir until smooth and thickened. Add the salt, white pepper, cayenne, and bay leaf. Cover and cook on low setting for 1 hour. Discard the bay leaf before serving.

Serve as a first course for Spicy Pot Roast (page 106).

Chicken Asparagus Supreme

Cooking time: 5 hours

Preparation time: 20 minutes

Attention: Medium

Pot size: 4–6 quarts

Serves 6

4 chicken breasts
½ cup water
½ cup dry white wine
4 hard-boiled eggs
¾ cup butter
½ cup flour
4 cups milk
½ teaspoon salt, plus extra for sprinkling on chicken
¼ teaspoon pepper, plus extra for sprinkling on chicken
1 cup grated Romano cheese
1 cup canned, chopped pimientos
1 pound fresh asparagus

1. Remove the skin and bones from the chicken breast. Sprinkle each lightly with salt and pepper, then place them in the slow cooker. Cover with water and wine. Cook covered on low setting for 4 hours. Remove the chicken from the slow cooker and discard the liquid.

2. Chop the eggs into ¼-inch pieces. Melt the butter in the slow cooker. Blend in the flour. Add the milk, salt, and pepper, stirring constantly. Add the eggs, cheese, and pimientos. Place the cooked chicken in the slow cooker on top of mixture. Wash the asparagus; cut off and discard the bottom 2 inches of the asparagus. Place the asparagus on top of the chicken. Cook on low for 1 hour, or until the asparagus is tender.

Sweet Potato and Apple Bake (page 274) is a perfect complement to this dish.

Pecan Mushroom Chicken Fettuccine

Cooking time: 5–6 hours

Preparation time: 45 minutes

Attention: Medium

Pot size: 6 quarts

Serves 4

*1 pound boneless, skinless
   chicken breasts*
1 cup green onions, chopped
2 garlic cloves
3 cups fresh mushrooms, sliced
1 cup chicken broth
½ teaspoon table salt
¼ teaspoon ground black pepper

*1 (10-ounce) package of
   uncooked spinach fettuccine*
⅔ cup half-and-half
½ cup grated Romano cheese
1 cup chopped, toasted pecans
*2 tablespoons fresh chopped
   parsley*

1. Cut the chicken into 1-inch cubes. Remove the roots and first layer of skin from the green onions. Chop into ¼-inch pieces, including the tops. Peel and chop the garlic into ¼-inch pieces. Clean the mushrooms by wiping with a damp cloth, then slice paper-thin. Place the chicken, chicken broth, mushrooms, onions, garlic, salt, and pepper in the slow cooker. Cook covered on low setting for 4 to 5 hours.
2. Add the pasta and half-and-half; stir gently. Cover and cook on low setting for 1 hour. Add the cheese once the pasta is tender. Stir until the cheese is fully melted and the sauce has thickened. Garnish with pecans and parsley.

Serve with French bread and Roasted Garlic (page 12).

Replacing Onions
Substitute leeks, rutabagas, or turnips for onions in your slow cooker recipes. They have a more distinct flavor that holds up longer than most onions. They also can turn a basic recipe into something more exotic.

Cooking time: 30 minutes

Preparation time: 15 minutes

Attention: Constant

Pot size: 2–4 quarts

Serves 2

Classic Swiss Fondue

1 garlic clove
1 tablespoon flour
½ cup vegetable broth
⅓ cup evaporated milk
¼ teaspoon brandy or
  brandy-flavored extract
1 tablespoon fresh Parmesan
  cheese

2 ounces (¼ cup) Swiss cheese
2 ounces (¼ cup) cream cheese
⅛ teaspoon ground black pepper
⅛ teaspoon ground nutmeg
1 loaf French bread, cubed

1. Peel the garlic and cut in half lengthwise. Rub the inside of the slow cooker with the cut sides of the garlic. Discard the garlic. Whisk the flour and 1 tablespoon of the vegetable broth in a measuring cup until it is well blended. Add the remaining broth and the milk to the slow cooker and cook, uncovered on high setting. Whisk in the brandy and the flour mixture. Cook, stirring constantly, for about 5 minutes.

2. Shred the Parmesan and Swiss cheeses using a vegetable or cheese grater. Cut the cream cheese into 1-inch cubes. Add the Parmesan cheese, Swiss cheese, cream cheese, pepper, and nutmeg to the slow cooker. Cook on high setting, stirring constantly until the cheeses melt and the mixture is very smooth.

3. Turn the slow cooker to the low setting for serving. Serve right inside the slow cooker to keep the fondue from solidifying. Use fondue forks or bamboo skewers to dip the bread.

Preventing Oily Fondue

Naturally aged cheeses tend to separate in the slow-cooking process. Try starting with a base of processed American cheese and adding small amounts of others for flavor.

Cooking time: 2 hours

Preparation time: 45 minutes

Attention: Minimal

Pot size: 3–6 quarts

Serves 2

Tenderloin of Veal

2 pounds veal tenderloin
1 teaspoon table salt
1 teaspoon ground black pepper
2 slices prosciutto ham
8 ounces Brie cheese
¼ cup flour
1 cup butter

4 ounces (½ cup) Morel
  mushrooms, sliced
4 shallots
1 cup cream
1 teaspoon lemon juice
1 cup parsley, chopped

1. Cut the veal into ¼-inch-thick slices and sprinkle each slice with salt and pepper. Pound each slice several times with a meat-tenderizing mallet. Chop the prosciutto ham into ¼-inch pieces and mix with softened and peeled Brie. Spread the Brie and ham mixture onto the veal slices; roll up.
2. Dust the roll-ups with flour. Melt the butter over medium-high heat in a large skillet. Cook the veal rolls until brown on all sides. Put the veal rolls in the slow cooker; retain the veal drippings in the skillet.
3. Clean the mushrooms by wiping with a damp cloth; remove the stems and slice paper-thin. Peel and mince the shallots with a sharp kitchen knife. In the skillet, sauté the mushrooms and shallots in the butter and veal drippings. Add the cream and bring the mixture to a boil, stirring constantly. Pour the sauce over veal rolls. Cook covered on low setting for 2 hours.
4. Coarsely chop parsley. Spoon the sauce over the veal rolls and sprinkle with lemon juice and chopped parsley before serving.

This dish is excellent with garlic spinach: Cook spinach in water with 1 clove minced garlic. Press the water out of the spinach before serving.

Roast Duckling with Orange Glaze

Cooking time: 6 hours

Preparation time: 20 minutes

Attention: Medium

Pot size: 3–6 quarts

Serves 2

2 cups prepared poultry stuffing
1 duckling, fresh or thawed
½ cup sugar
½ teaspoon salt
1 teaspoon cornstarch
1 (6-ounce) can frozen orange juice concentrate, thawed

1. Prepare the stuffing according to the package directions and stuff into the duckling cavity. Place the duckling breast side up in the slow cooker. Cook covered on low setting for 6 hours.
2. One hour before serving, combine the sugar, salt, and cornstarch. Add the thawed orange juice concentrate. Stir over moderate heat until slightly thickened. Brush the entire surface of the duckling with the glaze. Repeat every 15 minutes for the remaining 1 hour.

Fresh steamed asparagus tips give a pleasing complement in both taste and color to this meal.

Put It All in the Fridge
Food can be stored in the crockery container for up to four days in the refrigerator. However, never freeze food in the container because the crockery may crack.

Cooking time: 6 hours

Preparation time: 20 minutes

Attention: Minimal

Pot size: 3–6 quarts

Serves 2

Quail Baked in White Wine

2 quail, fresh or frozen (game
   hens can be substituted)
2 garlic cloves
1 small yellow onion
1 tablespoon shortening
2 whole cloves
1 teaspoon black peppercorns

1 bay leaf
1 teaspoon fresh chopped chives
1 cup white wine
½ teaspoon salt
⅛ teaspoon ground black pepper
⅛ teaspoon cayenne pepper
1 cup heavy cream

1. Thaw the quail (if necessary) and clean by running under cold water. Peel and chop the garlic and onions into ¼-inch pieces.
2. Melt the shortening in a medium-sized frying pan on medium heat. Add the garlic, onions, cloves, peppercorns, bay leaf. Cook for several minutes. Add the quail and brown on all sides.
3. Place the quail and the mixture from the frying pan into the slow cooker. Chop the chives into ¼-inch pieces. Add the wine, salt, pepper, cayenne pepper, and chives to the slow cooker. Cook covered on low setting for about 6 hours.
4. Remove the quail and set aside. Remove the bay leaf and discard. Strain the liquid, then add the cream to the liquid. Stir well for 5 minutes. Pour over the quail to serve.

Serve with Orange-Glazed Vegetable Medley (page 277) for a nice mix of flavors.

Replacing the Wine
If you don't have wine handy for your recipe, substitute one tablespoon of red or cider vinegar mixed with one cup of water.

Chicken Cordon Bleu

Cooking time: 4–6 hours

Preparation time: 30 minutes

Attention: Minimal

Pot size: 3–6 quarts

Serves 2

2 whole chicken breasts

4 small ham slices

4 small Swiss cheese slices

¼ cup flour

¼ cup grated Swiss cheese

½ teaspoon fresh or dried sage

¼ teaspoon ground black pepper

1 (10 ¾-ounce) can condensed cream of chicken soup

1. Remove the skin and bones from the chicken breasts. Cut each breast in half and pound with a kitchen mallet until about ¼-inch thick. Place a ham slice, then a Swiss cheese slice on each piece of chicken. Roll up and secure with toothpicks.
2. Combine the flour, grated cheese, sage, and black pepper in a small bowl. Dip the chicken rolls into the mixture. Place in the bottom of the slow cooker. Pour condensed soup over chicken rolls. Cook covered on low heat 4 to 6 hours.

Serve with Curried Vegetables and Garbanzo Beans (page 280) for a truly international meal.

Grate Your Own Cheese

As a time and money saver, buy blocks of cheese and grate them yourself. To keep the cheese from sticking together, add a little cornstarch and toss cheese until mixed through.

Game Hens in Red Wine

Cooking time: 6 hours

Preparation time: 20 minutes

Attention: Minimal

Pot size: 3–6 quarts

Serves 2

2 game hens, fresh or thawed
1 cup flour
½ teaspoon salt
¼ teaspoon ground black pepper
⅓ cup vegetable oil
1 cup sour cream
1½ cups red wine

1. Clean the game hens by running them under cold water. Combine the flour, salt, and ground black pepper. Roll the game hens in the mixture until lightly coated. Heat the vegetable oil at medium temperature in a medium-sized frying pan. Place the game hens in the frying pan and brown on all sides.
2. Place the game hens in the slow cooker on low setting. Pour the red wine on top of the game hens. Cook covered on low setting for 5 hours, add the sour cream and cook for another hour.

Serve with Grandma Dorothy's Peas and Rice (page 279) to make a complete meal.

To Prevent Curdling

To prevent curdling of milk, yogurt, or sour cream, mix it with an equal amount of cooking liquid from the dish being prepared. Consider adding milk products during the last hour of the cooking process and always cook them on the low setting.

Cooking time: 4–6 hours

Preparation time: 30 minutes

Attention: Minimal

Pot size: 3–6 quarts

Serves 2

Cheese Soufflé

14 slices fresh white bread
3 cups sharp Cheddar cheese, grated
3 cups milk
6 large eggs
2 tablespoons Worcestershire sauce
½ teaspoon table salt
Shortening, for greasing slow cooker
¼ cup butter
½ teaspoon paprika

1. Remove the crusts from the bread and tear the bread into small pieces, about ½-inch squares. Grate the cheese. Put the milk in a medium-sized pot on the stove and cook on high until slightly yellowed. Beat the eggs, milk, Worcestershire sauce, and salt until well blended.

2. Grease the slow cooker by putting the shortening on a paper towel and rubbing it on the inside of the pot. Place half of the bread in the slow cooker. Add half of the cheese and half of the butter. Add remaining bread. Put the remaining cheese and butter on top of the bread. Pour the prepared liquid sauce over everything. Sprinkle with paprika. Cover and cook on low 4 to 6 hours. Do not remove cover until ready to serve.

This is the perfect complement to Roast Duckling with Orange Glaze (page 294).

Using Condensed Milk

Instead of regular milk, cream, or sour cream, substitute sweetened condensed milk in slow cooker recipes. It tends to hold up better over the longer cooking times.

Poached Pears in Red Wine

Cooking time: 4–6 hours
Preparation time: 30 minutes
Attention: Minimal
Pot size: 3–6 quarts
Serves 2

1½ cups dry red wine
1 cup sugar

¼ teaspoon red food coloring
3 small pears

1. Combine the wine and sugar in the slow cooker. Cover and cook about 1 hour, until the sugar is dissolved. Add the food coloring.
2. Peel the pears and slice in half, removing stems and centers. Place in the slow cooker and stir slightly, so the pears are covered with the sugar and wine sauce. Cover and cook on low setting for 4 to 6 hours.

This is the perfect dessert for Classic Swiss Fondue (page 292).

Caramel Rum Fondue

Cooking time: 3–4 hours
Preparation time: 15 minutes
Attention: Medium
Pot size: 3–6 quarts
Serves 8

1 (14-ounce) package caramels
⅔ cup cream

½ cup miniature marshmallows
1 tablespoon rum

Combine the caramels and cream in the slow cooker. Cover and cook on low setting for 2 to 3 hours, or until the caramels are completely melted. Stir in the marshmallows and rum. Continue cooking covered on low setting for 1 hour. Stir before serving.

Serve with fresh sliced apple wedges.

Cooking time: 3–4 hours

Preparation time: 15 minutes

Attention: Minimal

Pot size: 4–6 quarts

Serves 8

Chocolate Pudding Cake

2 cups packaged chocolate cake mix
½ cup instant chocolate pudding mix
2 cups sour cream
4 eggs
1 cup water
¾ cup vegetable oil
1 cup semisweet chocolate chips

1. Combine the cake mix, pudding mix, sour cream, eggs, water, and oil in a medium-sized mixing bowl. Beat with an electric mixer or by hand with a wooden spoon until mixture is creamy. Stir in the chocolate chips.
2. Pour into a 2-pound coffee can. Place the coffee can inside the slow cooker. Cover and cook on low setting for 3 to 4 hours. Because this cake is more moist than others, a toothpick inserted into the center will never come out completely clean. Look for moist crumbs instead of batter to ensure it is done.

Make homemade whipped cream by beating whipping cream on a high speed with a hand mixer. Add a bit of vanilla and confectioner's sugar to give it more flavor.

Cooling Down

Let the slow cooker cool down on its own time. Do not pour cold water into it or immerse it in cold water, as this could cause the crockery pot to crack!

CHAPTER 22
Desserts

| Cooking time: 3–4 hours |
| Preparation time: 20 minutes |
| Attention: Minimal |
| Pot size: 4–6 quarts |
| Serves 8 |

Hot Fruit Medley

3 fresh grapefruit
3 fresh oranges
2 cups fresh or canned pineapple, cut into chunks
2 fresh pears
2 fresh peaches
3 fresh bananas
1 cup fresh cherries
1 cup seedless grapes
¼ cup sugar
¼ cup water
1 tablespoon lemon juice

1. Peel and section the grapefruits and oranges. Cut the pineapple into chunks about 1 inch square. Peel the pears, peaches, and bananas, then slice into pieces no larger than ¼-inch thick. Remove the pits from cherries.
2. Combine all the ingredients and place in the slow cooker. Cover and cook on low heat 3 to 4 hours, stirring occasionally.

Ladle over low-fat vanilla ice cream for a healthy treat.

Converting Recipes

When converting recipes from the oven to the slow cooker, plan about 8 hours on the low setting for every hour in the oven. Plan about 4 hours on the high setting for every hour in the oven.

Caramel and Peanut Fondue

Cooking time: 1 hour

Preparation time: 10 minutes

Attention: Constant

Pot size: 1–3 quarts

Serves 8

½ cup butter
½ cup light corn syrup
1 cup brown sugar
½ cup chunky peanut butter

1 can sweetened condensed milk
4 apples, sliced into ½-inch
   wedges

1. Combine the butter, corn syrup, brown sugar, peanut butter, and condensed milk in a medium-sized saucepan on the stove. Bring mixture to a boil, stirring constantly. Continue to boil for 3 minutes.
2. Pour the mixture into the slow cooker. Cook covered on low for 1 hour. Dip the fresh apple slices into the mixture.

This dip also makes an excellent ice cream topping.

Curried Fruit Bake

Cooking time: 3–4 hours

Preparation time: 20 minutes

Attention: Minimal

Pot size: 3–6 quarts

Serves 8–12

2 cups pitted prunes
2 cups canned or fresh apricots,
   peeled and pitted
1½ cups fresh or canned
   pineapple chunks

1½ cups fresh or canned peaches,
   peeled and pitted
1 cup packed brown sugar
½ teaspoon curry powder
1 (12-ounce) can Ginger Ale

Wash and cut the fruit into 1-inch pieces. Combine all the ingredients in the slow cooker. Cover and cook on low heat 3 to 4 hours.

In the summer, prepare this dessert the night before an event and put it in the refrigerator for a cool, refreshing treat.

Cooking time: 8 hours	
Preparation time: 20 minutes	
Attention: Minimal	
Pot size: 2–6 quarts	
Serves 6	

Raisin and Orange Baked Apples

6 medium-sized apples
½ cup raisins
3 tablespoons flour
⅓ cup sugar
½ teaspoon cinnamon
⅛ teaspoon salt
1 teaspoon grated orange peel
2 tablespoons butter (or margarine)
⅔ cup water
⅔ cup fresh orange juice

1. Wash and core the apples by taking a paring knife and "digging out" the center of each apple, leaving ½ to 1 inch on the bottom. Start at the top and peel the apples about a third of the way down. Fill the center of each apple with raisins and set the apples in the slow cooker. (You may stack them if necessary.)
2. Using a fork, mix together the flour, sugar, cinnamon, salt, orange peel, and butter (or margarine) in a small bowl until the mixture is crumbly. Sprinkle it over the apples.
3. Mix together the water and orange juice and pour around the apples. Cover and cook on low setting for 8 hours.

There is less chance of the apples falling into pieces if you let them cool slightly before removing them.

Cooking time: 1 hour

Preparation time: 15 minutes

Attention: Minimal

Pot size: 2–4 quarts

Serves 8

Grandma's Apples and Rice

1¼ cups uncooked brown rice
1 cup apples, peeled and cubed
4 tablespoons butter, divided
2½ cups chunky applesauce
¼ cup packed brown sugar
1¾ teaspoons ground cinnamon, divided
½ teaspoon salt

Cook the rice according to the package directions. Peel the apples and cut into 1-inch cubes. Stir 2 tablespoons of the butter into the hot rice. Add the applesauce, apples, brown sugar, 1½ teaspoons cinnamon, and salt. Pour into the slow cooker. Dot with the remaining butter and sprinkle with the remaining cinnamon. Cook uncovered on low setting for 1 hour.

Serve in bowls topped with whipped cream.

Seasonal Best

Because there are so many types of apples available year-round, you should always inquire about which ones are in season. This will insure that you are using the tastiest ones in the bunch. Also, try combining different kinds for added flavor and variety.

Cooking time: 1–2 hours
Preparation time: 15 minutes
Attention: Medium
Pot size: 2–4 quarts
Serves 8

Rice Pudding

2½ cups cooked white rice
1½ cup scalded milk
3 eggs
shortening for greasing the slow cooker
⅔ cup brown sugar
3 tablespoons soft butter
2 teaspoons vanilla
1 teaspoon salt
1 teaspoon nutmeg
1 teaspoon cinnamon
½ cup raisins

1. Cook the rice according to the package directions to yield 2½ cups cooked rice. Scald the milk by cooking it in a small saucepan on high heat on the stove until it slightly yellows. Beat the eggs in a small bowl with a fork until the whites and yellows are well mixed.
2. Lightly grease the slow cooker by putting shortening on a paper towel and rubbing it on the inside of the slow cooker. Combine all the ingredients. Pour into the slow cooker. Cook covered on high 1 to 2 hours. Stir after first 30 minutes.

Ladle into individual graham cracker crusts to make mini pies.

Cleaning Caution
Do not use detergents or scouring powders with slow cookers. The porous clay cooking crock with soak up the detergent, tainting the flavor of future dishes.

Chocolate
Peanut Butter Cake

Cooking time: 2–3 hours

Preparation time: 10 minutes

Attention: Minimal

Pot size: 4–6 quarts

Serves 8

½ cup chopped walnuts
2 cups chocolate cake mix
½ cup water
⅓ cup creamy peanut butter

1. Combine all the ingredients in a medium-sized bowl and beat with a wooden spoon for about 2 minutes.
2. Grease the inside of a 2-pound coffee can, then sprinkle the inside with flour. Pour the batter in the coffee can and cover with aluminum foil. Poke 3 sets of holes in the aluminum foil with a fork. Place the coffee can in the slow cooker. Cover and bake on high for 2 to 3 hours.

Spread a thin layer of peanut butter on each piece right before serving.

A Time-Saver
For an even quicker recipe, buy the walnuts already chopped!

Cooking time: 3–4 hours	
Preparation time: 15 minutes	
Attention: Minimal	
Pot size: 4–6 quarts	
Serves 8	

Cinnamon Streusel Pound Cake

1 (16-ounce) package pound cake mix
¼ cup chopped walnuts
¼ cup brown sugar
1 tablespoon flour
1 teaspoon cinnamon

1. Prepare the cake mix according to the package directions. Grease the inside of a 2-pound coffee can by putting shortening on a paper towel and rubbing it inside the coffee can. Sprinkle the inside lightly with flour. Pour pound cake batter into the coffee can.
2. Chop the nuts into $\frac{1}{16}$-inch pieces with a sharp knife. In a small bowl, combine the brown sugar, flour, nuts, and cinnamon. Sprinkle this mixture over the cake batter.
3. Cover the coffee can with aluminum foil. Poke 3 sets of holes in the aluminum foil with a fork. Place the coffee can in the slow cooker. Cover and cook on high setting for 3 to 4 hours.

This is the perfect complement to eggs and bacon for Sunday brunch.

Adding Frozen Foods

If you must absolutely use frozen foods, set the slow cooker to high for the first two hours then turn it to low to resume cooking. This reduces the chance that bacteria will grow.

Scalloped Fruit Cocktail

Cooking time: 3 hours

Preparation time: 10 minutes

Attention: Minimal

Pot size: 3–6 quarts

Serves 8

3 cups (24 ounces) canned fruit cocktail
8 slices white bread
2 cups sugar
3 eggs
¾ cup butter, melted
¾ cup milk

1. Drain and discard the juice from the fruit cocktail. Mash the fruit with a fork. Remove and discard the crusts from the bread. Tear the bread into ½-inch cubes.
2. Mix all the ingredients in a large mixing bowl, taking care that the eggs are well integrated pour mixture into the slow cooker. Cover and cook on high setting for 2 hours. Turn to low setting and cook covered for 1 additional hour.

Use any canned fruit, such as peaches or pineapple, instead of the fruit cocktail.

Don't Overfill!

Leave at least two inches of space from the food to the top of the slow cooker, especially if the recipe contains a lot of liquid. This will prevent the food from boiling over while simmering.

Pumpkin Pie Pudding

Cooking time: 6–7 hours
Preparation time: 20 minutes
Attention: Minimal
Pot size: 3–6 quarts
Serves 8

2 eggs
1 (15-ounce) can solid-packed
  pumpkin
1 (12-ounce) can evaporated milk
¾ cup sugar

½ cup buttermilk biscuit mix
2 tablespoons melted butter
½ teaspoon nutmeg
2 teaspoons vanilla

Beat the eggs with a fork until slightly frothy. Mix together all the ingredients. Pour into the slow cooker. Cover and cook on low setting for 6 to 7 hours.

Use this as dessert for Day-After Thanksgiving Soup (page 26).

Raisin Bread Pudding

Cooking time: 5 hours
Preparation time: 15 minutes
Attention: Medium
Pot size: 3–6 quarts
Serves 8

8 slices cinnamon raisin bread
4 eggs
2 cups milk
¼ cup sugar

¼ cup butter, melted
½ cup raisins
1 teaspoon cinnamon

Tear the bread into 1-inch pieces and place in the slow cooker. Beat together the eggs, milk, sugar, butter, raisins, and cinnamon. Pour over the bread. Cover and cook on high setting for 1 hour. Reduce heat to low. Keep it covered and cook an additional 4 hours.

Add a drizzle of confectioners' sugar mixed with milk and vanilla to the top of each serving.

Maggie's Favorite Oatmeal Raisin Cookies

Cooking time: 4 hours
Preparation time: 15 minutes
Attention: Frequent
Pot size: 3–8 quarts
Serves 30

½ cup shortening
¾ cup brown sugar
½ teaspoon salt
½ teaspoon cinnamon
½ teaspoon nutmeg
½ teaspoon allspice
1 egg
¾ cup flour
⅜ teaspoon baking soda
⅛ cup buttermilk
½ cup walnuts, chopped nuts
¾ cup rolled oats
¾ cup seedless raisins

1. Combine the shortening and brown sugar in a mixing bowl. Beat well with a wooden spoon or electric mixer, until the batter is smooth and creamy. Add the salt, cinnamon, nutmeg, allspice, and egg. Beat the mixture well, until the batter is smooth and creamy.
2. Mix together the flour and baking soda. Add half this mixture to the batter and beat until creamy. Add the remaining half and the buttermilk. Beat until well mixed.
3. Chop the nuts into about ¹/₁₆-inch pieces with a sharp kitchen knife. Add the nuts, oats, and raisins to the batter; mix well with a wooden spoon. The mixture should be firm but not dry. Drop onto the bottom of the slow cooker by rounded teaspoonfuls, about 4 at a time. Cook each batch covered on high for about 15 minutes.

Take two cookies and make a sandwich by spreading vanilla frosting in between.

Fruit Drop Cookies

Cooking time: 4 hours

Preparation time: 15 minutes, plus 1 hour of refrigeration time

Attention: Frequent

Pot size: 3–8 quarts

Serves 30

1 cup diced dates
1 cup candied maraschino cherries
½ cup soft shortening
1 cup brown sugar
1 egg
¼ cup buttermilk
1½ cups flour
½ teaspoon baking soda
¾ cup broken pecans

1. Cut the dates into ¼-inch pieces with a sharp knife. Cut the cherries in half. Beat the shortening, sugar, and egg until smooth and creamy with an electric mixer. Stir in the milk. Combine the flour, baking soda, and salt. Mix with batter, beating until creamy. Stir in the pecans, cherries, and dates using a wooden spoon.
2. Cover the bowl and put the batter in the refrigerator for at least 1 hour. Preheat the slow cooker on high setting. Drop the batter by rounded teaspoonfuls onto the bottom of the slow cooker. Cover and bake each batch 10 to 15 minutes.

Serve with Minty Hot Chocolate (page 178).

Microwave No-No

Don't put the crockery food container in the oven or microwave unless the manufacturers' directions say you can. It could crack or even completely break apart!

Chocolate Coconut and Peanut Clusters

Cooking time: 30–60 minutes
Preparation time: 15 minutes
Attention: Constant
Pot size: 2–8 quarts
Serves 24

2 pounds white candy coating,
   broken into small pieces
2 cups semisweet chocolate chips

½ cup sweet German chocolate
½ cup flaked coconut
3 cups roasted peanuts

Put the candy coating, chocolate chips, and German chocolate in the slow cooker. Heat on high setting, stirring every 10 to 15 minutes until the mixture is completely melted. Stir in the coconut and peanuts; mix well. Drop by teaspoonfuls onto waxed paper. Set in a cool area until the candy is hard.

Add pecans instead of peanuts.

Strawberry Rhubarb Sauce

Cooking time: 7–8 hours
Preparation time: 20 minutes
Attention: Minimal
Pot size: 3–6 quarts
Serves 12

6 cups fresh rhubarb
1 cup sugar
½ white grape juice

1 cinnamon stick
2 cups quartered strawberries

1. Wash the rhubarb and remove the leaves; chop the rhubarb into 1-inch pieces. Place in the slow cooker with the sugar, grape juice, and cinnamon stick. Cover and cook on low setting for 5 to 6 hours.
2. Remove the cinnamon stick. Remove the stems from the strawberries and slice into quarters. Add to slow cooker. Cover and cook on low setting for 2 hours.

Excellent served warm over homemade vanilla ice cream.

Cooking time: 3–4 hours

Preparation time: 20 minutes

Attention: Minimal

Pot size: 4–6 quarts

Serves 8

Beer Cake

²/₃ cup butter

1½ cup brown sugar

3 eggs, beaten

2½ cups flour

1½ teaspoons baking powder

¼ teaspoon baking soda

1 teaspoon cinnamon

¼ teaspoon nutmeg

1½ cups brown ale

1 cup walnuts, chopped

1 cup seedless raisins

1. Mix the butter and sugar in a medium-sized mixing bowl using an electric mixer. The mixture should be light and fluffy. Add the eggs one at a time, mixing well. Combine the flour, baking powder, baking soda, cinnamon, and nutmeg in a bowl; mix well. Pour half this mixture and half the beer into the batter and mix until smooth. Add the remaining flour mixture and beer. Mix until smooth. Fold in the walnuts and raisins.

2. Grease a 2-pound coffee can by putting shortening on a paper towel and rubbing the inside of the can. Lightly sprinkle the inside with flour. Place the batter in coffee can. Cover with aluminum foil. Poke 3 sets of holes into the aluminum foil with a fork. Put the coffee can in the slow cooker. Place the lid on the slow cooker slightly off center so that steam can escape. Cook on high setting for 3 to 4 hours. Remove the coffee can from the slow cooker and allow to cool 15 to 30 minutes before removing the cake.

Who could resist serving this on Super Bowl Sunday as dessert for Halftime Chili (page 175)?

Index

THE EVERYTHING ONE-POT COOKBOOK

By Lisa Rojak

What could be easier than cooking an entire meal using just one pot? One-pot cuisine is characterized by hearty, satisfying dishes that can be prepared using only one of a variety of conventional cooking techniques: a single baking pan, skillet, slow cooker, or conventional stovetop pot. *The Everything® One-Pot Cookbook* features hundreds of exciting recipes that are guaranteed crowd pleasers, with minimal mess. From appetizers to entrees and even desserts, these one-pot meals are quick, simple, and delicious.

Trade paperback, $12.95
1-58062-186-4, 288 pages

OTHER *EVERYTHING®* BOOKS BY ADAMS MEDIA CORPORATION

Everything® **Pregnancy Organizer**
$15.00, 1-58062-336-0

Everything® **Project Management Book**
$12.95, 1-58062-583-5

Everything® **Puppy Book**
$12.95, 1-58062-576-2

Everything® **Quick Meals Cookbook**
$14.95, 1-58062-488-X

Everything® **Resume Book**
$12.95, 1-58062-311-5

Everything® **Romance Book**
$12.95, 1-58062-566-5

Everything® **Running Book**
$12.95, 1-58062-618-1

Everything® **Sailing Book, 2nd Ed.**
$12.95, 1-58062-671-8

Everything® **Saints Book**
$12.95, 1-58062-534-7

Everything® **Scrapbooking Book**
$14.95, 1-58062-729-3

Everything® **Selling Book**
$12.95, 1-58062-319-0

Everything® **Shakespeare Book**
$12.95, 1-58062-591-6

Everything® **Slow Cooker Cookbook**
$14.95, 1-58062-667-X

Everything® **Soup Cookbook**
$14.95, 1-58062-556-8

Everything® **Spells and Charms Book**
$12.95, 1-58062-532-0

Everything® **Start Your Own Business Book**
$12.95, 1-58062-650-5

Everything® **Stress Management Book**
$14.95, 1-58062-578-9

Everything® **Study Book**
$12.95, 1-55850-615-2

Everything® **T'ai Chi and QiGong Book**
$12.95, 1-58062-646-7

Everything® **Tall Tales, Legends, and Outrageous Lies Book**
$12.95, 1-58062-514-2

Everything® **Tarot Book**
$12.95, 1-58062-191-0

Everything® **Thai Cookbook**
$14.95, 1-58062-733-1

Everything® **Time Management Book**
$12.95, 1-58062-492-8

Everything® **Toasts Book**
$12.95, 1-58062-189-9

Everything® **Toddler Book**
$12.95, 1-58062-592-4

Everything® **Total Fitness Book**
$12.95, 1-58062-318-2

Everything® **Trivia Book**
$12.95, 1-58062-143-0

Everything® **Tropical Fish Book**
$12.95, 1-58062-343-3

Everything® **Vegetarian Cookbook**
$12.95, 1-58062-640-8

Everything® **Vitamins, Minerals, and Nutritional Supplements Book**
$12.95, 1-58062-496-0

Everything® **Weather Book**
$14.95, 1-58062-668-8

Everything® **Wedding Book, 2nd Ed.**
$14.95, 1-58062-190-2

Everything® **Wedding Checklist**
$7.95, 1-58062-456-1

Everything® **Wedding Etiquette Book**
$7.95, 1-58062-454-5

Everything® **Wedding Organizer**
$15.00, 1-55850-828-7

Everything® **Wedding Shower Book**
$7.95, 1-58062-188-0

Everything® **Wedding Vows Book**
$7.95, 1-58062-455-3

Everything® **Weddings on a Budget Book**
$9.95, 1-58062-782-X

Everything® **Weight Training Book**
$12.95, 1-58062-593-2

Everything® **Wicca and Witchcraft Book**
$14.95, 1-58062-725-0

Everything® **Wine Book**
$12.95, 1-55850-808-2

Everything® **World War II Book**
$12.95, 1-58062-572-X

Everything® **World's Religions Book**
$12.95, 1-58062-648-3

Everything® **Yoga Book**
$12.95, 1-58062-594-0

*Prices subject to change without notice.

EVERYTHING KIDS' SERIES!

Everything® **Kids' Baseball Book, 2nd Ed.**
$6.95, 1-58062-688-2

Everything® **Kids' Cookbook**
$6.95, 1-58062-658-0

Everything® **Kids' Joke Book**
$6.95, 1-58062-686-6

Everything® **Kids' Mazes Book**
$6.95, 1-58062-558-4

Everything® **Kids' Money Book**
$6.95, 1-58062-685-8

Everything® **Kids' Monsters Book**
$6.95, 1-58062-657-2

Everything® **Kids' Nature Book**
$6.95, 1-58062-684-X

Everything® **Kids' Puzzle Book**
$6.95, 1-58062-687-4

Everything® **Kids' Science Experiments Book**
$6.95, 1-58062-557-6

Everything® **Kids' Soccer Book**
$6.95, 1-58062-642-4

Everything® **Travel Activity Book**
$6.95, 1-58062-641-6

Available wherever books are sold!
To order, call 800-872-5627, or visit us at everything.com

Everything® is a registered trademark of Adams Media Corporation.